"Gabriel Moran's book is a tour de force of practical theology. Beginning from a creative reappropriation of the meanings of 'faith' and 'revelation' as 'believing in a revealing God,' Moran establishes a lively and relevant theological basis for addressing problems of authority and responsibility in the Church, for identifying the distinctively Christian faith-response to divine revelation, and for questions of teaching and learning. This remarkably stimulating and thoroughly original approach to our ecclesial life today offers real guidance through the perils and pitfalls of today's Christian believing. Written with a clarity and attractiveness that should give it a wide readership, the book charts its own distinctive course through some very well-traveled waters."

—Paul Lakeland
Aloysius P. Kelley SJ Professor of Catholic Studies
Director, Center for Catholic Studies
Fairfield University, Connecticut

"Gabriel Moran, master-teacher, teaches us anew about old topics. He has fresh, insightful things to say about the God who reveals, the humans who accept and respond to this revelation, and the community in which the revelation is mediated. When a master teacher speaks, there is always much to be learned by all who listen carefully, and that is abundantly true in this book."

—Michael G. Lawler
Professor Emeritus of Catholic Theology
Creighton University
Omaha, Nebraska

"Once again Moran has shown he is one of the most underestimated Roman Catholic intellectuals of our time. No work is more timely. No project more important. The book is the summit of his life's work on the question of revelation. Moran's intention here is to be deeply conservative. He reclaims and restates wisdom from our Jewish and Christian past. His key question is: can the Christian church's tradition of profound ideas on revelation be made intelligible and relevant to today's problems and possibilities? Moran answers in the affirmative. However, everything depends on our interpretation of divine revelation. Moran's new work is our indispensable guide on this fundamental issue at this critical point in the twenty-first century."

—Dr. Kieran Scott
Fordham University

D1155424

Believing in a Revealing God

The Basis of the Christian Life

Gabriel Moran

A Michael Glazier Book

LITURGICAL PRESS

Collegeville, Minnesota

www.litpress.org

A Michael Glazier Book published by Liturgical Press

Cover design by David Manahan, OSB. Cover illustration © Rvs and Dreamstime.com.

Excerpts from documents of the Second Vatican Council are from *Vatican Council II: Volume 1, The Conciliar and Post Conciliar Documents*, by Austin Flannery, OP, © 1996 (Costello Publishing Company, Inc.). Used with permission.

Scripture texts in this work are taken from the *New Revised Standard Version Bible* © 1989, Division of Christian Education of the National Council of the Churches of Christ in the United States of America. Used by permission. All rights reserved.

1   2   3   4   5   6   7   8   9

Library of Congress Cataloging-in-Publication Data

Moran, Gabriel.
　　Believing in a revealing God : the basis of the Christian life / Gabriel Moran.
　　　p.   cm.
　　"A Michael Glazier book."
　　Includes bibliographical references (p.　　) and index.
　　ISBN 978-0-8146-5388-3 (pbk.)
　　1. Revelation—Catholic Church.   2. Christian life—Catholic authors.   3. Church.
　I. Title.
BT127.3.M668 2009
231.7'4—dc22   2008047361

Contents

Introduction

The Word of the Lord
Is Always Spoken Now

The Second Vatican Council initiated a series of changes in the Roman Catholic Church, the full extent of which may not be clear for a century. The changes reverberate in other Christian churches and in the secular world as well. Perhaps the single most important thing about the council was what it did not do: it did not define doctrines as previous councils had done; it did not condemn church heresies or secular movements. In the words of one historian, it moved "from threat to persuasion, monologue to conversation, ruling to service, exclusion to inclusion, the vertical to the horizontal."[1]

The immediate result of the council was to release a great deal of pent-up energy for church reform. Some movements reflected the council's concern for a "return to the sources" as a basis for proposed changes. Other attempts at reform may have been swept up in the fashions of the day. Already by the end of the 1960s there was movement by some church officials to put a brake on changes the council had initiated.[2]

The Catholic Church has entered a period in which inevitable change meets a constant resistance to almost all particular changes. From outside the church it is not a pretty sight. Inside the church there is a high level of frustration by many loyal members who recognize the need for a more radical rethinking of doctrinal, liturgical, moral, and organizational issues so that the church can be true to its best self.[3] The present pope said before his

1. John O'Malley, "Did the Council Change Anything?" in *Vatican II: Did Anything Happen?* ed. David Schultenover, 52–91 (New York: Continuum, 2007), 81; Giuseppe Alberigo, "Transition to a New Age," *History of Vatican II*, vol. 5 (Leuven: Peeters, 2006), 573–652.

2. Piero Marini, *A Challenging Reform: Realizing the Vision of the Liturgical Renewal 1963–75* (Collegeville, MN: Liturgical Press, 2007).

3. U.S. Religious Landscape Survey (Washington, DC: The Pew Forum on Religion in Public Life, 2008), 22–35.

election that "it seems certain to me that very hard times await the Church. Her own crisis has hardly begun."[4]

What distinguishes today's Catholic Church is that it faces a constant give-and-take with the surrounding world. It has to choose either to resist these influences or to enter into serious dialogue with other religious traditions and with secular institutions. If dialogue is the choice, then that means acknowledging that the church does not control the language it uses. It has to negotiate religious terms with Jews, Muslims, and other groups. In addressing the whole world it cannot simply decide on its own what the words mean. The church needs "scanners," people who are removed from official positions and are comfortable in both the language of insiders and the language of outsiders.

The Second Vatican Council took a great step forward by inviting Protestant, Orthodox, and Jewish observers to its proceedings. They provided a respectful but critical view of the Roman Catholic Church's inner language. I would particularly note Orthodox writers, even though most Roman Catholics in the United States are barely aware of the Orthodox Church. This Eastern Christianity has a theology distinctly different from that of the Latin Church and could offer a corrective to emphases in the authority pattern and sacramental practices of Roman Catholicism. Some very pointed criticism of the council's document on the church was provided by Orthodox theologians.[5]

Orthodox Christianity has given a prominence to the Holy Spirit that is still notably lacking in the Roman Catholic Church. We do not need a separate "theology of the Holy Spirit," but a transforming of the way that faith in God and the revelation of God are perceived as the basis of all theology. The present pope has expressed the desire for dialogue with the Eastern half of the church.

The Second Vatican Council opened a window for the Spirit to blow through every office, corridor, and corner of the church. It encouraged further thinking on the most basic issues of church life. The reflections in this book are based on respect for official pronouncements, including the documents of Vatican II, but the reflections are not always in complete agreement with official documents.

4. Robert Moynihan, *Let God's Light Shine Forth: The Spiritual Vision of Pope Benedict XVI* (New York: Doubleday, 2005), 144.

5. John Zizioulas, *Being as Communion* (New York: St. Vladimir's Seminary Press, 1985); Nikos Nissiotis, "The Main Ecclesiological Problems of Vatican II," *Journal of Ecumenical Studies* 2 (1965): 31–62.

The title and theme of this book, "believing in a revealing God," is a simple idea: it is the relation between divine activity and human response. But simplicity in life comes from going beyond complexity rather than trying to avoid it. The complexity is due to the fact that the human mind divides things. Even though human life is all about relations, the human mind thinks in concepts, not relations. We *live* relationally—body/soul, individual/community, past/present, human/nonhuman, creature/creator—but we struggle at the limits of language in trying to describe any of these relations.

The relation that is the topic of this book is usually described with the words "faith and revelation." But two nouns with a plus sign between them do not capture what is, in fact, a single relation composed of two activities. It is not surprising that in Christian history faith and revelation have so often been treated as two separable things. They are taken to be essential building blocks in the foundation of Christian theology, church authority, and Christian instruction.

The choice is a simple one. Either faith is a thing directed to something in the past called revelation, or faith is an act directed toward what is revelatory in the present. In the first case faith is imagined as a "cognitive" question: that is, its concern is with assent to truths. In the second case faith engages the whole person and is concerned with today's life. The first version of faith, as I have described it, no longer has many defenders, but if one really wishes to get free of it one has to be ready to live with the consequences of believing-revealing.

The sign that faith and revelation are imagined as things is the use of "Christian" as an adjective modifying the nouns "faith" and "revelation." To speak of "the Christian faith" may seem like an obvious way to distinguish the Christian block of material from other faiths, particularly Jewish and Muslim. But each of these religions intends "faith" to be the act that unites their members with God. A person has faith in God or is lacking such faith. The Jewish Bible, the Christian Bible, and the Qur'an know of only one faith. Many people think that what is different in our day is the recognition of a multiplicity of faiths. We do have to find a way to accept a religious diversity or plurality, but "many faiths" is not the best way to do that.

The term "Christian faith" does have a place in church tradition. It most often has referred to the fact that the Christian believes in God with a Christ-focused faith. Thomas Aquinas occasionally uses "Christian faith" in this way, but far more often he refers to "faith" without a modifier.[6] The choice

6. For a statistical comparison of the uses of "faith" and "Christian faith" in Thomas Aquinas's writings see Wilfred Cantwell Smith, *Faith and Belief* (Princeton, NJ: Princeton University Press, 1979), 299.

is not between something specific and something general, as if "faith" alone were vague, while the word "Christian" makes it more concrete. The choice is rather between noun and verb. The adjective "Christian" throws the emphasis onto faith as a thing located in the past and preserved by the church. In contrast, "faith" without a modifier can express a concrete demand for an activity in the present.

In Jewish, Christian, and Muslim religions the act of faith is a radical choice. Either one believes or one does not believe. I should add that when saying that the Bibles and the Qur'an know only faith or lack of faith one must also say that these documents remind the reader that we—the humans—are not the final judges of who are the true believers. From a Muslim perspective only true Muslims are saved, but someone who professes to be Muslim may turn out to be a false Muslim. Conversely, some true Muslims might be Christians or Jews. In a similar way, Christians claim that all genuine faith is "in Christ," but God is the final judge of who are the true Christ followers. The New Testament picture of the last judgment (Matt 25) warns that there could be big surprises.

If there is some justification for talking about "Christian faith," there is none whatever for "Christian revelation." There is no "Christian revelation" any more than there is Christian creation, Christian grace, or Christian redemption. The phrase "the Christian revelation" was coined in the late sixteenth century and ever since then it has been a major obstacle to thinking about both faith and revelation. "Revelation" in a religious context is a claim of God acting: a revealing of the divine. Whatever can be put into human speech is not divine revelation. At best it is a human response to that divine activity.

It may seem like a sign of modesty to refer to "the Christian revelation" in contrast to a Jewish or a Muslim revelation. But none of these religions believes that it is referring to only a part of divine revelation. If the word refers to divine activity, there is no multiplicity of things called divine revelations. There is one God, one creation, one revelation, one redemption.

Each religion has a right to claim, and does claim, to have the most accurate interpretation of God's revealing activity. But no religion can claim to possess God's revelation. "Woe unto the possessed who fancy that they possess God."[7] When each religion is understood to have an interpretation of divine revelation, that language allows different religions to live together peacefully and makes it possible for one religion to learn from another without abandoning the truth it knows.

---

7. Martin Buber, *I and Thou* (New York: Scribner's, 1970), 106.

There is then no "deposit of revelation" established for the Christian church in the first century. There is a deposit of testimonies to what has been seen and what has been heard. Among the testimonies of faith—human responses to divine revelation—the body of Sacred Scripture holds a special place. However, calling Scripture the "revealed word of God" is misleading.

Thomas Aquinas always refers to "articles of faith," not "articles of revelation," as the basis of Christian theology.[8] He usually uses the word revelation with a preposition; we know through, by, or from revelation. Articles of faith follow *from* revelation.[9] A resistance to following Thomas in this understanding of revelation may be explained by the fact that it leads to such startling conclusions as his statement that "revelation does not tell us what is, and thus joins us to him as an unknown."[10]

It is not just the timid, the lazy, or the unenlightened who look for stability in fixed truths. In fact, scholars and church officials are likely to be more attracted to "the Christian revelation." Scholars in various branches of theology assume that theology as a whole has a stable basis, and when Roman Catholic bishops enunciate a position, or issue a decree, they regularly appeal to the revealed truths in the deposit of revelation that they are preserving and defending.

I sympathize with Catholic bishops because they are doing their job as they understand it. Unfortunately, they are trapped within their own language and there is a continuing erosion of church authority. A more aggressive insistence on the truths of "the Christian revelation" will likely only worsen the erosion. The third chapter of this book is a defense of authority, with suggestions for a more tenable pattern of authority than is currently found in Catholic and Protestant churches, but such change would not come easily.

My argument that there is no body of revealed truths will seem to some people an attack on church authority. The language I advocate, although based on church tradition, involves an uneasy transition, but the alternative is to defend what is increasingly indefensible. Nothing is proposed in this book that does not have historical backing. Of course, there is more than one way to read history, so many points are debatable.

"Liberal" and "conservative" are not the best alternatives for describing the Christian church's history and current problems. Conflicts within the church are most often between the superficially conservative and the deeply

8. Thomas Aquinas, *Summa Theologiae* I, q. 1, a. 8 and I, q. 1., a. 5.
9. *Summa Theologiae* I, q. 1, a. 6.
10. *Summa Theologiae* 1-II, q. 12, a. 13, ad 1.

conservative. The church needs people whose liberal thinking is based on being deeply conservative. Modern liberalism has too often pitted dreams of the future against the rigidity of the past, but much of what passes for conservative in the church is not conservative enough. "Conservative" often means attachment to sixteenth- or nineteenth-century formulas. Fundamentalism, for example, is not traditional doctrine, but a modern reaction to criticism of the Bible. The assumption that revelation consists of "propositions" is a nineteenth-century view that does not succeed in defending the basic doctrines of the tradition.[11]

My intention in this book is to be deeply conservative. The meaning of "revelation" presented here is consistent with the writings of Isaiah and Jeremiah, Mark and John, Augustine and Aquinas, Luther and Calvin. These authors do not all agree with one another, but each of them bears testimony to an understanding of divine revelation. They are still of relevance for a twenty-first-century understanding of revelation.

The Christian meaning of faith-revelation was especially influenced by seventeenth- and eighteenth-century writers: Edward Herbert, John Locke, Joseph Butler, Voltaire, and Jean-Jacques Rousseau, among others. In Georges Bernanos' *Diary of a Country Priest,* the Curé reflects on the absurd phrase " 'to lose one's faith' as one might a purse or a ring of keys," and concludes that "it must be one of those sayings of bourgeois piety, a legacy of those wretched priests of the eighteenth-century who talked so much."[12]

An Age of Revelation (or Enlightenment)

In listing some of the profound writers on revelation, I stopped at the sixteenth century, even though "revelation" became a more commonly used term after that time. Unfortunately, the term became equated with a set of truths that God has placed in the past. In Protestant circles revelation became equated with the scriptural texts. The Catholic attempt to keep open a wider meaning of revelation resulted in adding other truths from tradition. Protestants gave more emphasis to faith than did Catholics, but both imagined faith to be acceptance of a body of truths called revelation.

Given this language, the Christian churches were effectively segregated into a sphere of their own. What Mark Lilla calls the Great Separation was the arrangement whereby Christianity was tolerated and even encouraged,

---

11. George Lindbeck, *The Nature of Religious Doctrine* (Philadelphia: Westminster, 1984), 73–88.

12. Georges Bernanos, *Diary of a Country Priest* (Garden City, NY: Image Books, 1954), 95.

so long as it stayed away from public life. Religion was thought to be a private matter, a very useful discipline of the individual's life.[13]

At the end of the eighteenth century, Immanuel Kant proclaimed the age of enlightenment.[14] The term "enlightenment" carries the same image as "revelation." Both words refer to lighting up the darkness. If "revelation" had not been so closely identified with Christianity, the secular founders of the modern age could just as well have announced the age of revelation. Of course, their revelation/enlightenment was based on a trust in empirical science and the political arrangements that were assumed to follow from such enlightenment/revelation.

When it came to competing at revelation, empirical science was more successful than Christianity at producing practical results. For a brief period science was called a "natural revelation" in contrast to a supernatural or special revelation that was assigned to the church. Even after scientists abandoned the term revelation, the Christian use of the term remained linked with a special set of truths outside of reason. These truths were to be accepted on faith.

This arrangement of faith next to reason, religion next to politics, and churches free to exist in a zone of privacy seemed to be the formula for Western progress. Life was indeed improved for millions of people through science and technology. Instead of waiting for a restored paradise at the end of time, modern science set out to make life much better here on earth. "Technology" is a word invented in the nineteenth century to express a new logic, one that employs technical and mechanized means to transform human life.

To the amazement of many secular proponents of enlightenment, however, this arrangement has shown increasing signs of collapse during the last half century. Religion, which had been expected to slowly disappear, has come back with a new worldwide fervor. That renewed energy intrudes into political life with a refusal to confine religious beliefs and practices to the sphere of privacy.

Mark Lilla's *The Stillborn God* is one of numerous books exploring this collapse of the Great Separation. In the opening paragraph of the book he writes: "Today we have progressed to the point where we are again fighting the battles of the sixteenth century—over revelation and reason, dogmatic purity and toleration, inspiration and consent, divine duty and common

13. Mark Lilla, *The Stillborn God* (New York: Knopf, 2007).
14. Immanuel Kant, "What Is Enlightenment," in *Kant: Political Writings* (Cambridge: Cambridge University Press, 1991), 54–60.

decency. We find it incomprehensible that theological ideas still influence the minds of men, stirring up messianic passions that leave societies in ruin."[15]

It is significant that in this passage Lilla's first pairing is "revelation and reason." That is indeed to go back to the sixteenth century and earlier. In the modern period the discussion has been about the relation between "faith and reason." That pairing usually has the effect of turning the question back inside the human head. Is there a faculty of the mind called "faith" that is next to reason? An inquiry into faith and reason that does not have an adequate meaning of revelation to work with locks faith into a private world. Faith, as something alongside reason, is then directed to "the Christian revelation." The position is invulnerable to scientific criticism, but the price of that invulnerability is the isolation of faith from the world of nature, politics, and daily life.

In contrast, Lilla's "revelation and reason" immediately leads to all of today's crucial questions about religion's relation to politics, societal upheavals, and the individual's search for meaning. The relation of revelation and reason was the ancient and medieval way to talk not about the individual's thinking but about the human relation to the universe. Reason was a power that humans participated in; revelation was divine activity in history, politics, and daily life.

There is no going back to an enchanted world before the rise of modern science, but neither can Christian religion be a force for good if it equates divine revelation with a store of truths from the past. If the churches are intent on preserving "the Christian revelation," they cut themselves off from today's religious and spiritual searching.

The way the term "revelation" is used in Christian theology today indicates a suspicion that the word has little connection to anything outside theology. Christianity is in danger of ceding its own idea to entrepreneurs in today's religious market. In any Barnes and Noble or Borders bookstore today the section on "New Age" religion is likely to be two or three times the size of the section on Christianity. That fact may be testimony to individual delusions and the corruption of the marketplace, but it does indicate a problem that Christianity has in its relation to the present (or new) age.

Much of what heralds itself as a new spirituality is in fact heavily dependent on Christianity, but it comes from the underside of Christian history, the part that is attractive to the suffering and the poor, displaced individuals, and disturbed visionaries. Christian churches that consider themselves re-

---

15. Lilla, *The Stillborn God*, 3.

spectable establishments are inclined to look the other way and think that they have nothing to do with spiritual seekers, religious visions, and messianic movements that often end in violence. In this case renouncing one's relatives is not helpful, either for reducing violence or for learning about oneself.

In recent decades there has been worldwide concern with terrorist violence inspired by Islam. Young, disaffected Muslims are willing to die for a paradise they believe is brought on with the use of violent means. There is a rightful demand that responsible Muslim leaders speak out in opposition to violence, and that they engage in the political, economic, and educational reforms that would ameliorate conditions that breed violence.

Christians have a right to condemn Islamic violence, but they have to be mindful of a similar strand in Christian history. A Christian vision of the end time has been at the root of violent political movements in past centuries and the wound has never been entirely healed. Muslim terrorism in the twenty-first century does not so far measure up to the peasants' revolt in the Christian Germany of the sixteenth century.[16]

What is called a millenarian movement started early in Christian history and has never disappeared. "Millenarianism" (or millennialism) refers to a thousand years, part of the vision of an end of history when Christ will reign. As the year 2000 approached, there were fears of a special outbreak of millenarian uprisings. The violence did not materialize. Nonetheless, such millenarian groups exist throughout the Christian world and are a continuing potential for violence.

Christians who dismiss millenarian groups as disturbed fanatics should be aware that the Christian movement as a whole began as an announcement of the end of time. For two thousand years the Christian church has had to struggle with its being in an awkward position between the announcement and the fulfillment of what the Bible calls "the kingdom of God." There is an undeniable truth to Alfred Loisy's statement that "Jesus promised the Kingdom of God but it was the church that came forth."[17]

Apocalypse

The basis of millenarian groups is revelation. The term "revelation" had its origin in the vision of the end. Used first by sects in the Near East, "revelation" was adopted by the church for its own version of a final judgment.

16. Norman Cohn, *The Pursuit of the Millennium: Revolutionary Millenarians and the Mystical Anarchists of the Middle Ages* (New York: Oxford University Press, 1970).

17. Bernard Lee, *The Becoming of the Church* (New York: Paulist Press, 1974), 285.

This fact is largely hidden by the use of the word "apocalypse," the original Greek word for revelation. Ernst Käsemann made the famous and controversial statement that "apocalyptic was the mother of all Christian theology."[18] If it were said that "revelation is the mother of all Christian theology," many scholars would take that statement to be self-evident. But, of course, "apocalyptic" has taken on special connotations distinct from "revelation."

The word "apocalypse" was not well known until recently. Historians and biblical scholars did know it well, and Catholics of an earlier generation knew the word as the name of the last book in the New Testament. Beyond the name, the book was hardly ever mentioned and certainly was not studied in school. A 1979 movie with the title *Apocalypse Now* probably had more to do with spreading knowledge of the word "apocalypse" than any piece of writing. Unfortunately, with influence from the movie, the word is now used to refer to total and violent destruction. The apocalypse in the New Testament does include a terrible time of transition, but the "apocalypse" itself refers to the "unveiling" of a new heaven and a new earth. If the movie had not skewed the meaning of the phrase, I could have given this book the title *Apocalypse Now*.

The desire for an apocalypse/revelation now is understandable, even desirable. The danger is that individuals who feel no stake in history and community are left to patch together their own version of a divine revelation from phrases in the Revelation of John, the book of Daniel, and a few other unusual sources. A contemporary scholar has written that "we are arguably in the throes of the most intense period of apocalyptic activity in recent history."[19] Ancient groups that were designated as apocalyptic expected the imminent end of the world and a final separation of good and evil. Contemporary apocalyptic or millenarian groups have a similar mind-set.

The modern secular arrangement that left such groups on their own creates a calm, rational, and well-ordered world—until a splurge of religious violence catches the population by surprise. We find it difficult to understand how there can be such violence in our enlightened world. Events such as the Jonestown massacre or the Branch Davidian violence in Waco, Texas, always come as a big shock. Almost every notorious school massacre has happened in a quiet suburb where the first reaction invariably is: we expect this kind of thing in other places, but not in our neighborhood.

18. Ernst Käsemann, *New Testament Questions of Today* (Philadelphia: Fortress Press, 1969), 102.

19. Michael Barkun, "Politics and Apocalypticism," in *The Encyclopedia of Apocalypticism*, ed. Stephen Stein, 442–60 (New York: Crossroad, 1998), at 442.

Achieving neighborhood or national peace involves more than the condemnation of violence and the exclusion of anyone who seems to be different. It involves social, political, and educational change to correct conditions that lead to violence, including the boredom and malaise that many young people feel. It also involves changes in religious concepts and religious institutions. Central to religious change is making certain that faith is not cut off from reason and that revelation is not left out of history, either as a deposit in the past or as the end of time.

Faith has to be an act of the person, neither controlled by the modern meaning of reason nor an irrational leap beyond all reason. The act of believing has to be directed to what is revelatory of the divine in the ordinary events of history and in artistic expressions of our time. The Christian tradition has a rich storehouse of interpretive tools, but they are not much help without a dialogue between institutions that brings past and present together.

The way faith and revelation are commonly used is an obstacle to any real dialogue. Christian writing makes claims that cannot be supported. A claim that anything finite is "absolute" seems to be idolatrous as well as a roadblock to dialogue. A claim to be "universal" is always premature when it is obvious that at most a potential for universality can be asserted. The claim of "uniqueness" for any person, thing, or event is a claim that can never be met within history (though I will argue in chapter 5 that some claims that something is "more nearly unique" may be defensible and helpful).

The Need of This Age

I repeat again that "believing in a revealing God" is a simple idea, but it means thinking through some phrases and claims that surround the ideas of faith and revelation. Many of these phrases are assumed to be traditional when in fact they are recent accretions that distort the power of the tradition. The process of recovery is not best imagined as stripping off a cover to discover the pure kernel of faith. That metaphor assumes that there is an unchanging core that holds answers for today. There are no fixed answers from the past; every formula needs to be critically examined. A truth from the past may need to be restated in the present simply to preserve the same truth.

No individual is wise enough to engage in such reformation by relying on his or her lights alone. The Christian church needs dialogue within itself as well as beyond itself with other religious institutions. Dialogue sometimes involves vigorous debate, which has not been a notable feature of the church.

Church councils have often excluded opinions that were judged to be outside the boundaries of orthodoxy but might still have been part of a continuing conversation.

The Second Vatican Council as a whole was an attempt to think through faith and revelation. The presence of Protestant observers was a step toward having a future council that would be more genuinely universal and ecumenical. (The almost total absence of women was not so hopeful.) The Catholic bishops, in preparing for the council, quickly discovered the need for expert advisers. Church officials had to listen to the word spoken now before they could make any pronouncements. Some of the advisers were men who had long lived under a shadow of suspicion that they were not quite orthodox.

Pope John XXIII gave a remarkable opening address to the council. Instead of assuming that this gathering was for the purpose of repeating eternal truths, the pope called for a new spirit of openness on the part of the Catholic Church. There has to be, he said, a continuous rereading of Christianity in light of the signs of the times. Before the church can be the teacher of all people, it has to attend to history as the "teacher of life."[20]

It was appropriate that the topic of revelation was taken up immediately at Vatican II. It was also the last topic that was addressed, because the first draft of the document was a disaster. The question of revelation thus served as bookends for the whole work of the council. If the original draft had not been rejected, there is no way to know how the council might have proceeded. The final document—which I will examine in chapter 2—was immeasurably better than the first draft. It is as good a document as was possible under the circumstances, but it is still only a first step toward a radical rethinking of the idea.

The first draft of the document on revelation was framed by the approach taken at the Council of Trent: How many sources of revelation are there? Is revelation contained in Scripture alone or in Scripture and tradition? The nature of revelation itself was not thought to be in need of examination.[21]

A small group of bishops decided to take an early stand on the direction of the council and the documents it would publish to the whole world. A coalition developed, made up of bishops from countries with theological experts and bishops from missionary lands. The two groups did not know

20. Giuseppe Alberigo and others, eds., *Reception of Vatican II* (Washington, DC: Catholic University of America Press, 1988), 332.

21. Joseph Ratzinger, "Commentary on the Constitution on Divine Revelation," in *Commentary on the Documents of Vatican II*, Herbert Vorgrimler, ed., vol. 3, 155–66; 181–98 (New York: Herder & Herder, 1967–69), at 170–71.

what should be said about revelation, but they knew that the document initially proposed would not do.

One of the leaders of this group was Cardinal Joseph Frings of Cologne. He was advised by a young theologian named Joseph Ratzinger. In a later interview Ratzinger, who is now Pope Benedict XVI, referred to his modest role in this event: "When the text on revelation was prepared for discussion, Cardinal Frings—and there, admittedly, I did play a part—explained that the text as it was then worded was not an adequate starting point. It was, he said, necessary to start from the ground up, to rework the document within the council itself."[22]

A majority of the bishops, but not the needed two-thirds, voted to return the document to committee. Fortunately, the pope intervened on the side of the majority; otherwise the will of the majority would have been thwarted from the beginning. The document was in fact returned to committee and underwent radical revision "from the ground up." The resulting document was a great improvement and the final draft received little debate during the last session.

A Look Ahead

Chapters 1 and 2 of this book set out the fundamental ideas of faith and revelation so that their relation constitutes the basis of Christian life. In the first chapter the several meanings of faith in both secular and religious contexts receive attention. The second chapter asks whether or not "revelation" is a term that Christianity is wise to use. "Revelation" needs to be intelligently and effectively articulated or else abandoned.

Chapter 3 examines a central problem in today's church: authority. To some extent the church is simply experiencing a distrust that affects all institutions. The Christian church lays claim to its own special basis of authority. Nonetheless, authority ultimately resides in those who accept it, not those who try to impose it. A pattern of church authority has to be made intelligible to members, drawing on the richness of the tradition while open to the best of modern political reforms.

Chapter 4 considers the moral stance of today's Christian. The Christian life is a response to what Christian tradition offers in dialogue with today's complex moral concerns. People in offices of authority have to create settings in which discussions and debates can occur, so that premature conclusions are avoided.

---

22. Joseph Ratzinger, *Salt of the Earth* (San Francisco: Ignatius Press, 1997), 72.

Chapter 5 places the Christian understanding of faith and revelation in an interreligious context. Muslim and Jewish religions give a prominent place to both faith and revelation. The Christian choice is whether to condemn these two religions as false or else to enter into serious dialogue with them. The benefits of dialogue are an understanding of fellow citizens of the world and a better understanding of Christianity itself.

Chapter 6 develops the theme that particular religious practices can embody a nearly universal meaning. The logic of religion is similar to the way of the arts: that is, particular people, events, and symbols can be revelatory of profound truth. The literature of Jewish, Christian, and Muslim traditions, as well as some modern fiction, exemplifies this principle. The Christian liturgy, in the joining of word and action, embodies a profound understanding of time, body, and power.

Chapter 7 brings all the themes of the book under the aegis of education, understood not as courses in school but as the lifelong journey of response to a divine teacher. Believing in a revealing God can be construed as a form of teaching-learning that begins at birth and continues until death. In a sacramental universe everyone and everything can share in divine teaching. The church needs people thoroughly versed in Christian teachings who can relate those teachings to contemporary situations.

The Christian church is the rich source of spiritual meaning in much of modern ethics and contemporary religious movements. The question is whether this tradition of profound ideas can be made intelligible and relevant to today's problems and possibilities. The Christian ideas of faith and revelation will either be the chief obstacle to dialogue with the contemporary world or else the main foundation to a Christian spiritual life that can give substance and direction to religious searching.

Chapter One

Believing in . . .

This chapter and the following one comprise a single unit. "Believing in a revealing God" contains two distinct but inseparable poles: "believing in" and "revealing God." In order to examine each of the elements it is necessary to break the relation into two parts. However, even while I do that the reader should keep in mind that each side implies the other. While I will make little use in this chapter of the words "reveal," "revealer," "revealing," and "revelation," most of what I say about "believing in" makes sense only in its relation to "a revealing God." The order of the two chapters could be reversed. Neither sequence can entirely avoid the danger that faith and revelation may be understood as two separable things instead of one relation composed of two actions.

My intention is not to state an idiosyncratic position on the use of the terms "faith" and "revelation." Instead, I am trying to point toward a broad and relevant basis of Christian existence today. I am not interested in contradicting church doctrines but in affirming what I take to be the more expansive spirit of these teachings over against some formulas that run counter to that spirit.

The Catechism of the Catholic Church presents a good example of the tension between an expansive spirit and formulas that undermine that intention. The *Catechism* is well structured; the first chapter is on "man's capacity for God" and the second is on revelation. The two concerns are brought together in the third chapter, titled "Man's Response to God." Those chapters are preparation for the main task of a catechism that follows: "The Profession of Christian Faith."

The *Catechism* finds the right context for faith and revelation. Using a reference to Vatican II, it says: "By his Revelation, the invisible God from the fullness of his love, addresses men as his friends, and moves among them in order to invite and receive them into his own company. The adequate response to this invitation is faith."[1] In this passage, God addresses, invites, and receives human beings; their response is faith. The addressing is called "revelation," and the human act of responding is "faith."

Unfortunately, there are many other passages that subvert this clear, compact statement of humans believing in a God who reveals. Revelation is regularly referred to as a thing from the past that is preserved in documents and handed on by church officials, and "faith" is often used interchangeably with that meaning of revelation. The meanings of faith and revelation—believing in a revealing God—cannot be completely developed in catechisms or conciliar documents. These documents can do no more than point toward the communal, liturgical, and moral life in which God reveals/humans respond.

Faith: Its Many Meanings

The term "faith" is more commonly used than "revelation." In secular writing, "faith" is regularly used for anything to do with religion; in church writing, faith is often used where revelation or doctrine would be a more accurate term. Not much progress in understanding is possible if the word is used so indiscriminately. The short, old words in the language—such as person, freedom, love, life, faith—are usually ambiguous. It is their ambiguity that makes them so rich in connotation. The task is not to eliminate the ambiguities but to be aware of them as one uses words to carry an intended meaning.

That task is never entirely successful; a listener or a reader may find meaning in a word that the speaker or writer did not intend. Sometimes the listener or reader has simply misunderstood the spoken or written word. More often the listener or reader picks up on the meaning others have given the term, perhaps in the distant past. Individuals and groups try to control the meaning of what they are saying by defining their terms, but for all the old words, rich in meaning, defining a term is overrated. Nietzsche's comment that "any word that has a history cannot be defined" applies to most words.

The examination of the meaning of words may seem to be an esoteric undertaking, one of interest only to linguists, historians, philosophers, or

---

1. *Catechism of the Catholic Church* (Washington, DC: United States Catholic Conference, 1994), chap. 3, sec. 142. Nicholas Lash, *Theology for Pilgrims* (Notre Dame, IN: University of Notre Dame Press, 2008), 229, says that "the *Catechism*, deplorably, begins not with God but with our 'search' for God." He seems most opposed to the word "search," but starting with some human experience—for example, listening—is more realistic for an educational work than starting with God.

anthropologists. Actually, this question of meaning roots us in ordinary conversation. Writing that deals only in "ideas" without noticing the ambiguity of the words employed is what leads to esoteric studies burdened with four-syllable words ending in -ism or -ity. To attend to the meaning of our words requires us to notice that other people are using the same words but with different meanings. Individuals or groups can wall themselves in and insist that they have the right meaning and other people are wrong. The alternative, which admittedly has risks, is to listen to a wide range of voices in the past and present that challenge one's assumptions. One need not abandon the meaning one has been holding on to, but one might discover a more comprehensive and consistent meaning.

The word "faith" is one of those old and simple-looking words that are extraordinarily complex in meaning. If one quickly skips over that fact it is possible to use "faith" within a carefully blocked-off area of life. The use of some theological terms in this manner is not a problem. If terms such as eschatology, mystagogy, pneumatology, or soteriology are used exclusively by students of Christian theology, the words may serve a useful if limited purpose. Every profession invents terms that are of interest only to the practitioner of the profession. Some of the technical language is undoubtedly necessary for the smooth working of the profession, even if one might suspect that other terms have the purpose indicated by a character in a G. B. Shaw play who says: "Every profession is a conspiracy against the laity."[2]

Technical language may be needed in Christian theology, but the Christian life has to have roots in ordinary language. There are border terms that link the whole of Christianity to other religions and to the secular world. If one does not explore the religious and secular meanings of words such as "faith," "spirit," "forgive," "hope," and a few dozen other such terms, the Christian religion will not be intelligible to the non-Christian world. Even more important, Christian doctrine and practice will have a very limited effect within Christian lives.

An inherent weakness or limitation of church documents, including conciliar documents, is an assumption that church leaders are in charge of the language they are using. For the intramural terms the assumption works, at least to a high degree. But for key terms that have ordinary secular meanings the assumption that one can simply stipulate a Christian meaning is an illusion. The First Vatican Council published a document that declared the meaning of faith and included a chapter on revelation. The Second Vatican Council published a document in which bishops with the help of biblical

---

2. George Bernard Shaw, *The Doctor's Dilemma* (New York: Echo Library, 2006).

and theological scholars pronounced the meaning of revelation. They also assumed a meaning of faith without directly addressing it.

Both Catholic and Protestant uses of "faith" are inextricably tied to contemporary secular meanings of the term. There is no fixed starting point for sorting out these meanings. Referring to our use of ordinary language, Hanna Pitkin writes that "we are like fishermen who can never put into port to fix their nets."[3] The Christian tradition does have one fixed point of reference in the books of the Bible. It might seem that all we need is an expert in Hebrew and Greek to determine a Christian meaning of "faith." And indeed, translators and exegetes are indispensable for Christian doctrine.

There remains the intractable problem of controlling the meaning of today's words. Is it clear that the meaning of a Greek or Hebrew word translated by the word "faith" is adequately conveyed by that contemporary English word? That is not a question solely for experts in ancient languages; it is a question about contemporary connotations of "faith" in secular as well as religious uses. Even if there is consensus that "faith" is the best translation of both a Hebrew and a Greek word, one should not forget that some of the connotations of "faith" capture well what Jesus, Paul, Amos, or Jeremiah intended; some connotations are less successful and possibly misleading.

What can we say then of "faith" as used in past and present, in secular and religious contexts? A first thing to note is that the English word "faith" is a noun, the name of something. In the Bible the word or words translated as faith are usually verbs. Faith refers to doing or acting. Although verbs becoming nouns is a frequent occurrence, this fact about "faith" poses a sizable problem and is a constant diversion from a Christian use of "faith." James Fowler, in his writing on "faith development," suggested we invent the verb "faithing" as a verb, but awkward inventions of words seldom succeed.[4]

What we do have in the English language is the verb "to believe," which is closely related to "faith." That solves one problem while it introduces another. There are actually two verbs "to believe": "believe that" and "believe in." In the first case, "believing that" has for an object a belief. Someone might say "I believe that virtue is its own reward." Here, the object of believing that something is true is a belief in the form of a proposition, namely, "virtue is its own reward." It is a daily, even hourly, occurrence for each of us to express a belief—that is, to hold that something is the case even though

---

3. Hanna Pitkin, *Wittgenstein and Justice* (Berkeley, CA: University of California Press, 1972), 297.

4. James Fowler, *Faith Development* (San Francisco: Harper, 1981).

we do not have firsthand knowledge of the matter. Given this frequent use of believe and belief, it may seem logical to assume that faith is just another word for belief or perhaps a general noun for the totality of one's beliefs.

There is, however, a second verb of believing: "to believe in." This meaning of believing is especially important for Christian use but is not exclusive to Christian or religious contexts. The verb "believe that" has an object—that is, facts, statements, or propositions held to be true. But the verb "believe in" does not have an object. What most often follows this verb is a person, cause, or symbol. Both of the verbs, believe in and believe that, are closely related to the noun "faith," but it is crucial to note the difference between faith as the holding of beliefs as true and faith as believing in someone or some cause. The ambiguity has been there at least since early in Christian history. The English language cannot eliminate the ambiguity, but it does have the resources to work with the diversity of meaning.

The early church in confessing *credo in unum deum* was not stating a belief that there is one God. It was shaping a Latin usage that had echoes of both Hebrew and Greek words. "*Credo* in" or "believe in" was directed toward a person as expressive of a trusting relation. Believing in a person includes that one is strongly inclined to believe what that person says. But to reduce faith to the act of holding statements as true is to miss the context that makes beliefs intelligible. Faith can include belief(s), but belief is not an adequate synonym for faith. The somewhat mysterious act of "believing in" someone or something needs more exploring. For the present, simply recognizing that there is an ambiguity in faith's relation to "believe that," "believe in," "belief," and "beliefs" provides a first step.

An Example of "believe that" and "believe in"

To illustrate how these words are used when neither religious nor secular context is specified, I use a book of eighty essays titled *This I Believe*.[5] The authors, some famous and some not, were asked to respond in a few hundred words to "this I believe." The collection of essays published in 2007 included some in response to a similarly worded invitation in the 1950s. Some of the authors took the question to be a religious one; most did not. About half of them answered by saying what they believe in; the other half expressed their beliefs—that is, they stated things they hold to be true.

The people who answered by saying who or what they believe in were much more succinct in their answers. Most of these answers were not

---

5. Jay Allison and Dan Gediman, eds., *This I Believe* (New York: Holt, 2007).

religious, although the boundary between religious and nonreligious meanings is sometimes unclear. Only one of the eighty essays begins "I believe in God." The author, John Fountain, quickly adds: "Not that cosmic, intangible, spirit-in-the-sky that Mama told me as a little boy 'always was and always will be.'" Despite distancing himself from what his mother had taught him, the author later says, "I believe in God, God the Father, embodied in his Son Jesus Christ."

The other authors who express "believing in" direct their attitude to a wildly diverse array of people, causes, and symbols. What each person cites in a single word is for him or her an all-embracing concern or powerful symbol about the whole of life. Here is a sample of what or who this group of individuals said they believe in: people, my mother, the sun, jazz, barbecue, the subway, politics, life, liberty. Some of those answers may seem trivial, but for the individual the choice is a lens through which all reality is grasped.

The other authors, who interpreted the question as asking for one's beliefs, were much less compact in their answers. Some of them, for example, Eleanor Roosevelt, express frustration at having such a limited space in which to cover what one believes. Here is a sample of their beliefs—that is, a proposition the author believed to be true: that everyone deserves flowers on their grave; that what we often call survival skills is simply creativity at work; that it is possible for ordinary people to achieve extraordinary things; that religious faith will continue to be an essential part of being human.

That last example, by novelist and critic John Updike, may seem to be a religious statement, but its religious character is doubtful. Believing that religious faith will continue does not require any exercise of religious faith; it is the usual stuff of sociology or anthropology. Some authors do not formulate what they believe. Thomas Mann begins with the statement: "What I believe, what I value most, is transitoriness." If one removes the phrase "what I value most," it is obvious that he does not have a statement of what he believes. Perhaps he means that he believes *in* transitoriness, though that would be a peculiar reality to put one's trust in.

One author, Penn Gillette, begins: "I believe that there is no God." That statement may seem to be the opposite of saying "I believe in God." But it is really the opposite of the speculative proposition "I believe that there is a god." Gillette is compelled to insist that there is no god, no gods, nothing that might get the name god. The reason for his insistence that there is no such being as God is found in the essay's conclusion: "Believing there is no god gives me more room for belief in family, people, love, truth, beauty, sex, Jell-O and all the other things I can prove and that make this life the best life I will ever have." He has placed *believe that* there is no god in opposition to *believing in* family, love, beauty, and so forth. His list includes just the kind of concrete realities the believer in God might also cite.

My intention in distinguishing the several meanings of "faith" is not to find the true meaning of the term and declare the others false. "Faith" used in both religious and secular contexts has those meanings. No one, not even the Christian church, can legislate one meaning. The ambiguity of a word becomes a problem when statements conflict with one another because the speaker is drawing on different meanings of the word while being unaware of how the meanings are related. Unfortunately, this problem regularly affects church documents when they use the word faith.

I advocate a pattern of usage that would draw out the full richness of the word and lead to effective practical results. The metaphor I suggest for handling the diversity is drawn from the theater. I advocate that one meaning be brought to center stage and other meanings be moved to the wings. The multiple meanings remain, but with a difference of importance and emphasis. It is not a matter of simply stating the case, but of individuals and institutions using that pattern consistently over a long period of time. In the church's history such changes can take centuries, though with our speeded-up means of communication some fundamental changes may now take only decades.

Christian Uses of "Faith"

How to use the word "faith" is not a new problem for the Christian church. From the first years of its existence it staked its claim on faith. But while the word has a central role in the Synoptic Gospels, the Fourth Gospel, and the letters of Paul, there are considerable differences in what the word means in those different sources. I note again that a range of meanings is not a bad thing so long as differences are acknowledged and the meanings are held in a fruitful tension.

The preaching of Jesus in the Synoptic Gospels draws on the religious meaning of the Hebrew Scriptures, in which "faith" is mainly about trusting in and relying on God. The true is the sure and the steady.[6] Faith—the act of turning over one's life to God—requires a conversion of the whole self.[7] Our English word "amen" has its origin in the Hebrew word for faith. Saying "faith" is saying "amen" or "yes": with one's life.

---

6. Thorlief Boman, *Hebrew Thought Compared with Greek* (New York: W. W. Norton, 1960), 202.

7. Martin Buber, *Two Types of Faith* (New York: Harper Torchbooks, 1961), 26.

The letters of Paul and subsequently the Fourth Gospel give a decided twist to this simple act of trusting in God. A more complex description was perhaps inevitable as the Jesus movement spread out in place and time. Jesus, as the Christ, was now the preached not the preacher; Jesus did not replace God but became the way to God.

A fundamental change happened simply by the use of Greek, which, in Paul's day and even today, is the source of philosophical vocabulary. Paul's use of the word *pistis* was a daring challenge to philosophy. Plato had used the term to refer to an inferior kind of knowledge, or rather what is merely opinion, not real knowledge. For Plato and most of Greek philosophy the truth is what I see, what comes out of the darkness and into the light; to them, knowing is a visual metaphor.

Paul tried to reverse the relation of knowledge and faith, claiming a superiority for faith. In the Pauline world seeing the truth can only take place within the activity of believing in. Faith now involved oral and tactile metaphors as well as visual. Faith comes by hearing and by touching the truth.

Like any attempt to single-handedly turn key terms upside down, Paul's could only be partially successful. He introduced new possibilities within the word "faith," but the former meaning continued on its way in the church and elsewhere. For two thousand years the Christian church has continued to struggle with the complex meaning of faith the New Testament introduced.

What adds to the complication is that Paul did not write an essay on faith. He wrote letters to a variety of people in diverse circumstances, emphasizing different aspects of faith according to what he saw as strengths and weaknesses in the people he was addressing. It is possible to quote Paul as saying that faith is what the philosophers had said it was, namely, holding statements as true on the basis of someone else's testimony.

A Christian meaning of faith, however, cannot be based on isolated texts of Paul. While his letters brought out particular beliefs, they were set within a "believing in Christ." While the result of his writing was an emphasis on the individual, he did not deny the corporate character of the church. Jewish writers have been particularly hard on Paul for inventing a new religion. The relation of Christian religion to ancient Jewish religion has always been a central question for the church.

By the early years of the church the word "faith" had the complex set of meanings it continues to have. Not surprisingly, people who are not Christian may think that faith still means secondhand opinion, even though the word is used otherwise in plenty of secular writing. Christians often do not make their own case well when they overuse "faith" or inappropriately use "faith" as a general noun.

E. R. Dodds points out that if a second-century pagan had been asked the difference between paganism and Christianity he would have said that Christianity, while having many virtues, lacked that of intellectual insight. Drawing on the Greek philosophical meaning of "faith," the pagan would have thought of Christianity as a set of beliefs or opinions.[8] Critics, such as Galen and Celsus, saw the issue as a simple choice between "blind faith" and "sober reason."[9]

Augustine of Hippo was the most influential writer in shaping the Latin language's use of "faith." His distinctions are still evident in today's English. Augustine used the verb *credere* for distinguishing three meanings of faith. The primary or central meaning for Augustine is *credere in Deum*, to believe in God. "What is it therefore to believe in him, *credere in eum*? It is believing to love, to delight, in believing to walk toward him, and be incorporated amongst the limbs or members of his body."[10] Augustine acknowledges two other uses of *credere*. One of these, *credere Deo*, believing what God says, is clearly embraced by the basic meaning of believing in God. Augustine's third meaning, *credere Deum*, is believing God to be God.

In Thomas Aquinas's commentary on Augustine's three meanings of faith he says that the three constitute a single act, not three different acts.[11] The act of believing in always involves something we hold to as a belief. While the unity of those elements is an important principle that remains significant to this day, the third element—believing that there is a God—became split off at the beginning of modern times. For Augustine, Aquinas, and most of the Middle Ages, God was not a proposition for belief. The reality of God was simply implied in the act of believing in God and what God reveals.

In modern times the word faith is often reduced to Augustine's third meaning. Faith is taken to mean believing that a being called God exists. Such a meaning of faith is not what Christian life is based on. There is probably no religious group that begins by asking whether God exists. As Martin Buber says, for anyone who asks that question in the absence of all experience, the answer has to be "no."[12]

8. E. R. Dodds, *Pagan and Christian in an Age of Anxiety* (Cambridge: Cambridge University Press, 1990), 120.

9. John Gager, *Kingdom and Community* (Englewood Cliffs, NJ: Prentice Hall, 1975), 118.

10. Augustine as cited in Nicholas Lash, *Believing Three Ways in One God* (Notre Dame, IN: University of Notre Dame Press, 1993), 20; Augustine, *Commentary on the Psalms,* 77, 8.

11. Thomas Aquinas, *Summa Theologiae* II-II, q. 2, a. 2, ad. 1.

12. Martin Buber, *The Eclipse of God* (New York: Harper, 1959), 44.

While the verb "believe that" is directed to a belief, the verb "believe in" is an attitude of openness and trust. There is no way to state an object for such believing in, which is directed to All/Nothing. Even God as the name of one thing among many is not the object of believing in. Buber notes that the absence of "God" after "believe in" is not just a permissible omission of a word that is assumed. The word "God" can limit the act of believing in to what is thought to be an object. The New Testament often uses the word faith without an object.[13]

Christians do not believe in a being named God; they direct their prayers to "the Father of Our Lord and Savior Jesus Christ." That is, the All/Nothing finds expression in very particular and concrete symbols. No language can completely capture a God who is revealed everywhere. The religious act of believing in finds the revealing God in any and every particularity. "First," wrote Rainer Maria Rilke, "you must find God somewhere, experience him as infinitely, prodigiously, stupendously present—then whether it be fear or astonishment or breathlessness, whether it be in the end Love with which you comprehend him, it hardly matters at all."[14]

Believing in a revealing God is an act of the whole person, not just a conclusion of the rational intellect. "Persons influence us, voices melt us, looks subdue us, deeds inflame us . . . no man will be a martyr for a conclusion."[15] Sometimes the act of faith or believing in is described as a leap beyond reason. That metaphor can suggest a closing of one's eyes and an irrational act of will and emotion. A more accurate image is that the believer opens his or her soul to a wider and deeper reality than concepts can ever encompass. It is an *intellectual* act deeper than reason. The human partner is not a disinterested observer, waiting for God to supply proofs, but someone attentive to the word spoken now.

The person who is not a religious believer has not necessarily rejected believing in. Much of the moral failing in the world is simply due to inattention. As Gabriel Marcel argued, conditions of modern life almost compel our inattention. What is most important in life can easily be swallowed by trivial details of ordinary life. Believing requires an act of volition. In this

---

13. W. Cantwell Smith, *Faith and Belief* (Princeton, NJ: Princeton University Press, 1979), 101–2.

14. Rainer Maria Rilke as quoted in Gabriel Marcel, *Homo Viator* (Chicago: Regnery, 1951), 222.

15. John Henry Newman, *An Essay in Aid of a Grammar of Assent* (Garden City, NY: Image Books, 1960), 89.

sense, hope and love are presupposed by faith. "Through faith the intellect apprehends what it hopes for and loves."[16]

The act of faith does not put the mind to rest. On the contrary, there remains "a searching of that which it believes—although it nevertheless assents to what is believed with the utmost firmness."[17] The person who has opened his or her soul to the whole of truth expects that there will always be more to know, since one cannot know the whole.[18] If faith were directed to something deposited in the past, the believer would know exactly what was required. Believing in a revealing God is a daily activity that leads to unpredictable consequences in the believer's life.

This central meaning of faith is obscured when church documents fail to distinguish between faith and its expressions, confessions, articulations, testimonies, and so on. A typical passage in the *Catechism* says: "The Church, 'the pillar and bulwark of the truth' faithfully guards 'the faith which was once for all delivered to the saints.' She guards the memory of Christ's words; it is she who from generation to generation hands on the apostles' confession of faith."[19]

The second sentence in this quotation states exactly what has been handed on from the beginning: "the apostles' confession of faith." The first sentence uses a traditional phrase that is misleading if taken literally. The faith could not be delivered once for all to the saints. Each of us has to do our own believing while surrounded by the company of saints. The individual and the whole church today "believe in" through the interpretive lens of the apostles' confession of faith. That confession or testimony is what is faithfully handed on across the generations and is indispensable for Christian life.

A tendency to refer to "Christian faith" when what is at issue is Catholic doctrine has the effect of giving certainty to church pronouncements that should be open to debate and are subject to error. The believer can be confident of the central teachings of the church, but not every doctrine is stamped with infallibility. Even those doctrines that are true leave out more truth than they can include. A person ought not to be called lacking in faith because he or she cannot accept one or several doctrines of the church. Believing in a revealing God has to be worked out in the course of a person's life. The

16. Thomas Aquinas, *Summa Theologiae* I, q. 2, a. 62, ad. 4.
17. Thomas Aquinas, *De Veritate*, 14, 1.
18. Josef Pieper, *Faith, Hope, Love* (San Francisco: Ignatius Press, 1997), 64.
19. *Catechism of the Catholic Church*, chap. 3, sec. 171.

person whose personal judgment is needed to be a Christian does not abandon that judgment when there is a question of an individual belief.[20]

One thing the Bible and Hellenistic philosophy agreed on was that faith is
an interior movement, an activity on the part of the believer. For the Greeks
it was a movement of the mind to acquire opinions that are something less
than real knowledge. For the Jews it was an interior movement of placing trust
in the God of the covenant. In neither case could one speak of a multiplicity
of faiths. In the Bible the opposite of faith is idolatry, which is a fraudulent
faith. To believe in an idol was to mistake a creature for the creator.

When the New Testament identified Jesus as Christ and Lord it seemed
to many Jews (and later to Muslims) that faith in God had been diluted. The
Christians seemed to be confusing a great prophet with the creator of the
universe. The Christian church tried to avoid idolatry by a series of careful
distinctions that resulted in the two central doctrines of the Incarnation and
the Trinity. Thomas Aquinas notes that the whole of Christian faith can be
summed up in these two doctrines. The complicated language of these beliefs
puzzles outsiders, and indeed, many Christians have found it nearly impossible to understand their significance. Mary Perkins Ryan used to say that
the success of a Christian education should be measured by how a Christian's
belief in the Trinity influences his or her behavior in the subway.

How Faith Has Fared

The Christian church's educational efforts have never caught up to the
needs of masses of converts. For tens of millions of Christians their religion
was a simple story: God appeared on earth, told us what to do, and after
mysteriously dying for our sins, returned to heaven. In this picture Jesus is
God, and the New Testament is God's word or words. Faith then found
concrete expression in the doctrines or beliefs surrounding God's appearance. By the second century the word "faith" was used for this set of beliefs
"which was once for all delivered to the saints." The act of believing in was
not eliminated, but it was obscured by the act of accepting "the faith," a
name for the teachings of the church's officials.

The great thinkers among the fathers of the church did not reduce faith
either to accepting church beliefs or to the beliefs themselves. Thomas
Aquinas followed Augustine's analysis of faith as believing in God revealed
in Christ. The theological virtue of faith is the activity that underlies the

---

20. Karl Rahner, "The Dispute concerning the Teaching Office of the Church," in *The
Magisterium and Morality*, ed. Charles Curran and Richard McCormick, 113–28 (New York:
Paulist Press, 1982).

whole of Christian life. "Things of faith," said Thomas, "are not proposed in themselves but by certain words and likenesses which fall short of expressing or representing them; consequently they are said to be known as through a mirror."[21] That sophisticated meaning of faith implies a need for education, but an education of all Christians remained a problem. By the late Middle Ages the church and its practices of faith were badly in need of reform.

Martin Luther initiated reform by clearing the ground of many superstitions and returning to the biblical source. One of his powerful cries was "faith alone" as the basis of salvation. It was the right word at the right time, even though sixteenth-century reformers lacked some of the resources for finding a full meaning of faith. Luther's great strength was the interiorizing of faith, a return to the primacy of faith as believing in. "My life has become addressed by the unconditional affirmation that not myself but my relationship to him constitutes the reason for living. I now live by 'faith alone.' "[22]

There was a danger in thinking of faith as an individual act without reference to the "we believe" of the community. In trying to purify the church, Luther accompanied his "faith alone" with the motto of "scripture alone." It was the right communal source for a Christian expression of faith. For Luther, faith would be expressed as a response to the preaching of the "word of God"; the individual "believing in" was nestled within the community.

Luther did not assume each individual sitting at home with his or her Bible. The printing press, invented just before Luther's reform movement began, had contrasting effects. It made possible a widespread knowledge of the Christian Scriptures and challenged the existing pattern of church authority. But the availability of the Bible also unleashed rebellions against the control of reform, as Luther himself eventually found. There was a tendency to think that the Bible contained "the faith." The preached word of God tended to become the printed words of God.

Luther took his lead on justification by faith from Paul's letter to the Romans. That was not a bad beginning, but it needs a larger context. Luther was aggressively antiphilosophical in trying to pierce through the desiccated concepts of late Scholastic philosophy, but faith as an idea in the modern era cannot completely escape philosophical questions.

In addition, Luther's reading of Paul created a sharp dichotomy between Jewish and Christian religions. Luther's third cry of "grace alone" implied a

21. Thomas Aquinas, *Commentary on the Sentences of Peter Lombard*, 24.1.

22. Eric Gritsch, *Martin Luther: God's Court Jester* (Philadelphia: Fortress Press, 1983), 170.

negative attitude to the "legalism" of the Jews. One might think that Luther's return to "scripture alone" and "faith alone" would have led to a revised understanding of the relation between Jews and Christians, siblings born of the same mother. Unfortunately, Luther failed badly on this central test of a Christian understanding of faith. Not that he was alone: the Catholic counter to the Protestant reform did not have a better understanding of the relation of Christian and Jewish religions, but it would be centuries before any serious conversation would take place between Christians and Jews. Even today that rethinking is still at an early stage.

The use of the word "faith" in the modern era has suffered from the opposition between Catholic and Protestant approaches. The Christian church needed a united front—together with the help of Judaism—as it wrestled with the claims of the new sciences. Instead, Catholic-Protestant controversy over faith and the "sources of revelation" weakened both parties in the face of the real challenge of modernity.

Protestant language did succeed in individualizing and interiorizing the meaning of faith. For sustaining that faith, the believer had the word of God. This language had the virtue of simplicity and it provided a powerful support for the Christian life. From the beginning Protestantism was suspicious of the word "religion," a name for external trappings of belief. Faith in the word of God seemed at odds with the elaborate belief system the Roman Catholic Church continued to maintain. A contrast of "Protestant faith" and "Catholic religion" seemed accurately descriptive on both sides.

The Catholic Church, of course, did not abandon "believe in," but it was resistant to emphasis on the individual's faith, except as a gift of the church. The result was that "the faith" became shorthand for the whole complex of church beliefs and practices. As Vatican II's Decree on Ecumenism (11) acknowledged, there is a hierarchy of Christian beliefs; some of those beliefs are very central to faith, while others are quite peripheral. In ordinary practice "the faith" was a mixture of many things, some of them a distraction from what is important about believing in.

The Catholic Church in recent decades, without adopting the formulas "faith alone" and "scripture alone," has emphasized faith as the individual's act of believing and Scripture as the chief testimony of faith the church relies on. Language changes slowly, and the Catholic Church is still burdened with formulas of faith and of revelation that interfere with a more intellectually stimulating and practically effective understanding of faith.

In the Middle Ages, especially after the tenth century, a distinction between natural and supernatural emerged. Far from trying to add a second story to the more obvious natural world, the language developed in order to affirm the relative independence of the natural within a supernatural world.[23] However, by the beginning of modern times, as a world of "nature" came under scientific scrutiny and control, a world of super-nature was left to those who wished to believe that there was a world above nature.

Faith and Reason

The key contrast for the modern idea of faith has been between faith and reason. In ancient philosophy and in some modern philosophy "reason" has a very comprehensive meaning and can even refer to the structure of the universe as a whole. In modern scientific thought "reason" tends to be located inside the human mind. It refers to the power to gather facts and to use that data to draw conclusions about the world. As such, it tends to lay claim to all that can be humanly known. "Science," a word meaning knowledge, has become equated with thinking that is in accord with facts known through the scientific method and arranged by the logic of mathematics.

A defense of faith within that context is a nearly impossible undertaking. A word's meaning can be grasped by asking what its opposite is. In this case, faith means "not reason," a nonrational or irrational way of trying to know the world. Faith gets directed to a special or supernatural revelation outside the "natural" flow of information and thinking that is available to everyone. Some people are comfortable with this restricted realm, but it has tended to shrink over time. Faith and reason in competition meant that an advance in science was a retreat for faith.

Reason set against faith was not healthy for either reason or faith. Faith was left as a nonrational or irrational claim to knowledge with no support outside itself. Reason, after dismissing faith as a fraudulent claim, was burdened with the responsibility for all knowledge (science). At the beginning of modern science its dependence on a believing-in attitude could remain hidden. Alfred North Whitehead notes that "the Middle Ages formed one long training of the intellect of Western Europe in the sense of order." Every detail in that order, Whitehead continues, implies the "rationality of God." Thus "faith in the possibility of science . . . is an unconscious derivative from medieval theology."[24] Faith in God was replaced by faith in man,

---

23. Marie-Dominique Chenu, *Nature, Man and Society in the Twelfth Century* (Toronto: University of Toronto Press, 1997); Lynn White, Jr., *Medieval Religion and Technology* (Berkeley, CA: University of California Press, 1986).

24. Alfred North Whitehead, *Science and the Modern World* (New York: Free Press), 17, 19.

faith in science, and faith in the created order. In Christian terms, believing in those symbols was not bad, but the danger was that faith in the creator had been shortened to faith in the creation.

The denial of faith in the name of reason was experienced as liberating. It wonderfully concentrated the mind on the solution of short-term problems by the gathering of hard data. The seventeenth and eighteenth centuries showed a new confidence in the power of "man" to control "nature." Pope Benedict XVI connects the idea of faith in progress with the seventeenth-century philosopher Francis Bacon.[25] As the pope argues, there is nothing within science itself that guarantees progress. Bacon was still influenced by a Christian view of history as having three stages: a paradise lost, a history in conflict, and a paradise reestablished. For Bacon, however, the future paradise will come about through "man's conquest of nature." Ironically, this language of human over nature is now an accusation made against Christianity in the context of ecological problems, even though that language was only invented in the seventeenth century.[26]

Despite the obvious successes of science, some doubts in the true faith of scientific progress began to arise in the nineteenth century. Faith in the power of humanity to perfect the world received further jolts in the twentieth century. When these doubts arose as to the supreme power of human reason, faith was not seen as an alternative. Beyond reason there was only an irrational and violent disorder. Friedrich Nietzsche, a harbinger of the twentieth century, explored the irrational roots of human reason. Instead of the limits of reason leading him back to a Christian outlook, Nietzsche says in *The Anti-Christ*: " 'Faith' simply means the refusal to know what is true."[27]

Some thinkers, beginning in the late nineteenth century, did try to rethink the relation between faith, understood as "believing in," and reason. The United States trailed Europe in the creation of grand systems, like that of Hegel's, in which the real is rational. But the practical bent of U.S. philosophy and a continuing religious environment led to an acknowledgment by some writers that our rational knowledge always has a context of bodiliness, emotion, culture, and personal attitude, all of which can be linked to "believ-

---

25. Pope Benedict XVI, encyclical *Spe Salvi* (November 30, 2007), sec. 17; see http://www.vatican.va/holy_father/benedict_xvi/encyclicals/documents/hf_ben-xvi_enc_20071130_spe-salvi_en.html.

26. Lynn White, Jr. "The Historical Roots of Our Ecological Crisis," *Science* (March 10, 1967): 1203–7.

27. Friedrich Nietzsche, *The Anti-Christ* (New York: Penguin, 1990), 205.

ing in." Charles Sanders Peirce, an influential logician and philosopher of language, posited that logic requires faith, hope, and charity.[28]

One of Peirce's successors was John Dewey, generally regarded as the leading philosopher in U.S. history. Dewey thought that facts should be seen as a case of belief. He was haunted by the need for a religious faith even as he distanced himself from his church upbringing. In 1930 he attempted to lay out the basis for what he called *A Common Faith*.[29] Partly due to Dewey's antichurch bias, which prevented his drawing from a rich Christian source, the book is shallow in its treatment of faith, and still more of religion. Nevertheless, Dewey's book is symptomatic of what became a spreading concern for the nonrational contexts and roots of scientific order. Twentieth-century philosophy, as well as psychology, sociology, and anthropology were forced to grapple with this question of believing in. "Nobody wants everybody not to believe in anything."[30]

The Christian church does not have an answer, but it could be a chastened partner in a conversation about where the world goes now. The church does not help itself by arrogantly assuming that it owns the word "faith" and by carelessly using the word where it does not belong. Faith as an act of believing in is simply a human necessity, a fact that would find widespread agreement if "faith" were not constantly used for a collection of beliefs that is assumed to be a synonym for religion. One of the many aggressively atheist books recently published is titled *The End of Faith*.[31] That is an inaccurate title for what amounts to an attack on religion. There is no sign of a disappearance of faith in its many forms.

The current problem of language is reflected in a controversy at Harvard University over the revision of the college's curriculum. A committee proposed a course called "Faith and Reason." A well-known professor and committee member, Steven Pinker, hotly attacked the proposal.[32] He wrote: "The juxtaposition of the two words makes it sound like 'faith' and 'reason' are parallel and equivalent ways of knowing, and we have to help students navigate between them. But universities are about reason, pure and simple.

28. Charles S. Peirce, *Writings of Charles S. Peirce* (Bloomington: Indiana University Press, 1982), 2:264–65.

29. John Dewey, *A Common Faith* (New Haven: Yale University Press, 1930).

30. Alexander Bickel, *The Morality of Consent* (New Haven: Yale University Press, 1975), 25.

31. Sam Harris, *The End of Faith* (New York: Norton, 2007).

32. Steven Pinker, "Less Faith, More Reason," *The Harvard Crimson*, October 27, 2006. Available at http://www.thecrimson.com/article.aspx?ref=515314.

Faith—believing something without good reasons to do so—has no place in anything but a religious institution, and our society has no shortage of these."

Pinker's definition of faith—"believing something without good reason to do so"—is particularly arrogant and ill-informed. And would that reason *were* a "pure and simple" alternative to believing things true without good reason. Pinker does make some good points. Reason and faith are not parallel ways of knowing, and as he says elsewhere in his essay, the committee really wanted a course on religion but it thought "faith" sounded like a more acceptable word. Pinker is opposed to a religion course, but at least a discussion of whether Harvard students should study religion—a study that does occur in numerous universities—would be on the right topic. The committee subsequently changed the name of the course to Culture and Belief, arguably an improvement but perhaps still an evasion of the question of a course on religion as that reality is found in history and in the lives of students.

Christian writers of the past and present are not the cause of today's intellectuals being ignorant of the meaning of faith, but they are a contributing factor. Early in the modern era Christian writers were all too ready to accept a place for faith as a private set of beliefs. Faith was reduced to the acceptance of "revealed truths." A series of British, French, and German thinkers provided the language of faith/revelation that affected Christian theology. One of the most prominent and influential of these writers, John Locke, wrote: "Faith is the assent to any proposition not thus made out by the deductions of reason but upon the credit of the proposer as coming from God in some extraordinary way of communication." Locke then linked this meaning of faith to a correlative meaning of revelation: "This way of discovering truths to men we call revelation."[33]

Within such a use of "faith" anyone was free to believe that such propositions were sent down by God, but there was no intrinsic connection between such faith and public life. In contrast, as Nicholas Lash points out, "believing in God" cannot be a private affair; it "requires comprehensive interest and engagement in questions of culture, politics and ecology."[34] But as Lash notes, "By the end of the seventeenth century, 'believing in God,' which for Augustine and Aquinas had been a matter of setting as our heart's desire the holy mystery disclosed in Christ toward whose blinding presence we walk

---

33. John Locke, *An Essay Concerning Human Understanding* (Los Angeles: Pomona, 2007), Book 4, chap. 18, par. 2; see also his *Reasonableness of Christianity* (Stanford, CA: Stanford University Press, 1958).

34. Nicholas Lash, *Believing Three Ways in One God*, 22.

in company on pilgrimage, had become a matter of supposing that there is, outside the world we know, a large and powerful entity called 'God.'"[35]

The attempts in recent decades to reappropriate that "heart's desire of blinding presence and company on pilgrimage" have often been timid and uncertain. The Catholic *Catechism*, in a section called "faith and science," unwisely cites Vatican I: "Though faith is above reason, there can never be any discrepancy between faith and reason."[36] This statement is unhelpful. It is true that faith as "believing in" does not conflict with reason, because the two do not compete. However, faith as beliefs, a regular usage in church documents, has constant conflicts with reason and is often shown to be wrong. What is most distressing here is locating faith *above* reason.

There is perhaps some atavistic tendency in human beings to assume that higher is better. Especially in morality and religion the movement upward is a tantalizing but misleading attraction. It leads to what Charles Taylor calls "excarnation," a religion above mere time, body, and community.[37] Moral development, as Maria Harris said, is better imagined as steps in a dance rather than steps up a ladder.[38] Similarly in religion, development ought to be circles inside of circles rather than going upward.

Spatial metaphors in religion are problematic but unavoidable. Praying to a God who is above in heaven is obviously a limited image given what we know of space. It is a harmless image provided we do not forget that God is in front, behind, underneath, and within. Saying that faith is above reason might seem harmless except for the modern history of the word, in which religious "propositions" sit above the rest of life.

If any spatial direction is attributed to "believing in," a location *above* reason is the most misleading. It can be argued that "believing in" is before reason in the sense of presupposition, or below reason in being a foundation, or in front of reason as ultimate purpose. No metaphorical direction need be totally excluded so long as one realizes that we are speaking metaphorically. A person who says that faith, as the most important aspect of his or her life, is higher in value than any other concern should be respected. That personal formula should not be equated with church pronouncements that speak of faith as a collection of truths above reason.

35. Nicholas Lash, *The Beginning and End of Religion* (Cambridge: Cambridge University Press, 1996), 169.

36. *Catechism of the Catholic Church*, chap. 3, sec. 159.

37. Charles Taylor, *The Secular Age* (Cambridge, MA: Belknap Press, 2007).

38. Maria Harris, *Dance of the Spirit* (New York: Bantam Press, 1989).

Reforming "Faith"

The reform of "faith" referred to here is not the reality of faith in people's lives but how the word faith should be used. Re-form presupposes an existing form. It is based on respect for the past and an appreciation of the many possibilities suggested in a detailed knowledge of the past. True reform is not an attempt to overthrow the past or to propose something radically novel. For an effective Christian use of the term, the proposed use needs support from the Bible, the early church writers, and the great saints and thinkers throughout the ages. The work does not belong exclusively to famous writers, church councils, and theological experts. The lives of ordinary people—hundreds of millions of them—are an indispensable source of reflection on how to speak about "faith."

What is the "content" of faith? A question about the "content" of interpersonal relations would be somewhat peculiar. In deep friendship or love between human beings, their two lives might be called the content of the relation, but there is no list of truths that the individuals themselves or an outside examiner could specify as the content of their love. Similarly with a religious idea of faith, Joseph Ratzinger writes: "In its core, Christian faith is an encounter with the living God. God is, in the proper and ultimate sense, the content of our faith. Looked at this way, the content of faith is absolutely simple: I believe in God."[39]

In saying that the content of faith is simply believing in God, the present pope is not denying the necessity or value of beliefs. Believing in is always accompanied by beliefs. But beliefs that issue from and provide guidance for believing in are not best described as "the content of faith." Beliefs are not what I believe in. Rather, the whole complex of Christian beliefs is the always inadequate attempt of the community to express its faith in words. These beliefs are a continual testing ground for the individual's act of believing in. The tendency to reduce faith to a set of beliefs follows from a naïve idea of revelation as a series of truths that make up the content of faith.

The most important need for reforming "faith" is to reform its relation to "revelation." There are many fine books on faith, some of which I have drawn material from. Often, however, they are limited by what they say—or do not say—about revelation. W. Cantwell Smith's *Faith and Belief* has excellent historical and comparative material on faith, but he admits toward the end of the book that he does not know what to do with revelation: "The *concept* of revelation has been part of the human response to what might be termed the

39. Joseph Ratzinger, *Gospel, Catechesis, Catechism* (San Francisco: Ignatius Press, 1997), 26.

fact of revelation, which in turn has yet to be understood and explained for our day."[40] John Henry Newman's brilliant analysis of the act of faith is restricted by a nineteenth-century idea of revelation in the last part of the book.[41]

The centrality of "believe in" cannot be achieved without the reform of "revelation," but the meaning of revelation is usually assumed in books on faith. I am trying to take seriously the Catholic *Catechism*'s description of faith: "With his whole being man gives his assent to God the revealer."[42] The primacy of faith as verb rather than noun is affirmed here. That in turn implies the present tense of the verb as primary. My believing in is in relation to someone or something in the present, "as assent to God the revealer."

A present, living faith does not exclude the reality of the past or the possibilities of the future. On the contrary, "I believe in God" surrounded by "we believe in God" entails an awareness of a past that we stand upon and an awareness that the future arises from the present response to the past. In Christian terms, "the confession of faith declares our present relation with God: God creator, God once born and crucified, now risen, God our present life and future peace."[43]

In weaving together the past-present and the future-present, Christian teaching at its best has not isolated faith as an assent of the mind to truths from the past. Faith has been an engagement of the person's mind, body, emotion, and will. Traditionally, faith was connected to hope and love as theological virtues. Hope is a word that connotes orientation to the future. Orientation means having direction without making predictions about the future. Pope Benedict XVI, in his encyclical *Spe Salvi* (Hope of Salvation) helpfully links faith and hope. He especially dwells on suffering and a final reckoning of one's life. From its origin in the Hebrew Bible, faith has always had a strong element of hope or trust. Isaiah 7:9 in the RSV translation reads: "If you will not believe, surely you shall not be established." Martin Buber translates the text as: "If you do not trust, you will not remain entrusted."[44]

Hope as a neglected connection between faith and love is perhaps an especially relevant virtue for the present. Many people have built a wall of skepticism against elaborate systems of propaganda and sales pitches for the latest product. Deep down, however, there remains a hope for something

40. Smith, *Faith and Belief,* 169.
41. Newman, *Grammar of Assent,* 318–79.
42. *Catechism of the Catholic Church,* chap. 3, sec. 143.
43. Nicholas Lash, *Believing Three Ways in One God,* 30.
44. Buber, *Two Types of Faith,* 29.

better out of life. Thomas Aquinas notes simply that "the difference between hope and despair is the difference between possibility and impossibility."[45]

The individual today wants to be in control of his or her life; suffering and death are shocking reminders of the power and forces that are far beyond the individual's control. The only choice in the end is between hope and despair, and as Gabriel Marcel says, "Hope is the will when it is made to bear on what does not depend on itself."[46] It is difficult to see how the acceptance of one's life is possible without the accompaniment of hope that "at the bottom of the heart of every human being, from earliest infancy to the tomb, there is something that goes on indomitably expecting, in the teeth of all experience of crimes committed, suffered and witnessed, that good and not evil will be done to him."[47]

Hope is directed to the future, but it is a present experience. "Believing in" is a hopeful act, a trusting that needs to be generated by a response in the first days of infancy and supported by a continuing trust in others throughout a final illness. The beliefs of a community are imperfect but helpful verbal expressions for human life, which begins and ends in silence.

45. Thomas Aquinas, *Summa Theologiae* II, q. 2, a. 40, ad. 1.
46. Gabriel Marcel, *Philosophy of Existence* (New York: Citadel, 1961), 32.
47. Simone Weil, *The Weil Reader* (Mount Kisco, NY: Moyer Bell, 1977), 315.

Chapter Two

. . . a Revealing God

At the base of Christian life is an act of believing in. But believing in what or whom? The obvious answer would seem to be "God." That answer is certainly not wrong, but it is neither specific nor practical enough. In the traditional way of speaking, Christians believe in God the Father, Son, and Holy Spirit. That specific language has meaning only within a historical narrative about particular people in particular places at particular moments.

That fact about the nature of Christianity is sometimes called the "scandal of particularity." Commenting on Gerard Manley Hopkins's *Wreck of the Deutschland*, Walter Ong writes: "Here the faithful waver. For it seems indecent that an Almighty God would tie himself so firmly into the flux of things, focusing his definitive visitation of man at one single brief period, the lifetime of Jesus Christ."[1] Modern thinkers attack Christianity on this point. For example, Ludwig Feuerbach states his objection to Christianity as an injury to the moral sense, that is, the belief that "God revealed himself once for all in the year so and so, and that, not to the universal man, to the man of all times and places, to the reason, to the species, but to certain limited individuals."[2]

Is Feuerbach correct in what he assumed to be the Christian meaning of revelation? It cannot be denied that something similar to that belief is asserted in much of Christian writing and official church teaching. Nonetheless, that meaning represents an insufficient grasp of the possibilities of the word "revelation."

The Second Vatican Council took on the idea of revelation as directly as it could. The Constitution on Divine Revelation is a valuable benchmark that I will examine later in this chapter. The council sparked a flurry of

1. Walter Ong, *In the Human Grain* (New York: Macmillan, 1967), 122.
2. Ludwig Feuerbach, *Essence of Christianity* (New York: Harper Torch, 1957), 209.

interest in reflecting on "revelation." But while Roman Catholics, like Protestants, now link Scripture and revelation, Christian writing still presupposes
an uncritical language of revelation.

Revelation is a difficult idea to examine because it is usually just assumed
in contemporary Christian writing. If one were to consider only what is
written by Christian writers, "revelation" would seem to be an unimportant,
perhaps disposable, idea. When a presupposed idea is seldom brought to the
surface, it could be that it is so obvious that it does not need exploring. An
alternative explanation is that there is an uncertainty that the idea can bear
scrutiny. Whichever explanation may be the case, the idea of revelation is
simply assumed in most Christian writing.

One glaring exception to this silence is interest in the book of Revelation,
the last book of the New Testament. The Internet has millions of web sites
on "revelation." Most of these sites are about the book of Revelation and
related literature. In contrast, the entry on "revelation" in theological dic-
tionaries and encyclopedias usually makes no reference to the book of Revelation. That holds true for Vatican II's Constitution on Divine Revelation,
which does not mention the book of Revelation. This fact indicates a deep
fissure in the middle of Christianity.

The part of Christianity that is described as "liberal" is dismissive of
obsession with "revelation" as found in the last book of the New Testament.
At the least, however, this obsessive attraction is a symptom that needs attention. Rather than this meaning of revelation being dismissed, it needs
integration within a comprehensive and consistent meaning of revelation.
Actually, the meaning of "revelation" that attracts millions of web users
today has a historical claim to the word prior to the meaning that came to
dominate mainstream theology.

One way to understand the problem of "revelation" in Christianity is to
recognize a split between its referring either to the past or to the future.
Much of Christian writing speaks of revelation as certain truths that have
been deposited in the past. By contrast, in the strand of Christianity that
takes its direction from the book of Revelation, revelation is all about the
future, a claim to know the end of history.

The way to overcome such a split and save the best on both sides is by
understanding divine revelation as situated in the present. Of course, this
present has to be understood not as a fleeting moment between past and
future, but as the present of a community with a sense of its past and a hope
for its future. A deep present that is ordered by respect for the past can cope
with visions and visionaries. Especially among the young, visions of the
future give zest to the present community. But it is the wise ones in the

community, rich in knowledge of the deep past, who must caution the visionaries that the future holds surprises beyond the secular imagining of prosperity or the religious claim to know how the human story ends.

Although the book of Revelation is supposedly the key to the future, it is still a text from the past. The choice, therefore, is not really between past and future. The choice comes down to how we understand the past in relation to the present. Either faith is holding to be true a message deposited in the past or faith is believing in a revealing God. The latter can include the former, but not vice versa. A full meaning of the "present" includes the past, but the past does not include the present. A full meaning of the present includes the possibilities of the future, but not without being anchored in the past.

There is much in Christian writing and preaching that affirms, encourages, and praises believing in a revealing God. Unfortunately, this fundamental act of Christian life is regularly subverted by the assumption that there is a "Christian revelation" deposited in the past. When words such as faith, belief, revelation, Scripture, and doctrine are used almost interchangeably, the Christian mind is pointed to the past. Scripture, doctrine, and belief belong in the present as distinct elements within believing in a revealing God.

The Metaphor of Revelation

Various metaphors have been employed for the use of language to express communication between God and humans. All speech about God fails badly, which is why seers, mystics, and poets have played key roles in the history of religions. At the limits of human speech we look for the least inadequate imagery and the figures of speech that might convey what humans are responding to.

In Christian history two metaphors are especially prevalent for divine communication: "showing" and "speaking." The two are sometimes used interchangeably, but there is considerable tension between the "word of God" and the "revelation of God." Christian history could be described as a constant struggle for supremacy between visual and oral metaphors. Do we primarily see the truth or hear the truth? Speech can be understood as leading to revelation, although revelation itself does not denote speech.

God speaking and God revealing are metaphors in tension with each other, but the tension can be fruitful. Even if one thinks that "believing in a speaking God" is a richer image than "believing in a revealing God," the metaphor of "revelation" has to be examined. Believing in has to be freed from a *thing* called revelation. That liberation can happen only if we restore the idea of revelation as a metaphor for God's activity to which humans respond.

Language may be the greatest gift humans have, but it consists of silence as well as sounds. At the beginning of life is silence, and at the end of life "all that is not music will be silence."[3] The metaphor of revelation can be a reminder that silence is between the sounds of speech and that all speech emerges out of silence. In this book I am caught in the paradox of using words to examine the silence that is revealing. The result is a set of forays into the inexpressible for words that do not do violence to sacred realities.

The term "revelation," like most words, can be stretched beyond its etymo-logical moorings. Nonetheless, if Christian writers are to have any chance of using the word effectively they have to take account of the origin and history of the term. The word "revelation" is less commonly used than "faith" in secular contexts today, but it has a clearer meaning. One cannot simply bypass that meaning on the way to a Christian meaning of divine revelation. The Vatican II document begins with the chapter heading "Revelation Itself," but the section has only a few brief articles that hardly begin to address the issue.

When used today in secular contexts, "revelation" usually refers to a secret that has become known. What is revealed is a secret and the result of the secret not being a secret anymore is called a revelation. ("In a revelation from the White House today . . ."; "the revelation of his drug use came as a surprise.") The etymological root of the word is to unveil, to remove the covering from what could not previously be seen. Usually a person does the revealing, though the verb can be extended to the inanimate world. ("The storm's damage revealed the inadequacy of the sea wall.")

A person usually is the revealer, but is a person the object of "reveal"? The direct object of "reveal" is not usually a person, but an object or fact that had previously been unknown or unseen. A partial revelation of someone occurs when some previously unknown fact, attitude, or activity of that person is made known. After a secret is uncovered, revelation ends; a secret revealed is a secret no longer. Of course, the person may have more secrets to be uncovered; those could be the objects of further revelations.

Religious Uses of "Revelation"

The ordinary meaning of "reveal"/"revelation" sets limits to its usefulness as a religious term. The uncovering of secrets about the gods might be a central activity of some religions. But that does not well describe the divine-human relation in Jewish, Christian, or Muslim religions. In the Hebrew Bible an aspect or activity of God might be shown, manifested, or uncovered. At no time does God "reveal himself."

3. C. S. Lewis, *The Screwtape Letters* (New York: Macmillan, 1959), 102.

"Revelation" in Jewish Tradition

In the two centuries before the Common Era the Greek word "revelation" made its appearance in Jewish tradition. The word reflects the influence of religions surrounding the Jewish religion, but also simply the use of the Greek language. The Septuagint translation of the Old Testament into Greek used the word for revelation—*apokalypsis*—a few dozen times in referring to what God would do: for example, lifting the skirt of a wicked city to reveal its nakedness (Nahum 3:5).[4]

Apokalypsis was not a commonly used word in Greek, though it existed at least as far back as Herodotus in the fifth century BCE. Plato uses it occasionally (Protagoras 352a; Gorgias 455d) without any technical meaning or special emphasis. The word could have taken on more prominence philosophically because it fit in with Hellenistic ideas of truth and knowledge. To know the truth was to bring it to light, to see what was once veiled in darkness. For Greek philosophy, words were a necessary instrument on the way to enlightenment. At the end, however, is a vision, a wordless gaze upon beauty, truth, and the good.

In the two centuries before the Common Era the word *apokalypsis* took on a special religious meaning that has remained to this day. "Apocalyptic" was used to describe a religious movement and the literary genre that resulted. Persian religion, embodied in the teaching of Zoroaster, was a powerful influence on ideas of good and evil, resurrection, the end of history, and a final judgment.[5] Apocalyptic literature divided the world into good and evil. Some people have a secret knowledge that has been revealed to them. This knowledge pertains to an imminent crisis when the good will be vindicated and freed from an evil world. That final conflict between good and evil is likely to be a violent conflagration.[6]

One cluster of Jewish writings, including 4 Ezra and 2 Baruch, had the qualities of apocalyptic literature. Some of this later Jewish literature reflected the destruction of the temple in 70 CE. When the Christians came to read the Old Testament, no apocalyptic work could match the importance of the book of Daniel, written near 165 BCE. Daniel's vision in chapter 7 is of a coming kingdom initiated by a messianic figure, "one like the Son of Man."

---

4. Morton Smith, *Apocalypticism in the Mediterranean World and the Near East*, ed. David Hellholm (Tübingen: Mohr, 1983), 10.

5. Norman Cohn, *Cosmos, Chaos and the World to Come* (New Haven: Yale University Press, 1993), 98–99.

6. James Vanderkam and William Adler, *The Jewish Apocalyptic Heritage in Early Christianity* (Philadelphia: Fortress Press, 1996), 8–13.

"To him was given dominion and glory and kingship, that all peoples, nations, and languages should serve him. His dominion is an everlasting dominion that shall not pass away and his kingship is one that shall never be destroyed" (Dan 7:14).

Apocalypse, the unveiling of a secret, thus made its way into religious literature, including Jewish writing, as a vision of the end, when the plan of history will be made known to all. The triumph of the good will be led by a powerful king or prophet. In Jewish history the idea was connected to restoring the line of David. The one anointed to be king was called messiah. Later Christian history would find in Daniel, Second Isaiah, and some other prophetic passages the foreseeing of this figure as one who transcends mere human kingship.

Early Christian Use of "Revelation"

The most obvious connection of apocalyptic literature and the New Testament is its last book, the Revelation of John. Contemporary speakers often call the book "Revelations," but the word is used only in the singular and only once in the book. This book is the only example of apocalyptic literature that announces itself as fitting that genre.[7] The question much debated in the twentieth century is the relation of Jesus of Nazareth to this revelation or apocalypse. An answer to that question largely determines how useful and accurate the word "revelation" is for describing the whole Christian movement.

When the question "was Jesus an apocalypticist?" is asked, the issue is whether he expected an imminent end of a dualistic history. There is no doubt that Jesus' preaching had some of the characteristics associated with "apocalypse."[8] He announced the coming of the kingdom or reign of God. He warned of God's judgment that would separate good and evil. He advised people to divest themselves of wealth and possessions in expectation of the end. There are set pieces within the gospels that are small apocalypses: "But in those days, after that suffering, the sun will be darkened, and the moon will not give its light, and the stars will be falling from heaven, and the powers in the heavens will be shaken. Then they will see the 'Son of Man coming in clouds' with great power and glory. Then he will send out the

---

7. John Collins, *The Apocalyptic Imagination* (New York: Crossroad, 1984), 3.

8. Dale Allison, "The Eschatology of Jesus," in *Encyclopedia of Apocalypticism,* ed. John Collins, Bernard McGinn, and Stephen Stein, 276–302 (New York: Continuum, 1998).

angels, and gather his elect from the four winds, from the ends of the earth to the ends of heaven" (Mark 13:24-27).

There is debate about how to interpret these aspects of Jesus' teaching. Did he see himself in line with the Jewish prophets who call for the renewal of the covenant, or was he breaking with the fundamental attitude of the Jewish community toward history? Did he presuppose, as Rudolf Bultmann wrote, "the pessimistic-dualist perception of the satanic corruption of the whole course of the world"?[9] Our difficulty in perceiving the "real Jesus" is increased by the fact that the picture we have was drawn several decades after Jesus' death when the synagogue and nascent church were in conflict. "Pharisee" became an especially negative word in Christian history, even though Jesus' teaching was similar to that of the Pharisees in many respects. The sharper the opposition between Pharisees and Jesus, the more Jesus appears to be an apocalypticist.

The occasional use of "reveal"/"revelation" in both gospels and epistles most often refers to a future judgment and "the day that the Son of man is revealed" (Luke 17:30). That will be "when the Lord Jesus is revealed from heaven with his mighty angels in flaming fire, inflicting vengeance on those who do not know God and on those who do not obey the gospel of our Lord Jesus" (2 Thess 1:7). Whatever the mind-set of Jesus, the term "revelation" found its way into New Testament writings with a meaning related to, if not directly derived from, the apocalyptic literature of the time. Secrets are made known (Matt 11:25; 16:17), but there is a final secret to be revealed on the last day when history is judged.

The last book of the New Testament, known simply as Apocalypse or Revelation, was not out of line with the apocalyptic writings that preceded it, but it did represent a different literary form in which there is a full-blown description of those last days. The author of Revelation was ready to provide names and numbers, but the writing is still wrapped in mysterious images. Augustine commented on the irony of the title, Revelation, while "there are in it many obscure passages to exercise the mind of the reader and there are few passages so plain as to assist us in the interpretation of others."[10] Despite this obscurity—or possibly because of it—the book has been a powerful stimulus to the apocalyptic imagination. Many passages are indeed obscure, but the main storyline is clear and simple: the saving of an elect few from the fires of damnation. With that key, the book lends itself to fanciful interpretations and implications. For many people the last book is the key to

9. Rudolf Bultmann, *Theology of the New Testament* (London: SCM Press, 1955), 3.

10. Augustine, *The City of God* (New York: Penguin, 2003), 20:17.

everything that precedes it in the Bible. If one knows how the mystery is resolved at the end of the book, one need not put much time into following the rest of the story.

The book of Revelation had a difficult time getting accepted into the canon of the New Testament. The idea of revelation, however—the vision of an imminent end to history—was a dominant theme of the early church. In one of the earliest Christian documents Paul writes: "for the Lord himself, with a cry of command, with the archangel's call and with the sound of God's trumpet, will descend from heaven, and the dead in Christ will rise first. Then we who are alive, who are left, will be caught up in the clouds together with them to meet the Lord in the air; and so we will be with the Lord forever" (1 Thess 4:16-17). The early Christians prayed for a speedy return of the Lord, something that could happen at any moment.

As the years and decades passed it became increasingly apparent that the revelation was not at hand. Was their expectation wrong or was it their interpretation of where and when revelation occurs? The possibility of looking at revelation differently is evident in the Fourth Gospel's announcement that the light had come into the world and the world had not received it. Instead of looking for a spectacular climax to history one should look inward to a transformation of body, mind, and soul. "But to all who received him, who believed in his name, he gave power to become children of God, who were born, not of blood or of the will of the flesh or of the will of man, but of God" (John 1:12-13). In this meaning of revelation the future tense has been replaced by the past tense.

The Fourth Gospel provided a brilliant reemphasis of the good news. It retained the Greek idea of a vision of the end and the church as a minority who save the true faith over against those who cannot or will not see. At the same time the church was embedded within history; it was not just a sect waiting out the clock.

Despite the Christian redirection inward, the expectation of an imminent end to history did not die out. Throughout most of the second century the belief remained strong and Christians prayed: Come, Lord Jesus. A significant change in prayer appeared near the end of the second century. Tertullian reports the words of a liturgical prayer: "We pray also for the Caesars, for their ministers, and for all in high positions, for the commonweal of the world; for the prevalence of peace; and for the delay of the end."[11] The entire substance of the prayer is surprising; its concern is for the workings of the

---

11. Tertullian, *Apology* 39:2, cited in Jaroslav Pelikan, *The Emergence of the Catholic Tradition 100–600* (Chicago: University of Chicago Press, 1971), 129–31.

secular world of politics and politicians. The last phrase is the biggest surprise: asking for a *delay* of the end. The main body of the church was no longer to be seen as an "apocalyptic sect," but as a transformative body within history.

Could the Christian movement simply divest itself of "revelation" without losing its drive and purpose? Especially among communities under threat, attachment to the book of Revelation was—and still is—a response to that question. Revelation, in its most obvious meaning as a final unveiling of the end, cannot be abandoned by Christianity. The clinging to revelation is a legitimate one, although believers in revelation have to remember that a vision of the end is not the end, and that the book of Revelation is not the same as revelation.

Adela Yarbro Collins, in her expert analysis of the book of Revelation, sets the proper balance: "The imagery and tone of Revelation may embody attitudes that are necessary in the struggle for justice under certain conditions. Those attitudes, however, have a dark side of which interpreters of the Apocalypse must be conscious and whose dangers must be recognized."[12] Collins's admonition is not merely speculative. Attachment to the book of Revelation has often left a bloody trail through the centuries. A word that starts out meaning a vision that uncovers the truth has acquired the connotations of unrestrained violence and complete destruction.

Collins nevertheless affirms that revelation or apocalypse may be necessary in the struggle for justice. She does not specify what the "certain conditions" are, but they could conceivably exist to some degree at any time and in any place. Jesus preached a nonviolent response to injustices in his world, which was a violent place. Martin Luther King, Jr., described faith as a "non-symmetric response to violence."[13] Much had changed between the first century and the twentieth, but violent surroundings and the need for resistance to injustice remained. King's most famous speech was recounted as a dream, the contents of that dream filled with biblical images of the end time. Even in a rich country where Christians are not persecuted for their beliefs, revelation can still be a driving force.

While the "apocalyptic element" has never disappeared from Christianity, it has tended to be overlooked or dismissed from official circles. There is a sense of embarrassment at apocalypse even though it was a central belief at

12. Adela Yarbo Collins, *Crisis and Catharsis: The Power of the Apocalypse* (Philadelphia: Westminster, 1984), 172.

13. Herbert Richardson, "Martin Luther King, Jr.,—Unsung Theologian," *New Theology No. 6,* ed. Martin Marty and Dean Peerman, 174–84 (New York: Macmillan, 1969).

the beginning of Christianity. "Apocalyptic sects" show no signs of disappearing. If apocalypse/revelation does not find healthy expression, it will take on corrupted forms that are frightening.

The early Christian church did not deny revelation, but it tried to impose controls. It was successful in this effort—perhaps too successful. The key tactic in the Western church was the use of two Latin words: *apocalypsis* and *revelatio*. The church adopted this second term that did not have all the religious connotations apocalypse had acquired. This word, "revelation," has the same etymological root as apocalypse—that is, the unveiling of a secret. The word *revelatio*, however, was not burdened with the connotations of apocalyptic literature. "Revelation" could be used for what was given to the prophets and found full expression in Jesus, the Christ. The veil had been lifted; the message was delivered. Revelation no longer occurs. The church's task was to preserve and deliver the truth to all the nations.

Revelation and the Spirit

The domesticating of "revelation" was probably inevitable. Apocalyptic sects that are composed of members who have visions of the future do not last long. Still, one has to be concerned with reaction as a strategy and overreaction as a result. People envisioning a much better world need guidance and restraint by a community that makes sure the ordinary tasks of life are fulfilled, but the community need not suppress visions of the future so long as they are solidly rooted in the community's past.

The word "revelation" should not be attached exclusively to a message from the past. What Isaiah saw may have been a revelation for Isaiah. What is written in the book called "Isaiah" is not revelation for a fourth-century or twenty-first-century person. It is a report of Isaiah's revelation. Of course, reading the book of Isaiah or hearing it preached might be revelatory for today's reader or listener. There is no revelation without a viewer or listener who believes in the one revealing. Referring to Scripture as "the revealed word of God" is misleading. The words of the text reveal only if there is a believing individual or community. As Joseph Ratzinger wrote in the 1950s, " 'Revelatio' refers not to the letter of Scripture, but to the understanding of the letter, and this understanding can be increased."[14]

From the third century to the early Middle Ages the main response to the book of Revelation was to treat it as allegory—that is, as a story about the life of the church, not a vision of the end of history. St. Augustine was es-

14. Joseph Ratzinger, *The Theology of History in Saint Bonaventure* (Chicago: Franciscan Press, 1971), 68.

pecially influential in interpreting "the thousand year reign of Christ" as referring to church history rather than the second coming of Christ.[15] Nevertheless, the expectation of the end—millenarianism—persisted in popular religion.[16]

Starting with the first Crusade at the end of the eleventh century and continuing to the middle of the sixteenth century, the millennial impulse was prominent. Not all of these apocalyptic groups were made up of illiterate peasants. Bernard McGinn has found that "the major apocalyptic thinkers of the twelfth century were figures situated in high echelons of intellectual and political power."[17] What united these disparate groups was a rebellion against present conditions in the name of a much different future.

The medieval religious order had many of the characteristics of the apocalyptic sect. It embodied a nonviolent waiting for the end rather than a violent thrust at bringing on the climax of history. In his study of Bonaventure, Ratzinger found that the saint "awaited a new and purer *revelation* which could become a reality for all practical purposes in the Ordo of the final age."[18] The early history of the Franciscans was split between those like Bonaventure who hoped for a "greater fullness of revelation" but kept within the boundaries of orthodoxy and a radical or spiritual wing of the Franciscans who followed where they thought the Spirit of God was leading.

The individual theorist who towered above medieval millenarianism and whose outline of history still influences us is Joachim of Fiore (1145–1202). Since Joachim's time Western thinkers have been fascinated by the idea that history has three stages and that the third stage in which "spirit" will replace institutions is just beginning. The New Age spirituality of the late twentieth century is a recent chapter in this story. Not surprisingly, Joachim took his lead from the book of Revelation, which for him was "the key of things past, the knowledge of things to come; the opening of what is sealed, the uncovering of what is hidden."[19]

---

15. *The City of God*, 20:9.

16. Norman Cohn, *Pursuit of the Millennium* (New York: Galaxy, 197), 30; Yonina Talmon, "Millenarianism," in *International Encyclopedia of the Social Sciences*, ed. David Sills, vol. 10, 349–62 (London: Macmillan, 2007).

17. Bernard McGinn, "Apocalypticism and Church Reform," in *Encyclopedia of Apocalypticism*, vol. 2, 85–86; see also Bernard McGinn, *Visions of the End: Apocalyptic Traditions in the Middle Ages* (New York: Columbia University Press, 1979), 32.

18. Ratzinger, *Theology of History in St. Bonaventure*, 70.

19. Joachim of Fiore, *Enchiridion Super Apocalypsim*, ed. Edmund Burger (Toronto: Pontifical Institute of Medieval Studies, 1980); McGinn, *Visions of the End*, 19.

In Joachim's reading of history the first age was that of the Father; it was an age of fear based on law. The second age was that of the Son; it was an age of faith based on the gospels. The third age is that of the Spirit; it is an age of love based on knowledge revealed directly to the heart. The final revelation had not earlier been made public, but it would soon be open to all. Joachim's own description of the third age retained some structures that prevented his teachings from being simply anti-institutional.[20] But those who ran with his teachings did not concern themselves with such niceties. A new age was beginning, and those who overthrew all legal restraints and institutional authority were the heralds of the Spirit.

The attraction of such rhetoric is almost irresistible to millions of people. The message is love, peace, and unity; who can object to that? However, since that is not the way things are, some individual or group is likely to be identified as standing in the way of the final triumph. The book of Revelation identifies that figure as the anti-Christ, friend or incarnation of Satan. In much of Christian history the Jews were assumed to be the natural fit for the role. But others, including the pope, have been called the anti-Christ, the last obstacle to revelation.

The need to vanquish the anti-Christ and all the forces of Satan has unfortunately unleashed frightening violence. Religious wars—and all wars perhaps have a religious dimension—call forth a passion for killing the infidels, who are not just other fallible human beings but the very embodiment of evil. Wars, however stupid and immoral, are not likely to cease until religions either disappear or find other outlets for the passion they generate. In Christian history the apocalyptic impulse—the desire for revelation—has fueled religious conflict.[21]

The complex doctrine of the Trinity was a brilliant insight into the experience of the divine in human history entwined with the rest of creation. Jesus, who is identified with the culmination of God's word, promises to send a "comforter," a gift of love. The Holy Spirit or breath of life is more elusive than the images of Father and Son. By the same token, the Spirit has the greatest experiential, ecumenical, and ecological possibilities.

A tragic result of heretical sects taking over the language of spirit was a downplaying of the role of the Holy Spirit in Christian theology. At least since the fourth century the Holy Spirit was recognized as a full member of

20. Marjorie Reeves, *Joachim of Fiore* (New York: Harper Torchbooks, 1977), 7.

21. Richard Landes, "The Apocalyptic Year 1000: Millennial Fever and the Origins of the Modern West," in *The Year 2000: Essays on the End*, ed. Charles Strosier and Michael Flynn, 13–29 (New York: New York University Press, 1997), 24.

the Blessed Trinity. The potential was there for developing an understanding of divine revelation as a present occurrence deep in the human soul and wide as all creation.

The potential was not developed in Christian theology of the past. There are hopeful signs of interest in contemporary writing, but there is a need to connect this new interest in the Holy Spirit to the history of "revelation."[22] What discouraged serious interest in the Spirit in the past and continues to be a problem is the teaching that "Christ is the fullness of revelation" and "there is no revelation after Christ." The Holy Spirit was given a few mundane tasks but has not been at the center of the human experience of the divine.

The relation of Christ and the Spirit is not a competition or a zero-sum game. The Spirit is the Spirit of Christ; the present Christ is experienced in the Spirit. The frequent assertion that Christ is the fullness of revelation is at the least incomplete. Christians believe that Jesus' life incarnates divine revealing and human response. The way Christians participate in the life of the risen Christ is by the Holy Spirit. The statement that there is no revelation after Christ is a Christian truism that tells us little about the present revelation. For Christians there is no revelation after Christ because there is no "after" Christ. There is no problem of revelation in a "*post-Christum* era" if "Christ" is not only a title for Jesus but also the foundation and end of the world.

Nearly all attempts at church reform make appeal to the Holy Spirit. The most radical reformers try to free themselves from tradition and from all but a select set of New Testament passages. More responsible reformers are aware of the church's living tradition and the testimonies of faith that make up the Bible. Martin Luther wrote that the doctrine of the apostles "was not restored without the Holy Spirit's revelation; for our predecessors also had the same Scripture, Baptism and everything. Yet it was all so soiled in the mud."[23] Although Luther appeals here to "the Holy Spirit's revelation," he quickly adds that "now no further words of revelation are to be expected." John Calvin says something similar, but with more emphasis on stability and doctrine. "The office of the Spirit . . . is not to feign new and unheard

22. For example, Dennis Edwards, *Breath of Life* (New York: Orbis Books, 2004), is a fine study of the Holy Spirit, but the term "revelation" is not in the index, and in the text "revelation" gets only passing reference.

23. Martin Luther, *Luther's Works,* ed. Jaroslav Pelikan (St. Louis: Concordia Publishing House, 1961), XXIV, 368.

of revelations but to seal in our minds the same doctrine which the Gospel delivers."[24]

Neither Luther nor Calvin, any more than the medieval church, could control the working of the Spirit and the groups that laid claim to the Spirit's guidance. The Bible was often sufficient as a guide to Christian living, but some groups gave greater play to what they saw as the movement of the Spirit within. The Quakers, for example, rely on silent meditation until someone, inspired by the Spirit, speaks to the assembly. There is no clerical authority insisting on continuity with the past. The Quaker community can be organizationally messy. Nonetheless, the Quakers have sometimes put to shame the larger church when it comes to a witness of nonviolence.

Both Protestant and Roman Catholic churches continue to struggle with outbreaks of people called spirituals. Intense piety can invigorate churches, but it always threatens to overflow the current ecclesiastical boundaries. Despite the antics of many rebels, those in charge of the church have to keep open the possibility that popular uprisings are a way the Holy Spirit is speaking to them.

Post-Reformation Uses of "Revelation"

In the Protestant and Catholic conflict over revelation the question was mainly about the "sources" of revelation. Protestants criticized numerous church practices from the standpoint of Holy Scripture; that criticism led to the Catholic reaction at the Council of Trent. Catholic-Protestant differences came to be expressed in a too-simple formula: Protestants hold that revelation is contained in Scripture alone; Catholics add a second source with the claim that revelation is contained in Scripture and tradition. The question of revelation itself was left largely unexplored in the debate over one source or two.

An interesting aspect of this debate was the use of the word "contain." Asking whether revelation is contained in one source or two presupposes that revelation is the kind of thing that can be put in a container. There is one positive value in saying revelation is "contained" in Scripture or in Scripture and tradition. A distinction is thereby implied between Scripture (or scriptural and traditional texts) and revelation itself. The Bible is not revelation; the human authors were inspired but the words are not the object of divine revelation. Saying that the Bible contains revelation allows for an

---

24. John Calvin, *Institutes of the Christian Religion* (Philadelphia: Presbyterian Board of Christian Education, 1960), I, 9, 1.

appreciation of historical and literary features of the Bible without such questions seeming to be an attack on divine revelation.

While a necessary distinction between Scripture and revelation is accomplished with the word "contain," the image of a "container" is inadequate and misleading. Scripture might be called a witnessing, a testimony, or a response, but Scripture is not well described as a container. Little progress can be hoped for in Catholic-Protestant relations if revelation is talked about as "contained" in sources.

As Christian apologists struggled with the wider knowledge introduced by the sciences they were attracted to the language of natural religion as a universal basis for a supernatural revelation. To natural religion Christianity would add truths not available to unaided reason. The phrase that was paired with "natural religion" in the seventeenth century was "revealed religion"; it is a phrase unthinkable early in church history. The object of the verb "reveal" is not religion. At the beginning of his book on revelation, Colin Gunton asks, "Why are theologians embarrassed by the concept of revealed religion?"[25] If they are, that would be a good sign, because the concept is unintelligible. If, on the other hand, theologians are embarrassed by the concept of revelation, that would be a different problem and one that needs to be addressed.

A dichotomy of natural religion and revealed religion had the effect of distancing Christian beliefs from the natural world. As the sciences advanced in their comprehension of "nature," Christianity was preserved in its own world of "revealed religion." The drawback was that any revelation of the divine in the natural world was separated from Christianity.

The one link to "revealed religion" was the capacity of the human mind to prove the existence of God. Whether or not one can prove that a being called God exists took center stage in discussions of religion. If one can establish this generic God, shared by other "theisms," then Christians could add their peculiar doctrines of Trinity, Incarnation, sin, grace, and redemption. Christian theology rested on a fragile connection to ordinary life. As science progressed, proofs for the existence of God came under threat.

Vatican I

In the nineteenth century "revelation" had come to mean for Catholics the package of truths deposited in the past; these doctrines constituted "the Christian revelation." It was in the nineteenth century that the phrase "deposit

---

25. Colin Gunton, *A Brief Theology of Revelation* (Edinburgh: T & T Clark, 1995), 1–2.

of revelation" came into use as a synonym or replacement for the traditional phrase "deposit of faith." The same century produced the phrase "revelation closed with the death of the last apostle." The vault was sealed; no more deposits were allowed. The "Christian revelation" was secure, but revelation was equated with a collection of revealed truths instead of divine activity inviting human response.

The First Vatican Council reflected the philosophical and theological currents of the nineteenth century. That was especially true of its document Dogmatic Constitution on the Catholic Faith, which included a chapter on revelation.[26] While much of what Vatican I had to say about faith and revelation was a repetition of the Council of Trent, a new twist was its concern that "God can be known with certainty from consideration of created things" (2:1). That concern is raised before the council turns to faith. Besides "the natural knowledge of God," the council says, God was pleased "to reveal himself and the eternal decrees of his will by another and supernatural way" (2:1). Notice the phrase "eternal decrees of his will," which made revelation consist primarily of such eternal truths.

When the council did get to "faith," the description was already determined by its assumption of a revelation of eternal decrees. Faith was a matter of accepting these decrees. "By divine and Catholic faith all those things are to be believed which are contained in the word of God as found in Scripture and tradition, and which are proposed by the church as matters to be believed as divinely revealed" (4:8).

Such a statement might not be a problem if it were set within a richly detailed and expansive view of faith and revelation. However, the whole story seems to be that faith is believing revealed truths. The eternal decrees of God's will having been revealed in the first century CE, the only choice offered is whether or not to believe these things. Revelation as revealed truths and faith as accepting those truths is a combination cut off not only from the natural world but also increasingly from the actual practice of religion. The liturgical and moral practices of the Christian life are nowhere adverted to in this idea of faith/revelation.

It should be noted that in a few places a different route for talking about faith and revelation is suggested. "Even when a revelation has been given and accepted by faith, they (the divine mysteries) remain covered by the veil of the same faith and wrapped, as it were, in a certain obscurity as long as in this mortal life we are away from the Lord, for we walk by faith and not

---

26. "Dogmatic Constitution on the Catholic Faith," in *Decrees of the Ecumenical Councils*, ed. Norman Tanner (Washington, DC: Georgetown University Press, 1990), II. 804–11.

by sight." (4:4). What the council points to here is faith as a journey or quest. The fullness of revelation is at the end of history. In the present we struggle to understand obscure mysteries. This teaching of Vatican I was a more modest but a more dynamic attitude to divine mysteries and to revelation still awaited.

The Twentieth Century

In the century between the First and Second Vatican Councils the world experienced revolutions of all kinds—in history, science, politics, philosophy, and technology. Religion changes more slowly than those concerns, but it nevertheless went through a transformation of its own. Until recent decades the magnitude of the religious change was more evident in Protestant than in Catholic Christianity. "Revelation" played a central role in Protestantism's split into liberal and reactionary wings.

The liberal Protestantism of the late nineteenth century found alliance with the evolutionary and progressive strands of science and politics. In that framework "revelation" became an ever-expanding light, a revelation that is continuing. That image kept religion up-to-date with science, which pictured itself as continuously enlightening human minds. The Bible was still spoken of with reverence, but much of its ancient teaching had to give way to scientific knowledge.

In reaction to theologians becoming too comfortable with the assumptions of modernity, some groups identified revelation with the text of the Bible— that is, with every text in the Bible. The doctrine of inerrancy, the belief that each statement of the Bible is without error, is a late-nineteenth-century doctrine. At least as far back as Augustine there had been recognition that the Bible uses various figures of speech and that the point of an allegory or a poem is not to make a series of true statements. But in the nineteenth century, as studies in history, biology, archaeology, and anthropology seemed to conflict with the Bible, some groups became more insistent on the truth of each statement in the Bible.

In Europe a new generation of Protestant theologians tried to transcend a split between liberal and fundamentalist approaches to theology and revelation. The assumptions of a liberal theology were challenged by scholarly study and committed Christian living. "Revelation" became identified closely with the biblical text, but now supported with modern scholarship. Some philosophical assumptions inevitably crept in, which made for wide differences among writers who supposedly were in agreement on "revelation alone."

The Roman Catholic Church was able to maintain a unity by resisting any sweeping changes in its philosophy and theology. The Catholic Church could speak with a strong and unified voice on such issues as social welfare and opposition to war. By the mid-twentieth century, however, it found itself increasingly isolated from much of contemporary scholarship. The Vatican was still expressing the greatest caution about New Testament studies. The seminaries were dominated by the nineteenth-century version of Thomism that Pope Leo XIII had put in all the seminaries of the world. Nevertheless, in some monasteries, universities, and centers of social action there were Roman Catholics quietly preparing the way for a reform of the church that would be deeply rooted in tradition.

Vatican II: Constitution on Divine Revelation

Pope John XXIII's announcement of an ecumenical council was not met with universal acclaim. The Vatican's main theological spokesmen set out to make sure that there would be no fundamental changes. The Catholic Church prides itself on continuity with its past. That stability is its great strength and cannot be abandoned without loss of its identity. When change is needed, the insistence on continuity is a formidable force to grapple with.

It was appropriate that the topic of revelation was addressed at the very beginning of the Second Vatican Council. Nothing else about the church could be rethought without a rethinking of revelation. Those who were most resistant to change prepared a document called *The Sources of Revelation* that simply reaffirmed what the Councils of Trent and Vatican I had said: namely, there are two sources of revelation; the revealed truths that the Catholic Church teaches are contained in Scripture and tradition.

This original document was rejected by the council. A revised document, approved only in the last session, was an immeasurable improvement over the first. It is clearly the product of biblical scholars and theologians who appreciate how the Scriptures could breathe new life into old formulas. It did not contradict either the Council of Trent or Vatican I; in the carefully chosen image of the constitution's Preface, it walked in the "footsteps" of those preceding councils. While the first document that started from Trent's "two sources of revelation" was rejected, its replacement could not entirely free itself from the framework set by Trent. Inside the finished product are signs of a more radical rethinking of revelation, but they are covered over by the language of compromise.

The Constitution on Divine Revelation is known by its first two words, *Dei Verbum*, which means "the word of God." The document never acknowledges the inherent tension between "word" and "revelation." In this document, shaped mainly by scriptural exegesis, the metaphor of word of God dominates. That was inevitable and probably fortunate unless the council was willing to explore the history and meaning of revelation. The biggest resulting drawback is a complete omission of the original meaning of revelation as an unveiling of the end time. The book of Revelation receives no mention in the treatment of revelation. In contrast, the Constitution on the Church has a chapter on the "eschatological character of the church."[27] That discussion more logically belongs in a document on revelation.

The first word of the Preface in most English translations is not "word" but "hearing": "Hearing the Word of God with reverence, and proclaiming it with faith, the sacred Synod assents to the words of St. John . . ." (*DV* 1). That is a promising start in which the council listens to the word and then proclaims. The council is not about applying revealed truths from a deposit of revelation, but about responding in faith to a word that is spoken now. To a considerable extent the promise of this first sentence was kept, though weighed down with other uses of "revelation."

One can appreciate subtle changes from previous councils that had to be fought for. For example, Vatican I's formula of "believing as true what God has revealed" became at Vatican II " 'the obedience of faith' . . . must be given to God as he reveals himself" (*DV* 5). There are implications here about faith and revelation that could have been further developed. But after a first chapter of five articles that are said to deal with revelation itself, the second chapter is headed "The Transmission of Divine Revelation." A more thorough inquiry into revelation itself would probably have led the council fathers to avoid using the word "transmission" in referring to revelation. There is plenty that the Christian church does transmit—the Scriptures together with teachings and practices consonant with the apostolic age—but revelation does not fit there.

The passing references to faith are good, but insufficient. Vatican I made the logical connection between faith and revelation in having a Constitution on Catholic Faith that included a chapter on revelation. In the case of Vatican I, the correspondence was between revelation as revealed truths and faith as believing those truths. A different relation between faith and revelation would require rethinking both ideas. Faith as an engagement of the whole self in a present encounter cannot be matched with the "transmission of divine revelation."

27. *Lumen Gentium*, chapter 7.

In one other respect Vatican I had the right topic, though with very inadequate contents. Its document begins with the "natural knowledge" of God, a starting point that acknowledged a world beyond church and Bible. Vatican II simply chose to avoid the issue. It rightly wished to be free of the dichotomy of natural religion and revealed religion. The solution, however, is not to give up natural religion and deal only with revealed religion. There has to be a rethinking of revelation in the natural world, in other religions, and in the whole of Christianity. If faith and revelation were described together as anchored in the natural world—as everyday occurrences in a secular context—then believing in a revealing God would have much greater support.

Where Vatican II greatly improved on Vatican I was in its focus on Christ rather than eternal decrees. However, "Christ as the fullness of revelation" remains a very ambiguous phrase. At one point (*DV* 4) Christ is referred to as giving testimony to revelation, a role Vatican I had given to the church. Christ is not simply another name for God, nor is Christ a gathering of revealed truths.

At stake here is the nature of Christianity as a religion of incarnation, a religion that does not enter history in order to abolish it. Vatican I said that the church received what Christ had bestowed; faith was believing that those things are true. Vatican II suggested, but did not pursue, the alternative: namely, that "Christ" refers to God revealing and humans responding. Jesus is the model for believers, and a dialogue of revealing-believing is found in the Christ figure today. The council document repeatedly says that there is a dialogue, conversation, or colloquium between divine and human (*DV* 2, 8, 25). But the phrase "Christ is the revelation" does not convey that. What does support a colloquium is Jesus as revealer because he is first among believers. The dialogue between divine and human reached its greatest expression in the life of Jesus and continues today through participation in the living Christ by the work of the Spirit.

The document makes the customary bow to the Holy Spirit, but only as guardian of the revelation given by Christ. The authors did not intend to slight the work of the Spirit, but they did so by simply repeating traditional formulas. The Holy Spirit cannot be taken seriously without revealing-believing as a true dialogue that finds full expression within the Christ who is still being formed. The Spirit was at work in creation in the millennia leading up to Jewish and Christian dispensations; the Spirit continues to work throughout the whole of creation until revelation is complete. A healthy tension between the metaphors of speaking and showing is embodied in the relation between Jesus' words and the silent presence of the Spirit.

A recent document from the Congregation for the Doctrine of the Faith indicates a continuing resistance to acknowledging the relational character of revealing-believing, most prominently realized in Jesus as Christ. The Congregation in responding to the work of Jon Sobrino took issue with some of his formulas. They said it was impossible that Jesus can be "a believer like ourselves" because if he were "he would not be able to be a true revealer showing us the father."[28] That makes sense in Vatican I's meaning of faith directed to revealed truths. But in the sense of faith-revelation that Vatican II was struggling toward (believing in a God who reveals), it is impossible for Jesus to be revealer *except* as believer, as the one who perfectly submits to the will of his father.

Vatican II's treatment of tradition was a great improvement over what had been said and what was implicit at Trent and Vatican I. Vatican II incorporated a sense of tradition that had been developed in literature of the nineteenth and twentieth centuries. Tradition is not a collection of truths to supplement Scripture; instead, it implies the being and faith of the church. What the council said of tradition, however, shows the compromises that were made with those who wished to preserve the language of Trent. In some places tradition still sounds like a stream parallel to Scripture ("flowing out from the same divine well-spring," *DV* 9). And to say that they "come together in some fashion to form one thing" (*DV* 9) is to revert to an objectified revelation that church officials control.

As Protestant observers were quick to point out, there was a failure here to offer any criteria for distinguishing genuine and false developments within the church's tradition. Even Joseph Ratzinger in his commentary admits that the council failed to criticize tradition or even to point toward how to criticize it.[29] If there is no criticism of tradition, then it is still implied that tradition is simply truths revealed by God.

The Protestant principle has always been that Sacred Scripture is judge of church practice. Vatican II's constitution, largely a product of biblical exegetes, goes a long way toward agreeing with Protestantism. At the same time, the need for tradition was also affirmed. Catholics and Protestants need more conversation about how the Scriptures are to be read and which developments within church history are unacceptable distortions.

---

28. Congregation for the Doctrine of the Faith, "Notification on the Works of Fr. Jon Sobrino, S.J., March 29, 2007"; for discussion of the issue see Luke Timothy Johnson, "Human and Divine: Did Jesus Have Faith?" *Commonweal* 135, no. 3 (31 January 2008): 10–16.

29. Joseph Ratzinger, "Commentary on the Constitution on Divine Revelation," in *Commentary on the Documents of Vatican II*, ed. Herbert Vorgrimler, vol. 3, 155–66; 181–98 (New York: Herder and Herder, 1969), at 192.

A danger lies in forgetting that "word of God" is a reference to inspired texts that admit of a variety of interpretations. The constitution says toward the end: "Sacred theology relies on the written Word of God" (*DV* 24). I pointed out earlier that "contain," while not a very felicitous way of distinguishing revelation and Bible, does preserve a needed distinction. The word of God as contained in the Bible means that the Bible is not "the written word of God."

A more modest image is used when tradition and Scripture are said to be "a mirror, in which the Church, during its pilgrim journey here on earth, contemplates God, from whom she receives everything, until such time as she is brought to see him face to face as he really is" (*DV* 7). There is an echo here of several New Testament passages (1 Cor 13:12; 1 John 3:23) as well as Vatican I's image of the church on a journey, with the fullness of revelation still to be realized.

Present and Future

The Constitution on Divine Revelation was, on the whole, a great achievement and a rousing success. It moved the Catholic Church into a new world of dialogical possibilities. It focused Catholic piety on Scripture and the centrality of Christ. I have pointed to a few places where there are awkward compromises and some questions yet to be explored. One could hardly expect the council to have done more, and the authors of the document were surely aware of the limits of their work. In his talk at the conclusion of the council, Pope Paul VI said that the council had not intended to resolve all problems that had been raised: "Some were reserved for further study by the church, some were presented in general and restricted terms, and therefore they remain open to further and deeper understanding."[30]

The pope thus invited further thinking on the issue of faith-revelation. It is dismaying that there has been so little follow-up in Catholic writing. Some philosophically minded Protestants have written books on the question of revelation, though in some quarters an interest in "revelation" still gets one classified as a follower of Karl Barth. Catholic writers regularly assume a "Christian revelation," mostly if not wholly found in the Bible and taught by the church. Theology has become a lot of subspecialties (ecclesiology, Christology, eschatology, pneumatology, soteriology, and other –ologies) in which the basis of a Christian theology is not usually a matter at issue. If a question about revelation does arise, it is given to biblical exegetes.

---

30. Quoted in Ormond Rush, *Still Interpreting Vatican II* (New York: Paulist Press, 2004), 29.

One exception to a complacent attitude about Vatican II's treatment of revelation was Karl Rahner. He had been a quiet force behind much of the council's intellectual journey. To the end of his life Rahner continued to ask probing questions, while not pretending that he or anyone else yet knows the answers. He thought that Vatican II represented the opening to a world church. His three-stage theory of church history bears no resemblance to the theory of three ages that has dominated Western thinking since Joachim of Fiore in the twelfth century.[31] Rahner thought that the first stage of church history was the brief Jewish-Christian era; the second stage has been a European-dominated Christianity. The Second Vatican Council, although still speaking the language of European Christianity, signaled an opening to Africa, Asia, and the rest of humanity. The church is at the beginning of the third stage of its history, a world Christianity.

If the church is to become a world church, universal or catholic in more than name, the idea of divine revelation needs a more radical rethinking than Vatican II could manage. Rahner pressed the issue of revelation between the time of the first humans and Abraham. The question demands more than a sentence or two. The issue of a "primitive revelation" leads Rahner to "revelation" beyond the present church and a revelation accessible in Africa and Asia. The Christian church testifies to a divine revealing throughout the world.

The last article of the Constitution on Divine Revelation returns to the universalism professed in the Preface of the document, the hope that "the treasure of Revelation entrusted to the Church may more and more fill the hearts of men" (*DV* 26). But that the "Word of God may speed on and triumph" everywhere, the Catholic Church has to avoid the posture of *possessing* the treasure. While holding on to the best in its own tradition, it has to be a learner in relation to other traditions.

Those other traditions include the Eastern church or Orthodoxy. Joseph Ratzinger credited Eastern Orthodoxy with correcting a bias in the Western church's view of revelation, which Ratzinger called too narrowly incarnational.[32] The Western church still has much to learn about the importance of the Holy Spirit. Joseph Ratzinger, now Pope Benedict XVI, is in a position to carry further the East-West dialogue.

Protestant scholarship on the Bible was an indispensable part of the preparation for Vatican II. The cooperation between Catholic and Protestant

---

31. Karl Rahner, "Basic Theological Interpretation of the Second Vatican Council," in idem, *Theological Investigations*, vol. 20 (New York: Crossroad, 1981), 77–89.

32. Ratzinger, "Commentary on Constitution on Divine Revelation," 190.

Scripture scholars has been an admirable development in modern church history. However, it would be unrealistic to expect a rethinking of revelation from scriptural exegetes. A wider conversation of historians, philosophers, educators, theologians, and artists is needed to stimulate Catholic-Protestant thinking on revelation. Protestant observers at Vatican II were important for keeping the conversation open and honest.

All Christian reforms include a return to the Jewish roots of Christianity. This principle holds in relation to "faith" and "revelation." Despite the obvious differences over Jesus as the Christ, Jews have valuable lessons for Christians to learn about both "word of God" and "revelation." The treatment of Jews and Jewish religion remains the single best test of whether Christian theology has gotten beyond the idea of revelation as truths deposited in the first century.

As soon as feasible, Islam has to be a full partner in dialogue with the other two descendants of Abraham. Christian differences with Islam are no doubt profound, but the world does not yet know where the irresolvable differences lie and where mutual learning could occur. Christianity and Islam are only two of the world's religions, but with over a billion people in each camp and with passionate commitment demanded of believers on each side, world peace largely depends on Christians and Muslims getting a better understanding of each other.

Whether "revelation" can be a central idea beyond the three Abrahamic religions is not clear. We cannot know that unless the three religions come to some understanding, even while continuing to have their disagreements.

Chapter Three

Authority in a Believing Church

The question of "church" is not an afterthought to a description of believing in a revealing God. All Christians, despite differences over the meaning of church, would agree that the church is a necessary context for a Christian believing in a God who reveals. The church is supposed to be helpful for this believing, but it can also be a problem. Joseph Ratzinger, as a young theologian in 1968, wrote: "For many people today the church has become the main obstacle to belief. They can no longer see in her anything but the human struggle for power, the petty spectacle of those who, with their claim to administer official Christianity, seem to stand most in the way of the true spirit of Christianity."[1] Those words are harsh criticism from a future pope.

The question of authority that Ratzinger highlights in his criticism is one way of approaching differing understandings of church and the need to reform the church so that it helps rather than obstructs believing in a revealing God. This chapter is about church authority, although that subject will unavoidably raise issues about church structure as a whole. Discussions of the church are confusing because Christians move between a language that sees the church empirically as a sociohistorical institution and language that views the church from the inside, a mix of theological theories and actual experience.

In Roman Catholic discussions of the church during the past half century it has regularly been said that Vatican II changed the perception of the church from "institution" to "people of God." Those terms are not alternatives within a common framework. "Institution" is an abstract concept for viewing the church from the outside. "People of God" is a biblical metaphor that makes sense only within a theological narrative; to an outsider the description either has no meaning or appears to be arrogant.

---

1. Joseph Ratzinger, *Introduction to Christianity* (San Francisco: Ignatius Press, 2004), 340.

For Vatican II the biblical metaphor became the rich starting point for a properly theological reflection on believing in God who reveals. Unfortunately, the church since then has neglected to change much of its institutional language and procedures, especially around the issue of authority. Theological language can have the effect of blocking out questions that may be obvious to an outside view, a view that can be taken not only by non-Christians but also by the ordinary Christian.

The Second Vatican Council did its best in navigating the contrasting languages. No one would expect the bishops of the Roman Catholic Church to have examined the church as if they were outsiders, although an occasional view from outside would not have been a bad idea. Protestant and Orthodox observers did have some helpful comments from beyond the boundaries of the Roman Catholic Church and the assumed language of Roman Catholicism.

To view the church as an institution is simply to acknowledge that it has a place in human history. Not only is it an institution: it is one of the largest, oldest, and most impressive institutions in history. It necessarily has a complex pattern of authority that needs more explaining than saying God ordained it so. The authority pattern varies in institutions according to the nature and purpose of the institution and the conditions surrounding a particular institution.

Authority

Authority is a question for every institution. Every group, community, organization, or society has a way of deciding things. Authority refers to how the power to decide for a group can be exercised in a way that is accepted as legitimate. "Whether a decision has authority depends on the person to whom the order is addressed, not on 'persons of authority' who give orders."[2]

As soon as a group gets to a size only slightly larger than a family there is a need for clearly understood rules of procedure. Rules need not oppress anyone's freedom, although undeniably they place restrictions on particular actions. As the pattern of authority becomes more explicit and detailed, individuals take on roles or exercise offices of authority. The person is neither the role nor the office.

It was an important contribution of the Christian church—but one often neglected in the church today—to make such a distinction and to recognize

---

2. Karl Weick, *The Social Psychology of Organizations* (Reading, PA: Addison-Wesley, 1969), 3.

that the exercise of authority in an organization is attached to an office and not to a person. If a president, CEO, or bishop is inept, the criticism ought to be directed at that person's exercise of the office. Sometimes the pattern of authority itself may need criticism and change. That situation should be clearly distinguished from individual inadequacies in office.

Understanding authority within the church may be helped by a comparison to other institutions. Some comparisons are unworthy, but others can produce insight. Is the New Testament more like the Declaration of Independence or the United States Constitution? Is the office of bishop more like the role of a father, a king, a president, a chief operating officer, or a coach? Is the authority pattern of a church more like a business corporation, a think tank, a political town meeting, or a baseball team? If one's answer to all such questions is "none of the above," there still remains the question of how to think about authority in a way that does not lose the particular context of a believing church, yet functions in a world with numerous offices of authority.

In modern times the authority pattern of the Christian church has been based on a division within the church between laity and clergy. This language had emerged in the early church, but it was only in the twelfth century that a two-class system was firmly set in place. A third category, "the religious," was absorbed into the other two.[3] A two-class system is usually defined by one group having something the other group lacks. The term "laity" originally meant "people," but it came to be defined as a deficiency. To this day, both in church circles and in the world of secular professions, a layperson is someone who lacks competence, knowledge, or skill. Authority has to be exercised by the higher group directing the lower group.

Vatican II's Constitution on the Church could not overcome a language of negation in defining "laity": "The term 'laity' is here understood to mean all the faithful except those in Holy Orders and those who belong to a religious state approved by the Church" (*LG* 31). The council hastened to add that the laity participates in the People of God by baptism, but there was no available language for overcoming the clergy-lay division. One bishop has suggested that all church members be called "citizens" of the church. The adoption of that term is unlikely, even though he can cite a New Testament basis for the name (Eph 2:19-20).[4]

This neat division within the church meant that authority was invested in an upper division. The responsibility of the lower division was to obey what

3. Kenan Osborne, *Orders and Ministry* (New York: Orbis Books, 2006), 62.
4. Geoffrey Robinson, *Confronting Power and Sex in the Catholic Church: Reclaiming the Spirit of Jesus* (Collegeville, MN: Liturgical Press, 2008), 293–96.

was commanded. There was a "church teaching" and a "church taught." In the Middle Ages the emerging universities offered some counterweight of teaching, although in theory they were obedient to the teaching of the bishops. The future Pope Boniface VIII complained to the faculty of one university: "You Paris masters at your desks seem to think that the world should be ruled by your reasonings. . . . It is to us that the world is entrusted, not to you."[5] It was in the nineteenth century that "the church teaching" was exclusively reserved for the bishops. That language remains firmly in place under a Latin term regularly used without much critical examination: *magisterium.*[6]

The Catholic Church's pattern of authority up to Vatican II generally corresponded with its meaning of faith-revelation. "Revelation" or "revealed truths" was the content of what was taught. Faith was the acceptance of those truths taught by "the church." Authority was not personal and idiosyncratic; it was the church that taught and had to be obeyed. "Church" regularly referred to the system of offices established by "holy orders." The bishop was supreme in his own diocese, where he exercised authority, assisted by the "lower clergy." Especially after Vatican I, the papacy took over as the seat of church authority; the diocese was treated as a branch office by the curia in Rome.

Change in Church Authority

The Second Vatican Council almost inadvertently upended this long-standing authority pattern in the Roman Catholic Church. The revolution was not in what the documents said but in the way the event occurred. When the council was called it was assumed by nearly everyone involved that it would be a brief meeting that would clarify and reaffirm what the councils of Trent and Vatican I had taught. The preparation for the council in documents drawn up by the curia proceeded on that assumption.

On October 13, 1962, the first general congregation of the council met. A single bishop, Cardinal Lienhart of Lille, objected to the rules and forced a delay until bishops could get to know one another and invent new rules.[7]

---

5. Alfred Crosby, *The Measure of Reality: Quantification in Western Europe 1250–1600* (Cambridge: Cambridge University Press, 1997), 59.

6. Yves Congar, "A Semantic History of the Term *Magisterium,*" in *The Magisterium and Morality,* ed. Charles Curran and Richard McCormick, 297–313 (New York: Paulist Press, 1982), 210.

7. Giuseppe Alberigo and Joseph Komonchak, eds., *History of Vatican II: Toward a New Era in Catholicism* (New York: Orbis Books, 1995), 2:26–31.

Once they got started there was no stopping them. Three years later it was a different church. The Holy Spirit was claimed by the change agents who did not agree with the way authority was exercised from the top of the organization.

What had happened with shocking speed was a de-divinizing of church structures. The whole world, including all Roman Catholics, could see that if the Holy Spirit was in charge it was through the arguments between people in positions of authority. The manner, style, and dynamics of the council meant that authority could never again be exercised by such mottos as "Rome has spoken; the case is ended."

The fact that a divinized structure had suffered a fatal blow was not recognized and accepted by everyone. There are still church officials who try to rule by fiat. It may even still seem to work, but an erosion of that kind of exercise of authority has been constant. The Roman Catholic Church has been in a confusing transition for the last forty years. The crisis is likely to continue for many more decades. The collapse of one pattern of authority did not automatically produce another. The Catholic Church badly needs conservatives who are not just trying to reestablish a church of the sixteenth or nineteenth century. It also needs the help of loyal critics who could introduce institutional reforms that are not dictated by theology but are not incompatible with some form of theology.

It is not clear that the sexual scandal involving many clergy has opened the door to reform. What began as a sexual scandal quickly morphed into a crisis of authority. How could bishops have allowed all that to happen? Through ignorance, incompetence, deliberate deception? None of the explanations is helpful in shoring up confidence in the way the church is run. The Catholic Church cannot muddle through this crisis. Various defensive strategies only make things worse. The Catholic Church has had to pay out hundreds of millions of dollars even while its reputation has been damaged by a refusal to candidly admit the failures.

The clearest case of Vatican II's de-divinizing of church structure was the change in religious orders. During the 1950s and early 1960s these congregations of men or women seemed to be at their zenith. Along with the seminaries, novitiates were filled with bright, enthusiastic vocations. For centuries religious brothers and sisters had dedicated themselves to church work and had lived simply, as dictated by a rule of life approved by the church. "Keep the rule and the rule will keep you" was the assurance given to every young person admitted to religious or evangelical vows. Everything depended on order, the discipline of the individual within a pattern that had changed little over the centuries. An ancient saying was that "the voice of the prior is the voice of God." There was no ambiguity about the nature and exercise of authority.

Between 1965 and 1975 this authority pattern collapsed. The religious order was an advance party of what would eventually work its way through the whole church. Despite the council's rhetorical praise of what is called "the religious life," the religious order was an unintended casualty of Vatican II. It became obvious that the prior or religious superior was not receiving orders directly from God. The rule was a fallible instrument, reflecting practices of another century that might be unhelpful and unhealthy today.

Many religious orders responded quickly to the effect of Vatican II and tried to devise new forms of authority. But they were caught between the slow pace of institutional change and the exodus of thousands of members who decided to change their own lives. A worse sign for the future was that young people were not entering novitiate training, even as novitiates tried to become up to date. Some Catholics saw conspiracy in the emptying of the convents, but what happened was almost the opposite of a conspiracy. An openness to rethinking old patterns of authority produced results no one could control. As the old pattern collapsed, many religious sisters and brothers continued to do admirable work while looking to construct a viable form of authority. Their efforts, even if only partly successful, might have lessons for the larger church, and especially for church officials who have often lacked appreciation of the dedicated work of sisters and brothers.

The secular clergy did not suffer the same immediate effect. The trappings of authority continued in place after Vatican II: dress, title, respect for the office, living arrangements, and patterns of work remained as before. The voice of the bishop, if not the voice of God, was still the unchallenged and unchallengeable voice of authority in the diocese. When a man became a pastor of a parish he could still find considerable satisfaction in the exercise of authority at the local level. The Catholic priest was still in a position of honor; thousands of priests continued to do good work in parishes and other church settings.

Until Vatican II the system limited but also sustained the individual priest. After Vatican II the system did not offer the same support, but it continued to isolate the individual. The temptations for the pastor and the assistant were different, stemming from the difference in the exercise of power, but both suffered from a lack of community. The religious order's one great advantage in its crisis was community that restricted but supported the individual religious brother or sister. As the de-divinizing effect of Vatican II slowly moved through the clerical system, individuals were on their own, many of them unprepared for a freedom from the structure accompanied by a lack of community support. The sexual scandal of the Catholic Church was predictable decades ago, but those in positions of authority seem to have been oblivious to the problem or just hoped it could be kept secret.

People who have felt oppressed by one system of authority can become antiauthority, mistaking authority for one pattern of its exercise. They say "authority" when they are referring to the people exercising power within that system. Faith-revelation needs a new or improved pattern of authority. In the world of Vatican I, revelation was a deposit of "eternal decrees." The faith that corresponded to that revelation was belief in the truth of the teachings of the church's bishops. In the world after Vatican II, revelation is better understood as the present activity of God, and faith is the obedience of the whole person in a relationship of trust and overflowing love.

For such a relationship to be effective, a more developed institutional authority has to emerge. A new pattern comes about when some key terms are changed, terms that have prevented the emergence of new ways of doing things. The usual process is not one of getting rid of the terms, but coming to be aware of how they are misused. The criteria for their proper use are intelligibility in the present combined with a rich meaning drawn from the deep past. The change of language should affect the authority pattern in important ways, but that fact need not be immediately apparent. The reaction of some people will be that the change is trivial. That reaction can actually be helpful because other proposals for large changes in the system are likely to cause a stand-off between opposing factions.

There are two words, "faithful" and "hierarchy," that are a key to the authority pattern of the Catholic Church. The two words are paired and are regularly—and unthinkingly—used together. The Vatican II document on the church showed some awareness of the misuse of these terms, but the council's efforts had little overall effect on its own documents or on commentaries on those documents. The meaning of each of these two words depends on the other. So long as the Catholic Church divides itself into the faithful and the hierarchy, the question of a better authority pattern cannot be seriously raised.

Vatican II, in discussing the church, wisely tried to find a starting point from which to look at the church as a whole. Many terms were available: mystery, sacrament, body of Christ, people of God. Such unifying images, however, do not overcome the language used and misused for the main elements of institutional authority. Here is a typical passage from Alois Grillmeier's commentary on Vatican II's Constitution on the Church: "The 'people of God' does not mean here the mass of the faithful in contrast to the hierarchy, but the Church as a whole, with every group of its members."[8] While Grillmeier is celebrating the affirmation of church unity, he cites as a standard way to describe the inner division of the church "the faithful" in contrast to "the hierarchy." However popular the phrase "people of God" has become, the components are still called "the faithful" and "the hierarchy."

The Faithful

The more glaring misuse of language is "the faithful" as a term to describe the laity. The Vatican II document insisted in several places that "the faithful" are coextensive with the church. However, the document itself slips back into the common way of referring to the laity as "the faithful," especially when they are taught or shepherded by people called "the hierarchy." In the chapter on the laity, pastors are said to understand "that it is their exalted office so to be shepherds of the faithful" (*LG* 30).

References to the faithful are taken to be a positive and complementary way of church officials referring to the laity. What is seldom noticed is that if the laity are "the faithful," where does that leave the clergy? Are they the faithless? Being faithful or unfaithful is hardly a minor issue in a church context. Presumably there should be no objection to including bishops and priests in those who are faithful. A vote on that question in any church body would likely find unanimous approval. Why, then, in at least nine out of ten cases of church usage, does "faithful" exclude the clergy or at least the bishops?

The answer is obvious if faith means accepting truths taught by the bishops. The use of the term "faithful" fits perfectly with revelation as a deposit of truths from the past and faith as assent to those truths. The "church taught," that is, the laity, need faith to grasp church doctrine as truths that have been revealed by God and preserved by church officials. Those who have the truth already do not have to rely on faith.

If, in contrast, faith is believing in a God who reveals in the present, then the church as a whole is the believer. The faithful are all church members who respond to a speaking and revealing God; they are all the followers of Jesus who believe in God as guided by the Holy Spirit. Church officials have to listen to the movement of the Spirit and respond as faithful. For such

---

8. Alois Grillmeier, "Commentary on the Constitution on the Church," in *Commentary on the Documents of Vatican II*, Herbert Vorgrimler, ed., vol. 1, 153–85 (New York: Herder & Herder, 1967–69), at 153.

faithfulness a great variety of church offices is needed to preserve the tradition within which believing in a revealing God occurs. The New Testament already gave names to such ministries in church life.

Hierarchy? Yes

"Hierarchy" is the single most important term that obstructs needed reform in the Roman Catholic Church. There is nothing wrong with the word itself. The Catholic Church is a hierarchic institution and always will be. Rethinking the pattern of authority in the church can only proceed by accepting the importance of hierarchy. Garry Wills, after quoting Jesus, "that everyone lifting himself up will be abased, and anyone abasing himself will be lifted up" (Luke 14:1), concludes: "there could not be a clearer injunction against hierarchy of any kind."[9] However, seeking "high rank" is what is forbidden, not necessarily hierarchy of any kind.

The problem is the constant misuse of the term "hierarchy," a word that describes an authority pattern in an institution. One cannot begin to rethink the hierarchical structure of the church until writers stop using "the hierarchy" to refer to the bishops. That first step would then make it possible to imagine a pattern of church hierarchy as other than a pyramid of power. The Catholic Church seems to be the only prominent institution in which hierarchy is almost totally identified with a group of people. Having taught the modern world what a hierarchy is, the Catholic Church seems to have forgotten what its own word means.

Vatican II made a valiant effort to situate the question properly. The first draft of the Constitution on the Church started with "the church militant." When that first draft was revised, "mystery of the church" came first, followed by the "hierarchical constitution," and then "people of God." In the final version of the document, "people of God" moved up to chapter 2. Chapter 3 was given the interesting title: "The hierarchical structure of the church, with special reference to the episcopate" (*LG* 18).[10] That is a promising recognition that hierarchy refers to church structure within which the episcopate is one element.

The natural question is: what else is in the hierarchy besides the episcopate? One might have presumed that the next chapter of the Constitution would be titled "the hierarchical structure of the church, with special reference to x." But that following chapter is called "the laity." It begins: "Having

9. Garry Wills, *What Jesus Meant* (New York: Viking Press, 2006), 45.
10. The title in the Flannery translation is simply "The Church Is Hierarchical."

made clear the functions of the hierarchy, the holy Council is pleased to turn its attention to the state of those Christians who are called the laity" (*LG* 30). The Council seemed to forget the title of the preceding chapter, and that hierarchy is the structure of the church that includes episcopal functions.

By the fourth chapter, on the laity, the document is back to speaking in the way that has become standard: ". . . the laity can be called in different ways to more immediate cooperation in the apostolate of the hierarchy . . . [and] appointed by the hierarchy to some ecclesiastical offices" (*LG* 33). In the sixth chapter "it is for the hierarchy to make wise laws . . . the hierarchy accepts rules of religious life which are presented for its approval" (*LG* 45). Critics inside and outside the church complain that "the hierarchy" still has nearly all the power, but the underlying problem is that "hierarchy" is referred to as a who rather than a what.

The term "hierarchy" was coined by Pseudo-Dionysius, a Syrian monk of the fifth century who had an extraordinary influence on the theology of the Middle Ages. He described hierarchy as "a sacred order, a state of understanding and an activity approximating as closely as possible to the divine."[11] Bringing together Neoplatonic philosophy and the New Testament, Dionysius was one of the chief inspirations of Thomas Aquinas. The Neoplatonic image of descent from the One was transformed by the image of Christ at the center of creation.[12] In early medieval portrayals of hierarchy God is above but surrounded by choirs of angels, a circling about the throne that was inspired by Dionysius and the biblical visions of Isaiah 6:2 and Revelation 4:4. Hierarchy was a metaphysical and mystical description long before it was applied to organizations.

Hierarchy need not imply an exertion of power from the top to the bottom. A "sacred order" can be a sharing of power. Rebellion against a pyramidal structure is often in the name of equality, but egalitarianism is not a workable proposal for the universe or for any organization of more than ten people. For example, the solution to our ecological problem is not an equality of all the animals, a formula that denies human responsibility. The needed image is circles within circles, a hierarchy in which men and women are imagined at the center of life. The humans are responsible for caring for other creatures to the extent they are capable. Christian theology sees the incarnated power

---

11. Pseudo-Dionysius, "The Celestial Hierarchy," in *The Complete Works* (New York: Paulist Press, 1987), 164D; Ronald Hathaway, *Hierarchy and the Definition of Order in the Letters of Pseudo-Dionysius* (The Hague: Nijhoff, 1969), 37.

12. Pseudo-Dionysius, "Letter Three," in *The Complete Works*, 145B.

of God at the center, a fact that would restrain humans in their tendency to think that they have the power to do whatever they wish.

When the idea of a holy order was applied to church organization as it emerged in the twelfth century, the historical and cultural conditions were not well suited to a church imagined as Christ and Spirit at the center surrounded by circles of believers. The Christian church might have embodied a genuinely religious organization with all humanity equal before God and dedicated to caring for human and nonhuman worlds, but the split within the church into two classes made a demonstration of "people of God" impossible.[13] The holy order was translated as holy orders, imagined as a series of steps upward. The laity had no place within these orders; the clergy were divided into higher and lower status.

The modern world absorbed "hierarchy" in the image of a pyramid. In the nineteenth century hierarchy became practically interchangeable with "bureaucracy." These days, hierarchy is mostly disparaged. Business leaders regularly make proclamations, such as this one from Jack Welch, former head of GE: "Hierarchy is dead. The organization of the future will be virtually layerless and increasingly boundaryless."[14]

It might be thought that secular objections to hierarchy would be due to its meaning a "holy order." That would be understandable, but the complaint is never raised. Objections to hierarchy are directed at a particular form of organization that emphasizes a superior-inferior relation, an exercise of power from top to bottom. People on the bottom understandably dislike being in that position. They feel exposed to the exercise of power over them so that they must either submit to the commands of a superior or quit and go elsewhere.

Mike Abrashoff, after long experience in the United States Navy, described the institution this way: "The Navy is like a tree full of monkeys. If you're at the top of the tree, all you see when you look down is a bunch of smiling faces looking up at you. When you're at the bottom of the tree and you look up, you have a different view."[15] In a culture obsessed with equality, the man (and now woman) who is on top does not necessarily relish the position. Some people do enjoy having the power to dictate orders to others, but many people in those positions long for some human give-and-take. They do not trust all those smiling monkeys. The higher up they go in the chain

13. Kenan Osborne, *Orders and Ministry*, 118; Michael Lawler and Thomas Shannon, *Church: A Spiritual Communion* (Collegeville, MN: Liturgical Press, 1995), 78.

14. Jack Welch, *Jack: Straight from the Gut* (New York: Warner, 2001), 433.

15. Mike Abrashoff, *It's Your Ship* (New York: Business Plus, 2002).

of command, the more isolated they feel. At the pinnacle of the pyramid there is no one to carry on a regular conversation. Presidents complain that no one will tell them the simple truth. Loyal lieutenants whose employment depends on the top man are not inclined to deliver bad news.

The constant criticism of bureaucratic hierarchy in business literature has not produced a realistic alternative.[16] In the last two decades some educational reformers have referred to "flat hierarchy." To many people that would sound like a contradiction in terms. "Flat" is indeed the wrong word to emphasize in describing an alternate form of hierarchy. What is needed is a description of small communities interacting with each other. Proponents of a "flat hierarchy" describe a school organized into several houses or communities. The teaching teams in these communities are the administrative units. The school principal is the principal teacher. The large size of an institution can be an advantage if it is designed as interacting communities organized around a center.[17] There are schools that do operate on this basis, but they need help from reform at regional and national levels.

What educational writers are groping toward as "flat hierarchy" should be evident to Christian writers who draw on the history of theology.[18] Christ is the center from which power radiates in the church. Each local church is not an administrative unit of a bureaucracy but the whole church in miniature. Where a few are gathered in Christ's name, the church of God exists. A bishop is not the top man in control of "his" diocese. A bishop is a collegial partner to other bishops. In a pyramid, the other bishops are always going to be one step below the bishop of Rome. In a hierarchy of circles inside circles, the bishops are a community with the pope at the center. The bishop of Rome, not as the "supreme pontiff" but as the "servant of the servants of God," can be a powerful symbol of church unity within the college of bishops.

Vatican II moved in the direction of a Christ-Spirit–centered church. The roots of that theology start with the New Testament, and a focus on Christ and Spirit has never disappeared in the prayer life of the church, even though

---

16. Katherine Newman, "Incipient Bureaucracy: The Development of Hierarchies in Egalitarian Organizations," in *Hierarchy and Society: Anthropological Perspectives on Bureaucracy*, ed. Gerald Britain and Ronald Cohen, 143–63 (Philadelphia: Institute for the Study of Human Issues, 1980).

17. Theodore Sizer, *Horace's School: Redesigning the American High School* (Boston: Houghton Mifflin, 1992), 180.

18. I agree with Terence Nichols in *That All May Be One: Hierarchy and Participation in the Church* (Collegeville, MN: Liturgical Press, 1997) that hierarchy should be based on participation in power. Unfortunately, Nichols does not challenge the image of up and down that precludes meaningful participation.

its administrative apparatus could obscure God's revelation in Christ through the Holy Spirit. If the Council of Trent had followed the Christ-centered theology of the Greek Fathers or that of Erasmus instead of simply reacting against the Protestant reformers, the Catholic Church would have presented a different institutional form to the world.[19] It is not too late for the Roman Catholic Church to draw on its tradition and show the secular world what a hierarchy looks like when it is based on community, the sharing of power, and respect for the individual creature.

The Constitution on the Church

Vatican II as a whole and its Constitution on the Church attempted to rediscover a richer strand of theology. To a large extent the bishops succeeded, although when they got beyond biblical phrases they reverted to language of top administrators speaking to the masses below. The Constitution on the Church is thought by many observers and commentators to be the most important achievement of the council. Fortunately, it was not just bishops reflecting on the nature of the church. They were aided by experts in Catholic theology as well as Protestant observers. It is no disparagement of the bishops to point out that bishops talking about the church could provide only one (clerical) perspective. It is important that dialogue continue between the Eastern and Western churches, as well as Catholic and Protestant versions of Western Christianity.

At several points the council was deliberately ambiguous because there was no consensus on the language to be used. Several of those points are hotly debated today, as I note below. The long-range effects of the Constitution still hang in the balance. Christopher Butler's judgment on the Constitution at the end of the council stands up more than four decades later: "I have no hesitation in saying that the Constitution is a great document, even though being the fruit of the Holy Spirit, working in imperfect human beings, it is a stepping stone and not a final accomplishment."[20]

I have already noted that the first draft of the document on the church, with its eleven chapters, was straight out of the sixteenth century: church militant, necessity of the church for salvation, episcopacy. . . . A second draft, which was reduced to four chapters, started with the mystery of the church and then took up the hierarchic constitution of the church. A section

19. Marjorie O'Rourke Boyle, *Erasmus on Language and Method in Theology* (Toronto: University of Toronto Press, 1979), 101–08.

20. Christopher Butler, "Introduction," in *The Constitution on the Church* (New York: Deus Books, 1965), 8–9.

of its third chapter, people of God, eventually became the second chapter. In the final version of the Constitution mystery precedes people of God, and hierarchical structure follows.

This sequence of chapters was widely and rightly praised. The hierarchical structure is within the people of God; bishops are part of the people and serve the whole church within the hierarchy. There was not a choice between people of God and hierarchical structure. A sociologist, tracing the effect of the council, should know better than to say at the beginning of her book: "Most importantly, Vatican II changed the way the Church understood itself, as its identity went from being a hierarchical authority to a church conceived as the people of God."[21] The bishops had no intention of relinquishing hierarchical authority.

The title of the Constitution on the Church is *Lumen Gentium* (Light of the Nations). As the opening words of the document, "light of the nations" could be misconstrued as a self-description. The words actually refer to Christ as the basis of the church's belief. The Constitution quickly adds that the church wishes to spread *his* radiance, which it does by proclaiming the Gospel. A fundamental ambiguity is already contained in these first two sentences. The church claims to continue Christ's presence on earth, but on what kind of analogy is that to be conceived? Is the church a continuation of the incarnation, the "body of Christ," or is the church a witness to Christ? Protestants have emphasized the latter: the church as "witness of the Lord who alone is fully the sacrament of unity and beginning of the Kingdom."[22]

"Mystery," which is the title of the first chapter, is an answer to the question of the church's relation to Christ, or perhaps it is an ambiguous context for working out an answer. Mystery is an ancient word that was applied to Christ as early as the New Testament (1 Tim 3:16; Eph 1:11). Both liberals and conservatives can hang on to the word. Augustine's meaning of mystery as something that can always be understood further was later almost reversed so that mystery became what cannot be understood. Some contemporary authors, most prominently Gabriel Marcel, have reclaimed the ancient religious meaning.[23] Marcel's contrast between a problem (a technical question with an objective answer) and a mystery (a self-involving question with no single answer) restored a more positive meaning to mystery.

---

21. Melissa Wilde, *Vatican II: A Sociological Analysis of Religious Change* (Princeton, NJ: Princeton University Press, 2007), 1.

22. George Lindbeck, "A Protestant View," *Vatican II: An Interfaith Appraisal*, ed. John Miller (Notre Dame, IN: University of Notre Dame, 1966), 226.

23. Gabriel Marcel, *The Mystery of Being* (New York: St. Augustine's Press, 2001).

By the second paragraph the document has moved from mystery to sacrament. Most people would be unaware that "sacrament" originally translated "mystery"; the modern catechism and theology textbooks hide such a connection. Generations of Catholics grew up with a clear meaning of sacraments as the seven external signs of the conferral of interior grace. The Council of Trent had specified that there are seven of these sacraments amid many smaller external practices called sacramentals. The nature and number of sacraments was a central point of dispute between Catholics and Protestants.

In the 1950s some German and French theologians had explored the use of "sacrament" to refer to the church itself. That rather daring change opened up new possibilities for rethinking the Catholic practice of sacraments and sacramentals, as well as providing a new basis for Catholic-Protestant dialogue. In this framework "Christ *instituted* the sacraments" by instituting the church as the primary sacrament. The Holy Spirit *constitutes* the church in its relation to contemporary conditions.[24] The number and hierarchy of sacraments are open for discussion.

The council's use of this figure of speech was a surprise that had major implications; it asserted that "the Church, in Christ, is in the nature of sacrament" (*LG* 1). The council avoided the phrase "primordial sacrament," which had been used by theologians, but it nonetheless endorsed the idea of church as sacrament. A double analogy was thus set up: the church is like Christ; the church is like the sacraments. The idea of mystery was thereby given some specificity.

The document immediately adds to the church as a sacrament that it is "a sign and instrument, that is, of communion with God and of unity among all men" (*LG* 1). The idea of "instrument" is in considerable tension with "sacrament." The church as instrument in the hand of God was a common metaphor in the late Middle Ages, used, for example, by Savanarola.[25] "Instrument" does not fit well with Christ as sacrament of God and church as sacrament of Christ's presence.

The seven sacraments were often described as instruments of grace, but this language lent itself to impersonal, sometimes magical, views of the Eucharist or penance. The Christian church as an instrument of world unity suggests a church as an object in God's hands instead of a people that,

---

24. For the play between instituting and constituting the church see John Zizioulas, *Being as Communion* (New York: St.Vladimir's Seminary Press, 1985), 140.

25. Michael Walzer, *Revolution of the Saints: A Study in the Origin of Radical Politics* (Cambridge, MA: Harvard University Press, 1982), 166.

believing in God revealed in Christ and the Spirit, is a demonstration community for humanity.

Post-Conciliar Debates

This logic of sacramentality underlies most of the controversies that accompanied the Constitution on the Church and have continued ever since. The most pointed argument is probably the meaning of the eighth article: "This Church, constituted and organized as a society in the present world, subsists in the Catholic Church. . . . Nevertheless, many elements of sanctification and of truth are found outside its visible confines" (*LG* 8). It is obvious that the council avoided using the term "church" for any group other than the "organized society" of the Catholic Church. It is also obvious that the council avoided saying that the existing society of the Catholic Church is the one and only church. The wiggle word in the passage is *subsist*, which replaced *is* from an earlier draft. Neither in Latin nor in English does the word "subsist" have a clear technical meaning that would resolve the question of what counts as "church."[26]

Nearly all the attention was directed to whether "church" should be used of Protestant bodies. From the outside view that question had already been resolved. Roman Catholics, like everyone else, refer to Protestant churches. The council, however, was addressing the question theologically. Those who were opposed to referring to Protestant churches contended that Protestantism has serious deficiencies in the sacrament of orders; elements of sanctification and truth are there, but not a valid Eucharist.

It might be helpful to note a different distinction implied in replacing "is" with "subsist." However conscious the bishops were of another distinction, "subsist" can call attention to the difference between the present, imperfect form of church and a greater church to be revealed at the end of days. The seventh chapter of the Constitution is on "the eschatological nature of the pilgrim church and her union with the heavenly church." This chapter was inserted late in the evolution of the document because Pope John XXIII asked for something to be said on "the veneration of the saints."[27]

This seventh chapter proves to be more than some pious comments for a conclusion. An interesting use of language in the chapter is "heavenly church" in contrast to "pilgrim church." The distinction that is affirmed here

---

26. Nicholas Lash, *Theology for Pilgrims* (Grand Rapids, MI: Eerdmans, 2008), 271–74.

27. Otto Semmelroth, "Commentary on the Constitution on the Church," in Vorgrimler, ed., *Commentary on the Documents of Vatican II*, vol. 1, 280.

is not between church and kingdom or between church and "heavenly Jerusalem," which is a traditional phrase.[28] The use of "heavenly church" implies incompleteness in every form of church on earth. The danger in the phrase, not overcome by the contents of the chapter, is the image of a two-story universe with a heavenly church above. The chapter was put together hurriedly and deserved more development than it received.[29]

The Lutheran or Presbyterian Church is not the one, holy, catholic, and apostolic church. But neither is the Roman Catholic Church—at least not yet. The Roman Catholic Church can lay claim to its share of apostolic notes. However, on its own theological terms it has yet to achieve perfect unity and complete universality. The pilgrim church is not the heavenly church. "We need only look at real history to see that no single church is one, holy, catholic and apostolic. The four so-called marks of the church from the Council of Constantinople do not therefore seek to *describe* a reality but are an eschatological call for repentance."[30]

In 2007 the Congregation for the Doctrine of the Faith issued a "clarification" of the question in the form of five questions and answers.[31] This brief document was an addition to several of its previous documents that caused widespread consternation for seeming to pull back from what the council had begun.

This new document starts with the question: "Did the Second Vatican Council change the Catholic doctrine on the church?" A credible answer would have been that the council did not abandon past teaching, did not reverse its doctrine or invent something entirely new. Instead, the document's answer is nonsensical: "The Second Vatican Council neither changed nor intended to change this doctrine; rather it developed, deepened and more fully explained it." Whether in Latin or English it is silly to claim that the doctrine did not change; the whole world knows that it did. "Develop," "deepen," "more fully explain" are forms of change.

The four questions and answers that follow are all part of a denial of change. The document asks: "Why was the expression 'subsist' adopted instead of the simple word 'is'?" The answer offered is: "The use of this expression, which indicates the full identity of the church of Christ with the Catholic Church, does not change the doctrine on the church." That response

---

28. Henri de Lubac, in Miller, ed., *Vatican II: An Interfaith Appraisal*, 161.
29. Barnabas Ahern, "The Eschatological Dimension of the Church," in ibid., 293–300.
30. Edward Schillebeeckx, *On Christian Faith* (New York: Crossroad, 1987), 44.
31. Congregation for the Doctrine of the Faith, "Responses to Some Questions Regarding Certain Aspects of the Doctrine on the Church," *Origins* 37 (July 19, 2007).

does not even attempt to actually answer the question. The bishops of the council made a change for some reason.

A fundamental debate over the meaning of "church" is illustrated by a lively and detailed exchange between Joseph Ratzinger, who was then head of the Congregation for the Doctrine of the Faith, and Walter Kasper, a bishop and distinguished theologian. Their debate was civil, with no name calling or angry outbursts, but it revealed two different perspectives on church and church authority.[32]

Walter Kasper's original comments were in response to a 1992 document from the Congregation for the Doctrine of the Faith.[33] This "Letter to the Bishops" used a formula Ratzinger had already adopted in two of his books: "The universal church in its essential mystery is a reality ontologically and temporally prior to every individual and particular church."[34] Walter Kasper had no disagreement with the theology. His concern was a practical one: namely, that "universal church" in practice became identified with Rome and that "the bishop of the universal church has ontological priority over other bishops."

In response Ratzinger denied that the Congregation identified the universal church with the Roman church. He suggested that Kasper's doctrine of the church tended "to dissolve the church into purely sociological entities." Kasper denied the charge, agreeing with Ratzinger on the danger of a sociological reductionism. Both men cited Galatians 4:26, a text that refers to the heavenly Jerusalem above as the basis for the "ontological priority" of the universal church.

Ratzinger's concern was that the Catholic Church not be understood as a group of local churches that form a kind of Baptist Convention. He was defending a theology in which the origin of the church was not a response to the failure of the kingdom of God to arrive. The church was from the beginning a response to God's call; local churches are expressions of that "ontological priority."

---

32. Much of their debate can be found in three essays in *America*: Joseph Ratzinger, "The Local Church and the Universal Church" (Nov. 19, 2001): 7–11; Walter Kasper, "On the Church: A Friendly Reply to Cardinal Ratzinger" (April 23, 2001): 8–14; Walter Kasper, "From the President of the Council for Promoting Christian Unity" (Nov. 26, 2001): 28–29; for a summary of the whole debate see Kilian McDonnell, "The Ratzinger/Kasper Debate: The Universal Church and Local Churches," *Theological Studies* 63 (2002): 227–50; 711–29.

33. Congregation for the Doctrine of the Faith, "Letter to the Bishops of the Catholic Church on Some Aspects of the Church Understood as Communion," *Origins* 22 (June 25, 1992): 108–12.

34. Ratzinger, "The Local Church and the Universal Church," 9.

What Kasper seems to suggest is that "ontological priority" makes theological sense, but "temporal priority" unavoidably refers to the historical unfolding of events. There were already diverse forms of church in the New Testament, not a universal church in Jerusalem followed by particular churches. Kasper cites the patristic scholar Henri de Lubac in saying that a universal church existing by itself is an abstraction.[35] That implies the need for a temporal simultaneity of universal and particular. A universal church is not the temporal result of many particular churches, but neither can a universal church exist except to the extent that it is embodied in particular churches.

The way to carry through a practical embodying of the universal in the particular is illustrated by Kasper's proposal for the election of bishops.[36] A bishop is related to a local church, to a conference of bishops, and to the universal church. In a revival of the patriarchate, local churches would be gathered around a metropolitan see. The local church would choose a bishop with the cooperation of the bishops' conference. Rome would have the power of veto. In this hierarchic image the church is multiple circles of communities in which the bishop of Rome at the center of the college of bishops would be a symbol of universality.

The term "universal" always represents an extraordinary claim that can never be entirely met. We may call something universal because it seems to be moving in that direction, but if "universal" means extending to all people, in all places, at all times, those conditions never exist. Most obviously, the stipulation "at all times" cannot be fulfilled while history continues. As for a claim that something applies to all peoples and all places, we have a better basis now than in the distant past to determine whether that claim is defensible. But despite our better grasp of "humanity" than first-century Roman thinkers or eighteenth-century French *philosophes* had, our knowledge of everyone everywhere is still very limited.

As I shall take up in chapter 7, on the logic of Christianity, it is important to realize that the particular and (nearly) universal imply one another. A particular church embodies the universal church—to the extent that a universal church can be said to exist already. The universal church, in turn, can only exist in particular embodiments. As Vatican II said: "This Church of Christ is really present in all legitimately organized groups of the faithful, which, in so far as they are united to their pastors, are also quite appropriately called Churches in the New Testament" (*LG* 26). It would have been more helpful, however, to refer to the faithful, *inclusive* of the pastor.

35. Kasper, "From the President of the Council," 29.
36. Kilian McDonnell, "The Ratzinger/Kasper Debate," 232–33.

There is a hierarchy of such embodied particulars. Some communities come closer to a complete universality, though human judgment is fallible on such a point. A community inclusive of both genders, three generations, various ethnicities, and a variety of disabilities has a better chance of demonstrating the universal community than a group of middle-aged white men from one place. "Church" does not apply to only one group with a specified composition. Kasper pointed out that already in the Gospel of Luke there were several forms of church.

The papacy and the Roman church are today a powerful symbol of universality. What applies to the pope can be said of very few other people: namely, that he gets the attention of leaders around the world when he speaks in the name of the Catholic Church. There is a world of difference between a symbol of universality at the center and an administrative superior of an organization that claims universality. Pope John XXIII managed to shift into a role of speaking to humanity from within the centuries-old backing of tradition. One can sympathize with popes trying to navigate this change, for which there are few helpful precedents.

Catholic Tradition

Modern democracy, denounced by Pope Gregory XVI in an 1832 encyclical, is still spoken of with reserve by Catholic Church officials. When reforms in the hierarchic pattern of authority are brought up, the standard response begins: "Of course, the church is not a democracy." Joseph Ratzinger has written that "the Church of Christ is not a party, not an association, not a club. Her deep and permanent structure is not *democratic* but *sacramental*, consequently hierarchical."[37] Such statements are expected to receive unquestioned approval by all church members, but they raise a question about the meaning of "democracy," assumed to be incompatible with a sacramental church. If democracy is taken to mean a simple majority vote on everything, then the church is not a democracy, but neither is any complex organization today.

If the characteristics of democracy are respect for individual persons, provision for participation in the workings of government, and protection for minority views, it is unclear why "democracy" should be immediately banned from discussion of church reform. John Courtney Murray's description of democracy as "conflicting opinions locked in a civil conversation" was integral to his heroic effort and ultimate success in getting a Vatican II

---

37. Joseph Ratzinger, *The Ratzinger Report* (San Francisco: Ignatius Press, 1985), 49.

document on religious freedom.[38] For many people outside the Catholic Church, that document was the most important one for showing that the Catholic Church's insistence on its tradition is compatible with democratic desires in the contemporary world.

Vatican II was not ready to describe the church as democratic. Given the ambiguity of the term and its exploitation by dictators who claim to be concerned for "the people," the church has good reason to proceed cautiously. Polls of U.S. Catholic laity find a desire for more "democratic decision-making" in church affairs at the levels of the parish (66 percent), the diocese (61 percent) and the Vatican (55 percent).[39] Of course, polling is itself a democratic procedure.

The council did embrace the beginnings of democratic reform in its own procedures. Some further steps could be introduced in parochial, diocesan, regional, and transnational circles of the hierarchy. The church should have a system of checks and balances of the sort that is standard in any modern organization. There must also be genuine consultative forums for the people affected by appointments. Democracy need not mean that 51 percent of the congregation could evict the pastor for preaching an unpopular sermon, but as things are now, priests lack some elementary protections of their civil rights. Priests having a say in the election of their bishop would not be caving in to contemporary fashion; it would merely be treating priests as something more than cogs in a machine.[40]

The Catholic Church could do the modern world a service by showing that democratic procedures and tradition are compatible. In his book on the relation of tradition and democracy, Jeffrey Stout writes: "Commitment to democracy does not entail the rejection of tradition. It requires *jointly* taking responsibility for the criticism and renewal of tradition and for the justification of our social and political arrangements."[41] Who better than the Catholic Church to demonstrate and renew tradition within a democratic and hierarchic institution?

As religious leaders the college of bishops, including the pope, could call regular ecumenical councils. Eventually such meetings of Christian men

38. John Courtney Murray and J. Leon Hooper, *Bridging the Sacred and the Secular: Selected Writings of John Courtney Murray* (Washington, DC: Georgetown University Press, 1994).

39. William D'Antonio, *American Catholics: Gender, Generation and Commitment* (Lanham, MD: Rowman and Littlefield, 2001), 120.

40. On a bishop's experience of the lack of real consultation see Robinson, *Confronting Power and Sex in the Catholic Church*, 135.

41. Jeffrey Stout, *Democracy and Tradition* (Princeton, NJ: Princeton University Press, 2005), 152.

and women would really deserve the name ecumenical. Even Jewish and Muslim leaders would be responsive to an invitation from the pope to sit together and discuss their respective and respected traditions.

The Catholic Church has little choice except to rethink its authority pattern so that small communities can provide the main restraint and guide for the religious experience of individuals. In a hierarchy of circles inside circles each community provides its own teachers and its guidance for the immature. Each small community needs to be in communication with other similar communities as well as with the larger church hierarchy.

The role of an office for teaching the larger church is awareness of tradition at its widest and deepest. The full range of teachings has to be preserved in season and out. Part of its work is to guarantee that debates are not cut off prematurely, that all voices can be heard. The tradition as a whole has to be spoken for while allowing for new soundings that challenge present interpretation of the tradition. "Those who are the hosts, the ones inheriting the tradition, bear the responsibility of building and rebuilding a structure that is faithful to the gospel command of inclusiveness interpreted through the ambiguity of a loved yet flawed tradition."[42]

---

42. Rosemary Haughton, *Images for Change: The Transformation of Society* (New York: Paulist Press, 1997), 175.

Chapter Four

A Responsible Church

Believing in a revealing God provides the basis for a moral life. The term that most comprehensively translates "believing in" to the moral life is "responsibility." That term has some of the built-in ambiguity that "faith" has. "Responsible" is best used as a verb rather than a noun. And like believing *in* and believing *that*, "responsible" covers two verbs, responsible *to* and responsible *for*. Thus the parallel to "believing in a revealing God" is "responsible to a revealing (or speaking) God." Similarly, as believing that something is true follows upon believing in God, so also responsibility *for* one's actions follows upon responsibility *to* God. I will spell out the difference between the two verbs, responsible to and responsible for, and their reciprocal relation.

Responsibility is perhaps the best single entry point for a dialogue between Christian tradition and the contemporary secular world. In today's ethical discussions no term is more omnipresent than responsibility, but few terms are more obfuscating. On the other side, Christian tradition has resources that could help to clear up the confusion that surrounds responsibility. The idea of responsibility has deep Jewish and Christian roots. The modern world has tried to snip off the roots and retain the plant. The success of that project is in severe doubt.

Responsibility is assumed to be something good. No one praises irresponsibility. Individuals who consider themselves very responsible think the world needs more responsibility, and they wish the people lacking in responsibility would get more of it. The endless invoking of responsibility occurs among the circle of people who assume ownership of the term. The voices of those who are classified as lacking in responsibility are seldom heard. Those people may be trying hard to be responsible for their lives but are overwhelmed by the conditions that surround and pressure them. If that should be the case, telling them "to take responsibility for your life" may be very bad advice.

The Origin of "Responsibility"

It is more than coincidental that "revelation" and "responsibility" originated in the same period of history. Both are Western ideas whose ability to travel to the whole world is still an open question. "Western" generally refers to a confluence of philosophical and religious ideas. In this case, as is common, the philosophy is Hellenistic Greek and the religion is Near Eastern, with Jewish religion especially prominent. In the centuries immediately before Christianity, Jewish religion was influenced by Hellenistic philosophy and a mix of religions, especially Persian.

"Revelation" is a Greek word that acquired a special religious meaning not just of unveiling a secret, but of unveiling the secret of the universe. In contrast, "responsibility" is notably absent from Greek philosophy; it emerged from a Jewish concern with how an individual deals with good and evil leading to a final judgment on the person's life. The two ideas can be understood to converge at the end of history, but until then there is a tension between them.

Revelation is a visual metaphor; the truth is what you see. Responsibility is an aural/oral metaphor; the truth is a call that demands an answer. One advantage of revealing over speaking as the fundamental metaphor is that while both are present activities, revealing is a more explicit reminder of the future. "All revelation is a calling and a mission."[1] The fullness of revelation is still to come.

Two Verbs of Responsibility

I have noted the parallel between faith and responsibility in that each includes two verbs. Faith can mean believing in (someone) or believing that (something) is true. Responsibility can mean responsible to (someone) or responsible for (something). In order to use the word "faith," the Christian church with the help of the Old Testament had to invent the verb "to believe in." Not surprisingly, many people are oblivious to faith as "believing in," and they equate faith with secondhand knowledge of statements taken to be true.

Similarly, many people today equate responsibility with taking responsibility for one's life. But being responsible *to* is the original and basic meaning of responsibility. Through most of its history responsibility was not a commonly used term, but its meaning was clear: answering *to* someone. The consequence of the answering was action that one is responsible *for*.

---

1. Martin Buber, *I and Thou* (New York: Scribner's, 1970), 164.

Responsibility was not one of the virtues in Jewish and Christian histories. Like believing in, it is a presupposition for virtue. To be a creature is to be responsive; to be a human being is to have the ability to say "yes" for oneself and for all creatures who cannot speak for themselves. Responsibility is not first a moral term; it is an anthropological description. We are born responsible, with the vocation to become more responsible. A responsibility to the world of persons and things begins at birth, if not earlier. A (moral) responsibility for one's actions takes several years to develop.

The sense of responsibility arose only as the main image of God moved from that of king or warrior to loving father. Christianity was indebted to the Pharisaic revolution for the image of God the Father. The call to be responsible did not come from an impersonal force or a terrifying judge, but from a parent concerned with the welfare of sons and daughters. Responsibility to a God who addressed his sons and daughters with loving concern led to the development of personal conscience and responsibility for one's actions.

The life and teachings of Jesus provided a distinctly concrete image of who we are responsible to. The God who raised Jesus from the dead and will not allow human life to perish gives hope that life is not a meaningless struggle. "The good news of the Gospel was quite simply that man was not alone in his heartbreaking struggle against personal and social evil. . . . The cry of the first apostles was not 'love your fellow man.' It was 'He is risen.' This was the spring of hope that first rose in Jerusalem, from there to flow through the whole empire."[2]

Although the term "responsibility" is not prominent in the Bible, the biblical covenant has the form of call and response. Like "believing in," "responsible to" engages the whole person: past, present, and future. The individual's conscience is formed within the people of the covenant. In Jewish religion the community has a natural basis that is lacking in Christianity. But as individuals respond to the call, the corporate character of the *ecclesia*—a gathering of the called—becomes more evident. We come to God through and with others who believe and respond. Dietrich Bonhoeffer states that "responsibility in the biblical sense is, in the first place, a verbal response given at the risk of a man's life to the question asked by another man with regard to the event of Christ."[3]

2. Barbara Ward, *Faith and Freedom* (Garden City, NY: Doubleday Image Books, 1962), 70.

3. Dietrich Bonhoeffer, *Ethics* (New York: Macmillan, 1965), 222.

Responsible To

The Jewish and Christian contribution to anthropology was an understanding of the human as structured by responsibility. The term literally means a being capable of answering a word that has been spoken. Historically, the Christian form of responsibility was linked to Jesus, who was obedient unto death, and to the Holy Spirit, who is comforter and advocate. The meaning of life is not invented by the humans but is discovered in being responsible to Christ and the Spirit. There is a direct link between faith and responsibility. As Joseph Ratzinger wrote, "The little word *credo* contains a basic option vis-à-vis reality as such; it signifies . . . a fundamental mode of behavior toward being, toward existence, toward one's own sector of reality and toward reality as a whole."[4]

Beginning in the nineteenth century, the Christian claim that there is one God to whom humans are responsible was systematically denied. The denial was most often in the form of simply omitting the question. Without God to be responsible to, history, humanity, human rights, or the nation had to bear the weight of the moral life. Responsibility was identified only with the verb "responsible for." Thus the human being had to step into the place of the divine source of responsibility. Responsibility has been understood to begin and end with human autonomy.

Emile Durkheim writes in his influential book *Moral Education* that "one of the fundamental axioms of our morality—perhaps even *the* fundamental axiom—is that the human being is the sacred thing *par excellence*. He merits the respect that the faithful of all religions reserve for their gods."[5] Durkheim simply declares that the human being is "sacred." His next sentence, however, is not encouraging: "We make the idea of humanity the end and the *raison d'être* of the nation." Here Durkheim transposes the sacredness of the human being to *the idea of humanity* as the purpose of the nation. The twentieth century repeatedly demonstrated that the passions of nationalism were stronger than the idea of humanity. Tens of millions of individual human beings were made sacred offerings to the idol of the nation.

Like "believing in," which is not followed by an object, the verb "responsible to" would be restricted by adding an object after the verb. Responsible to, however, does need direction; it receives that by a word, image, or symbol. Both "believing in" and "responsible to" employ images, although they are ultimately directed to a reality that is not an "object," but a reality in the face

---

4. Joseph Ratzinger, *Introduction to Christianity* (San Francisco: Ignatius Press, 2004), 50.

5. Emile Durkheim, *Moral Education* (New York: Free Press, 1973), 107.

of which words and images fail us. While it is important to keep a personal dimension to our grasp of the ultimate, "person" may be too limiting an image and word.

For the person who asks to whom or to what am I responsible, an initial answer can be All/Nothing. That is, in principle responsibility is to everyone and everything. Except perhaps for some philosophers, that is not a very satisfying or practical answer. All of us need symbols, images, and particular historical events that embody the All/Nothing for us. The daily act of responding to has to rely upon trusted guides, such as a tradition, a body of literature, or a group of people.

Even a single person can be a lens to a universal morality, or a cause can embody the hope for a world beyond injustice. For some people today, care for the environment is the basis of their responsibility to everyone and everything, though "environment" needs some embodying in particular people, animals, and other beings. In Jesus' preaching those who are the peacemakers, those who hunger after justice, those who visit the imprisoned are respondents to the ultimate beyond words even if that is not in their immediate consciousness.

Love of a person or devotion to a noble cause are ways to be responsible to. However, turned in on themselves such actions may become idolatrous. Religious language consists of saying "this is not god, that is not god, nor that, nor that. . . ." Being responsible to is a reminder that the human being is not the creator but the creature, who receives whatever he or she has on loan. Today people are asked to be responsible *for* all kinds of things, a demand many find to be an insupportable burden. They often turn inward, giving pep talks to their will, and are frustrated when their resolve to be responsible for their life keeps crashing.

Some people who live in response to a greater reality are called atheists because they are opposed to modern theisms that imagine a great being in the sky. Vatican II's Constitution on the Church recognizes atheists who may be searching for God and are moved by grace (*LG* 16). People called atheists may have a "religious" attitude. As politicians, environmentalists, medical researchers, or artists they may live in response to a vocation of serving the good in striking ways. Without the guidance of a tradition, the call can go badly astray, but it does not always do so.

One of the most fateful statements in recent history was spoken by George W. Bush in a talk at Washington's National Cathedral the week of September 11, 2001. Bush said: "Our responsibility to history is already clear: to answer these attacks and rid the world of evil."[6] Bush invoked responsible to, which

---

6. Jim Wallis, *God's Politics* (San Francisco: Harper, 2005), 143.

he directed to "history." That would usually be too generalized a concept to be helpful. In this case history is indeed clear, but not in the way Bush claimed. If history has anything to teach, it is that no person or government can "rid the world of evil." The attempt to rid the world of evil can only end in some people being designated for destruction, while evil still remains. The events of the years that followed in the Bush presidency consistently if tragically flowed from taking on the divine task of getting rid of evil.

Christian history at its best is a responding to God revealed in Christ and the Spirit. But religious leaders who have claimed to be acting as responsible to God were often idolatrous. Church, doctrine, and ecclesiastical office have been among the idols, and as the medieval saying warned, "The corruption of the best is the worst." Responsibility to God requires a constant process of de-idolization. "Such is the need and such the demand of man for gods and absolutes, that it will often be wise to descend firmly but slowly from the throne. . . . The fact that there is one God and no more is for all of us, the well and the ill, the most difficult proposition in the world."[7]

There is one place in the modern world where the verb "responsible to" has survived, but any religious connotations are carefully excluded. In a bureaucratic pyramid each person is responsible to the next office above. In theory, the responsibility is not to a person but to an impersonal order dictated by the purpose of the system. The aim of the Enlightenment was to replace personal status with contractual relations.

A bureaucratic pyramid does protect individuals against idiosyncrasy and arbitrariness. One's job is defined as carrying out orders under specified contractual conditions. Responding to the next link up the chain guarantees a limit on personal liability when something goes wrong. In this case the relationship between "responsible to" and "responsible for" is almost the reverse of a Christian morality. Instead of responsibility to God focusing and energizing one's actions as responsibly one's own, the bureaucratic form of being responsible to almost eliminates responsibility for a person's actions.

A bureaucratic pyramid can be efficient for accomplishing well-defined tasks in a stable environment. If a worker has a lively personal life outside the bureaucratic world, following orders and doing one piece of work for some specified hours of the day may be fine. For most people most of the time, obeying instructions is justification for their actions.

What happens, however, when the whole enterprise is corrupt? Individuals may escape legal responsibility so long as their actions are not a violation

---

7. William Lynch, *Images of Hope* (Notre Dame, IN: University of Notre Dame Press, 1974), 108.

of a law. But the courts have ruled that "I was just following orders" does not exculpate a person if the action is illegal. As for moral responsibility, response to a wider, deeper, or greater reality may be needed when an organization is producing harmful products or destroying life. The "whistle-blower" feels compelled to go outside the chain of command and respond to some other moral guide.

Helen Prejean, in her extraordinary study *Dead Man Walking*, recounts a conversation with a head of a Department of Corrections regarding executions. She is told that the personnel in the department "don't have to take any personal responsibility for what they are doing. It's their job. They are told to do it. They are told how to do it. They are told how long it's going to take and what you do when you do it. It's like a drill, like an exercise so they have no personal responsibility."[8]

The people involved in state executions (euphemistically called capital punishment) can only function if they can feel they are not the cause of the death. Firing squads traditionally included one gun loaded with blanks; each person could have an escape hatch from personal responsibility. What the twentieth century showed is that horrendous evil can be perpetrated by rational and efficient systems in which everybody just does his or her job. In a bureaucracy each person is responsible to the next highest office. Responsibility, one might think, is at the very top. The most frightening thing about bureaucracy, as Hannah Arendt wrote in her brilliant analysis, is that when you get to the top you find that nobody is there. "No men, neither one nor the best, neither the few nor the many, can be held responsible, and which could be properly called rule by Nobody."[9]

A clear example of what Arendt is referring to is the Holocaust. A vast rational system was put in the service of systematic murder. Everybody in the system concentrated on doing his or her job. Adolph Eichmann was identified as the chief bureaucrat and was tried for his crimes. Hannah Arendt was the appropriate reporter, someone with profound insight into how bureaucracy and violence are related.

Arendt's book *Eichmann in Jerusalem* is a careful and clear-eyed study of Eichmann and the judicial proceedings. But she received harsh criticism from people who wanted her to report that Eichmann was an evil monster. Instead, she described him as a fairly typical bureaucrat who was proud of his "objectivity." His lawyer argued that Eichmann should not be held responsible for "the collection of skeletons, sterilizations, killing by gas, and

---

8. Helen Prejean, *Dead Man Walking* (New York: Vintage Books, 1993), 103.

9. Hannah Arendt, *On Violence* (New York: Harvest Books, 1970), 38.

similar medical matters."[10] These "medical matters" were all just part of a day's work with schedules to arrange, meetings to be held, and a budget to control. Whether or not Arendt's famous phrase "the banality of evil" captured her intention, her conclusion was that "lack of imagination and thoughtlessness can wreak more havoc than all the evil instincts taken together."[11]

Responsible For

The verb "responsible for" is easier to discuss than "responsible to"—at least it appears that way, because the contemporary world is awash in discussion of what people are responsible for. Despite all the talk about "taking responsibility," the verb "responsible for" is regularly misused in making vague or limitless demands on individuals. The verb "responsible for" needs to have its scope defined by the verb "responsible to." The deeper and wider sense we have about being responsible to, the clearer we can be about what we are and are not responsible for.

It may strike many people as paradoxical that being responsible to God can lighten the burden of what we are responsible for. People who call for responsibility today are often harsher taskmasters than the God of Christian tradition. We don't have to wait for the last judgment to be judged that we are not responsible enough. In contrast, God's commandment, Dietrich Bonhoeffer says, "allows the flood of life to flow freely. It lets man eat, drink, sleep, work, rest and play. It does not interrupt him."[12]

Erich Neumann, in a study of the unconscious, ridicules Augustine for "thanking God that he is not responsible to God for his dreams."[13] Augustine may have been naïve about the existence of the unconscious, but he did not have to bear responsibility for his dreams. Is the contemporary individual who is told to be responsible for everyone and everything, including his dreams, better off?

When it follows upon "responsible to," the second moment of responsibility—responsible for—can be precisely focused. An individual is responsible for actions over which he or she has sufficient control. The last phrase acknowledges that there are debatable cases of what constitutes "sufficient control." Some people are sick and are not in control of their actions. The more common case is that individuals have areas of life where, for a range

---

10. Hannah Arendt, *Eichmann in Jerusalem* (New York: Penguin Books, 1994), 69.

11. Arendt, *Eichmann*, 158.

12. Dietrich Bonhoeffer, *Ethics* (New York: Macmillan, 1965), 283.

13. Erich Neumann, *Depth Psychology and a New Ethic* (Boston: Shambhala, 1990), 74.

of reasons, the freedom to choose is impaired. We know now that genetics, early environment, parental attitudes, and a host of individual factors shape the possibility of "responsible action" at any moment. Some inclinations that cannot be directly changed in one's life can indirectly and gradually be brought under "sufficient control" for the action to be morally responsible.

At no moment in life can a person "take responsibility for my life." It is not there for the taking. One can only have sufficient control over particular actions. There are moments that can reorient a life; most often we recognize how important those moments were as we look back on our lives. That may seem discouraging, but freedom mainly involves looking back and examining where we have failed. Understanding the past is a chief ingredient of freedom to act in the present. The Christian call for conversion is one of those moments when the present and future of one's life can be reoriented.

We are free not when we have a wide range of choices but when the action is our own.[14] The great saint and the great sinner are likely to say something similar: "I could not do otherwise." The great sinner feels that life is beyond his or her control. In contrast, the saint gradually becomes the person who has eliminated the choices to do what is wrong. Daniel Dennett was surprised to discover that this fact had already been enunciated by Augustine and Aquinas.[15] As Karl Polanyi states it, "The freedom of the subjective person to do as he pleases is overruled by the freedom of the responsible person to act as he must."[16]

Those of us who are not yet saints have a range of choices that are responses to creaturely guides of the creator. Nearly everyone, including great sinners or people whose freedom is restricted by problems not of their own making, can take the next step as a responsible act. There is a proper demand that a person be responsible for doing in the present what he or she can sufficiently control.

The modern demand to "take responsibility for your life" is delusional for those who think they have succeeded and paralyzing for those who know very well that they cannot. Only at the end of life might it be possible to take—or more realistically, to accept—responsibility for the character of one's whole life. In Elisabeth Kübler-Ross's well-known stages of dying,

14. Mary Midgley, *Ethical Primate* (New York: Routledge, 1996), 182.

15. Daniel Dennett, *Elbow Room: The Varieties of Free Will Worth Wanting* (New York: Bradford, 1984), 157; see Augustine, *The Enchiridion: On Faith, Hope and Love* (Chicago: Regnery, 1961), 123; Thomas Aquinas, *On Truth*, 23, 4.

16. Karl Polanyi, *Personal Knowledge* (Chicago: University of Chicago Press, 1974), 309.

the culmination is "acceptance."[17] That act of freedom means "the struggle is over; this is who I have become; I accept that my call is to affirm the life that is mine."

There was a theological parallel to this acceptance, developed especially by Ladislaus Boros and Karl Rahner. As one dies there is a final option to accept or reject God. Rahner's brilliant essay *The Theology of Death* described life moving into the straits of death. The final option is "to die with Christ" or to die alone.

This theological description should not be taken as an empirical or psychological theory of how people die. A demand for life's most important decision at the moment of dying could be construed as a terrifying burden. It might suggest a throwback to the medieval imagery of a court proceeding at the deathbed and the sentiments in the hymn *Dies Irae*. Rahner's intention in describing the end of life was to affirm that anyone who has been responsible to the grace and love of God need not perform some extraordinary feat at the moment of death, but simply accept "dying with Christ."[18]

The contemporary rhetoric of responsibility not only advocates taking responsibility for one's own life but taking responsibility for other people's lives as well. How many other people? The demand seems to be limitless. It is assumed that being responsible only for oneself is selfish; the unselfish person is supposed to be responsible for other people. However, in the Christian framework the choice is not between selfish and selfless; it is to be a self in relation to God and neighbor. The moral demand is not to be responsible *for* other people but responsible *to* them, that is, listening to their voices and finding out how to share life with them. Then one's actions will be responsible in relation to people who have responsibility for their own actions.

In the claim that we should be responsible for other people, the constantly used phrase is "my brother's keeper." Even in secular ethics the biblical question "Am I my brother's keeper?" is cited to seal the case. The presumption is that any ethical person is bound to say that "yes, I should be my brother's keeper." The question "Am I my brother's keeper?" was first asked by Cain after murdering his brother Abel. It seems to be assumed that God's answer to Cain's question was yes, but God did not deign to answer. If God had answered, he might have said: No, I do not think you should be your brother's keeper. I asked you to be your brother's brother. Brothers are neither for killing nor for keeping.

---

17. Elisabeth Kübler-Ross, *On Death and Dying* (New York: Macmillan, 1969), 112–37.

18. Karl Rahner, *Theology of Death* (New York: Herder & Herder, 1964).

Dietrich Bonhoeffer writes that in the biblical perspective responsibility is always limited. It is especially limited by the freedom of the other person. I am not responsible for other human beings, because they are responsible for their own actions. "Responsibility differs from violence and exploitation precisely in the fact that it recognizes the other man as a responsible agent and indeed that it enables him to be conscious of his responsibility."[19]

Bonhoeffer's last reference in this quotation is to parents helping their children become responsible agents. A parent bears responsibility for a child's decisions to the extent that the child is not yet able to be responsible for its own actions. The infant has almost no responsibility for its actions, but each year, each day, the child can take on increasing responsibility for what it does. The parent's responsibility is not to be responsible for the child but to contribute to the child's becoming responsible for an increasing range of his or her own actions. While children should be responsible to their parents, it is just as important that parents be responsible to their children if they are going to help the children become responsible for their own actions.

There are times when one must act on another's behalf because the other person is temporarily or permanently incapable of acting. Sometimes the lack of competence is partial, as in a range of physical and mental disabilities. It is important that a person be responsible for his or her actions to whatever extent possible. Those who wish to help others in need of help have to exercise patience; the very old, the very young, and the severely disabled may need a lot of time to do what they are capable of doing.

There are now tens of thousands of people who are in irreversible comas (the term "vegetative state" is both insulting and misleading). In these cases another human being has to be the responsible agent. Each of us can only hope that if we are beyond all control of our life the decisions will come from someone who has our best interests at heart. Otherwise, the economics of the system will decide who lives and who dies. When a person has died, all responsibility passes to another. The word for "keeper" in the Genesis passage cited above is also used in the Jewish burial rite for the person who watches over the dead body until burial. I am my brother's keeper when my brother has died.

There are animals that manifest a degree of choice and decision. The degree of freedom possessed by cats, dogs, and other domesticated animals should be respected. If a human takes an animal into his or her home, the animal acquires some rights as a family member. Humans also have to

---

19. Bonhoeffer, *Ethics*, 234.

negotiate with other animals about the environment both of them share. We cannot expect bears, wolves, elephants, or alligators to obey our demands simply because humans decide to take over what had been the habitat of other animals. In this respect animals are like children in having limited responsibility for their actions. The grown-ups may have to decide, but they should show some respect for the freedom and responsible activity of others, even if the responsible actions by others are very limited.

Finally, there are nonliving things that apparently have no power to choose, but whose existence and nature deserve respect. It is not an extreme extension of the metaphor of responsibility to say that mountains, oceans, forests, deserts, and ice fields speak to humans if the humans are ready to listen. Responsibility to God includes responsibility to all of God's creatures. God is revealed in the small as well as the great. Correspondingly, responsibility for our actions may find guidance in our responding to the smallest, most vulnerable of God's creatures.

Humans have to be protective of the earth's goods. Our ecological problems reflect a confusion in the rhetoric of responsibility that says we should be responsible for people but not for things. A Christian view of responsibility is the reverse: We should *not* be responsible for other people (except to the extent that they are incapable of being responsible for their own actions), but we should be responsible for things—that is, our decisions and behavior should stand in for things that are vulnerable to exploitation. In the biblical image, the human being is the priest of all creation. Responding to all the other creatures, the man and woman at the center bring together the voices of all creation. The humans say "amen" for all the "non-two-legged creatures who are saints."

Personal-Corporate Responsibility

The one certainty about responsibility voiced from the mid-nineteenth century to the present is that it belongs to the individual. Some people see no problem with this principle. However, many have a nagging sense that individual responsibility is at least in some cases inadequate. Concentration on the individual seems to leave untouched the structures, organizations, and institutions as seats of power that control individual decisions, but any talk of "collective responsibility" seems to conflict with the first principle of responsibility.

The Christian church from its beginning tried to provide a doctrine of responsibility that was an alternative to both individual and collective. The fact that today's language includes only individual and collective is a sign that the Christian attempt has not been widely successful. The failure internal to the church was educational; that is, Christian believers did not grasp the significance of key Christian doctrines that link revelation, faith, redemption, and responsibility. As a result, Christianity offered some but not much resistance to the scientific and political movements that issued in individualism.

Some attempts today by church officials to offer an alternative to contemporary confusion about morality reveal a startlingly thin understanding of their own Christian tradition. In 2008 Gianfranco Girotti, regent of the Vatican Penitentiary, said of the Catholic Church's view of sin: "If yesterday sin had a rather individualistic dimension, today it has a value and resonance that is above all social because of the great phenomenon of globalization." In a front page story, *The New York Times* described the move as the Catholic Church updating to "social crimes bearing a collective guilt."[20]

Girotti assumes a choice between an individual or a social morality that would correspond to individual or collective responsibility. His "updating" is caught in the unworkable language of modern secular ethics. If he were going to offer a Christian alternative, he would do better to draw on the New Testament and the best of medieval theology. Christianity has the resources in its history to offer an understanding of responsibility as *neither* individual *nor* collective. Christians should indeed be concerned with political, economic, ecological, and military issues, but those issues cannot be addressed as individual or collective concerns.

A responsibility that includes responding to God and then acting in response to earthly realities is personal-corporate. Personal responsibility and corporate responsibility are not separate possibilities. Every human act has both personal and corporate dimensions. As personal, an act can vary in the depth of one's involvement, but the personal always implies a communal relation. And the corporateness (bodiliness) has many degrees of extension, but every human act has some bodiliness in its execution.

The word "person" is constantly tossed around, often just as a marker in a sentence or as a synonym for "individual." At times, however, there is a sense that "person" refers to an inviolate reality, one who is a bearer of rights. A person is not just one case in an actuarial table, but a someone who speaks and is addressed by others. The lawyers and the psychologists have the most control of "person" in modern times, but the word has its roots in the Christian doctrines of the Trinity and the Incarnation. There was no word for "person" in Greek philosophy. The early church had to carve out a new concept for its most important beliefs. It is hardly surprising that the doctrines

20. *New York Times*, 7 April 2008, 1.

of three persons/one nature and two natures/one person took time to be developed and involved strenuous controversies.

Christianity, like Judaism, insisted that there was only one God, but in light of reflection on Jesus' relation to God there was believed to be an interior life to God. God's Word and Spirit are called persons, not just attributes or functions. The one God is "triune." In the related doctrine, Jesus is so taken up into God that he does not have a human person. Who he is—his personhood—is said to be the Word or Son of God. The consequence of this doctrine is a recognition that nature refers to the *what*, person to the *who*. Each human being is alike in sharing a human nature, but each has his or her distinctiveness in being a person.

The term "person" was borrowed from the theater. A person is an actor speaking through a mask. Personal life is not transparent to others or even to oneself. The person's nature (what one is) always remains in tension with who one is trying to become. From the beginning of life, personal is linked with communal. The relation of personal and communal even applies to God. Every human person shares in the life of the divine persons and is within a human community. Every human person's existence is situated in a body interacting with other persons in and through the body.

For a human, the most specifically personal activities are thinking and willing, which are set deep within the person. An act of thinking or choosing becomes fully human only as it finds bodily expression in imagination and external behavior. Personal control of oneself has to be democratic; each cell of the body has to be heard from if choice is to orient the physical person. Authoritarian orders to one's body may work for a while, but eventually they bring on disruptive rebellion.

Personal responsibility, therefore, begins with listening to God in creation, especially as found in the movements of one's own body. If one is in tune with the depth and breadth of oneself it is much easier to hear guidance from other humans, past and present. Other bodily creatures, sometimes only by the stubborn resistance of existing, are what persons must be responsible to.

Every personal act has a bodily aspect, beginning with one's own body and extending to each natural and artificial thing with which a person interacts. With other persons the aim is to share life through the sharing of material goods. The biology of the family provides the most intense and lasting bond among persons. It is also the metaphor for recognizing that the human race is the "family of man"; other humans are sisters and brothers, or at least distant cousins. Nonhuman animals may be difficult to recognize as our kin, but we all share a fragile, bodily environment that needs to be cared for by responsible human action.

Humans also construct organizations or institutions to extend the effect of their actions through space and time. Each of these material constructs is a corporate extension of the human body. Corporations can have a life of their own (as "artificial persons") and they can outlive the human individuals who started them. That is the power of corporations and their danger. A corporation needs an executive structure that allows and encourages a group of people to guide the corporation responsibly.

In the twentieth century, "corporation" got taken over by the business organization. Behind that isolation of the business corporation was the contention that business has to have its own ethic. However, other organizations remain legally and morally corporations and, together with business corporations, have to be directed responsibly by personal choice. Like the human body it magnifies, a political, religious, educational, or business corporation has to listen to its members and be responsible to its environment if its actions are to be effective and morally responsible.

At the center of Christianity is the doctrine of incarnation, the belief that the divine finds corporate expression. The corporateness found in Jesus as the Christ is extended through history in the "body of Christ." To be a Christian is to be a member of that body, as St. Paul's striking metaphor first articulated (1 Cor 12:12-31). It is no less a real body for being a mystical body, most mysteriously symbolized in the sacrament of the Eucharist.

The doctrine of incarnation had two corresponding doctrines: original sin and the resurrection of the body, both of which are testimonies to the personal-corporate nature of responsibility. "Original sin" was a poor choice of words for the Christian insight into the human race's unity together with its experience of restriction and conflict throughout human history. Jean Piaget gets it mostly right in saying that "only in theology, that is to say, in the most conservative of our institutions, does the idea of Original Sin keep alive the idea of collective responsibility."[21] If Piaget had said "corporate" instead of "collective" he would have hit the mark.

Piaget, like numerous other writers, was attacking the doctrine of original sin. He was advocating an individual as opposed to a collective responsibility. Given the connotations that the term "original sin" acquired, it is difficult to defend the doctrine, particularly because of Augustine's fateful linking of the doctrine to transmission by sexual intercourse. The doctrine has been ridiculed even by Jews and Muslims. Rightly understood, however, the doctrine is a profound insight into the nature of responsibility as both personal and corporate.

21. Jean Piaget, *The Moral Judgment of the Child* (New York: Free Press, 1965), 331.

The story at the beginning of the Bible was a projection from the experience of conflict within the family of humankind and of conflict that runs deep in each person. One can imagine a world where humans are not killing each other (or even other animals), but as far back as memory and memorials go the actual record is one of bloody conflict.[22]

Humans fail personally and corporately; the line is blurred between failings that are "natural" and ones that are a result of human choice. However one imagines that relation, the result is that each person is born into a mess not of its own making but that has been left by previous generations. Humans quickly discover that their "free will" is not as free as they would like it to be.

Original sin—human failure all the way down—does not have to be imagined as a black mark on the soul. It is evident in the shanty towns at the edge of rich cities, in a million infants dying of malaria for want of a net that costs fifty cents, and in the lack of clean drinking water for more than a billion people. No matter whose "sin" these conditions are, they are signs of failure in personal-corporate responsibility.

Jean-Jacques Rousseau, a central figure in modern thought, both secular and Christian, set out to eliminate the doctrine of original sin. Rousseau begins his treatise *Emile* with the proclamation that "everything is good as it leaves the hands of the Author of things." But he still has difficulty explaining why "everything degenerates in the hands of man."[23] Rousseau provides a brilliant psychological analysis of how the fear of death and the individual's self-deception infect human love. He borrows from Augustine even while opposing him.

Rousseau's "theism" ends as a flattened-out Christian theology that loses a sense of incarnation. Rousseau professed a great admiration for Jesus, but he saw no point to the church. His denial of "original sin" leads to a different myth, a view of "society" as individuals held together with a social contract. The evils that affect the world are left at the individual level. Conor Cruise O'Brien, surveying the wars at twentieth-century's end, asks whether Augustine's doctrine of original sin or Rousseau's denial of the doctrine looks more realistic today. O'Brien concludes that there is "far more evidence extant in favor of the Christian doctrine of Original Sin than of Rousseau's doctrine of Original Virtue."[24]

---

22. George Ovitt, *The Restoration of Perfection* (New Brunswick, NJ: Rutgers University Press, 1986).

23. Jean-Jacques Rousseau, *Emile* (New York: Basic Books, 1979), 37.

24. Conor Cruise O'Brien, *On the Eve of the Millennium* (New York: Free Press, 1995).

Parallel to the personal-corporate responsibility of original sin at the beginning of time is the doctrine of bodily resurrection at the end of time. Both doctrines originate through the lens of Jesus' death-resurrection. "Jesus died for our sins" was a way of saying that sinfulness and failure from the beginning found their counterweight in Jesus' acceptance of death as symbol of innocence in the midst of conflict and hatred. His death was a confirmation of his life, which is why death was necessary for "redemption."[25]

Christianity, however, is not a religion of death but a triumph over death. Jesus' resurrection is the "first fruits" or "down payment" of the resurrection of the whole body, human corporateness. Jesus begins his resurrection from the center of the world, carrying earth's bodily life with him. Jesus only completes his resurrection when the members of his body complete "what is lacking in Christ's afflictions for the sake of his body, that is, the church" (Col 1:24).

The creedal phrase "resurrection of the body" would be better translated as "resurrection of the person." The person as bodily and communal is the seat of resurrection. It is not a salvation of souls but a restoration of the unity of personal center and bodily expression. Peter French, a strong advocate of collective responsibility, complains that "the grand individualistic tradition that characterizes much of our moral thought has its taproot in Western religion's conception of personal salvation."[26] French's complaint is ironic because it was "personal" salvation that provided a sense of corporateness and a corporate dimension to responsibility. French would have a case if he had complained that personal (and corporate) salvation was largely replaced by salvation of the disembodied and isolated soul. The centrality of the incarnational principle that distinguished Christianity from most surrounding religions was obscured by a focus on "immortal souls."

Augustine was largely responsible for introducing an individual judgment of the soul at the death of each person. A "final judgment" then seems to be superfluous and with it the very meaning of resurrection. Thomas Aquinas, while not contradicting Augustine, nonetheless argued that a human is not a person without a body. The church is the body of believers, the sacrament of sisterhood-brotherhood, moving toward revelation-redemption in its fullness. Personal-corporate responsibility that began with Adam and Eve in the garden is realized with the resurrection of the whole earth in the City of God.[27]

25. Rahner, *Theology of Death* is here again most helpful.

26. Peter French, *Collective and Corporate Responsibility* (New York: Columbia University Press, 1984), viii.

27. Augustine, *City of God* (New York: Penguin Books, 2003) 20:8; Thomas Aquinas, *Summa Theologiae* I-II, q. 75, a. 4; Caroline Walker Bynum, *The Resurrection of the Body in Western Christianity 200–1336* (New York: Columbia University Press, 1995), 266–69.

Confess-Forgive

The contemporary world is flooded with demands for apologies and with a stream of apologies that on close scrutiny are revealed to be not apologies at all—at least they are not apologies in the modern meaning of the term. "Apology" is one of those strange words that have two nearly opposite meanings. The original meaning of apology, which has not completely disappeared, is a defense of some policy or action of one's life: "This is why I am right." Today's meaning is to admit that one was wrong, that the policy or action is indefensible. Perhaps the phony apologies of the kind "I am sorry that people had the wrong reaction" are simply a return to the older meaning of apology; the apparent admission of wrong is really a defense and justification of one's actions.

In a religious context, in which the whole self is at issue, neither meaning of apology is especially helpful. What people want deep down is to be forgiven. An apology is a way to ask forgiveness, but it always gets entangled in self-justification. And even when "I am sorry" is responded to with "I forgive you," the feelings of failure and guilt do not usually disappear. The phrase "forgive and forget" is commonly used, but the two do not go together. Forgiveness involves remembering. The human psyche does not forget; it just keeps burying memories more and more deeply. If we are asked to forget something we cannot do so. In a court, the judge does not say to the jury: "forget the last remark," something that is not possible. The judge says to "disregard" the statement in considering the evidence.

Human beings want to have their lives forgiven, but no individual is able to give that. The process of seeking forgiveness begins with confession to the source of the self. The formula at the very beginning of the liturgical service is: "I confess to almighty God and to you my sisters and brothers . . . ." The "almighty" refers to the power to forgive. At times it might be useful to alter the formula to "I confess to you my sisters and brothers and through you to God almighty." In either case, the confession of the person is always in the company of one's sisters and brothers, living and dead.

Confession is a personal-corporate act of responding to God and thereby accepting responsibility for actions that I can sufficiently control. I and we ask forgiveness for what is beyond our direct control—unholy thoughts that cross the mind, words that unintentionally wound, actions with unforeseeable consequences. We do the best we can at enumerating our faults, but confession to God goes beyond the individual failings that are clearly stamped on the memory.

The church has to confess its failures to carry out its vocation to be a sign of human reconciliation. The claim is still often made in official documents that Christians sin but the church itself is spotless. The "heavenly church" the council referred to is beyond sin, but the existing pilgrim church has corporate faults that are obvious to everyone. The Christian church need not endlessly apologize to every group it may have wronged, but a believing and confessing church would act with humility, candor, and openness to dialogue.

The individual Christian confesses to God as a member of the confessing church. The Catholic Church has a sacrament that used to be called Penance, a word that put the emphasis in the wrong place. Today it is called by the better name Reconciliation, which describes a hoped-for result but not the process itself. The popular name for this sacrament was "confession," an accurate name, though the part about telling your sins to the priest was exaggerated. Outsiders found it to be an odd procedure. Why not just ask God for forgiveness?

Confession and forgiveness involve personal-corporate responsibility. Similar to the sacrament of matrimony, where the officiant is the witness of the larger church to the persons marrying each other, the priest is the witness for the larger church to a person's confessing to God. The priest who "hears" a confession is not the intended recipient of the knowledge, nor is the knowledge for his use. Even most non-Catholics have heard of the "seal of confession," a secrecy concerning a person's confession that exceeds the promise of confidentiality in other professions. The priest cannot "absolve" sins, although as representative of the church the priest's sacramental absolution expresses God's forgiveness.

I think it must be admitted that the Catholic Church has never found the proper form for a sacrament of confession/forgiveness. The frequency of the ritual (from every week to once in a lifetime) was unclear and the physical arrangement (talking face to face or going into a dark box) was either too intimate or too impersonal. The attempts at reform after Vatican II came too late and the sacrament seems to have all but disappeared. However, the drive to confess has not disappeared, as the growth of psychotherapy and much of "reality" television testify.

The Catholic Church had a good idea, but it did not fit into a two-class system of clergy and laity. Despite what theology may have said, what appeared to both insiders and outsiders was a ritual in which one of the "faithful" asked for forgiveness and a priest granted it. The little dark box was a fearful place in which the individual struggled with formulas that could not get at the deeper problems. The strength of the confessional box was that it did retain an impersonal element; confession was to God in the presence of a silhouette.

The attempt to make reconciliation a warm and personal experience was a quick jump that could not work very well. Whatever aura the sacrament had was lost in general confessions and general absolutions. If the sacrament is to be renewed—or reinvented—it can only be as an element in the restructuring of church authority. A church of circles within circles, of small communities interacting as cells in a transnational body, would experience confessing/forgiving as a regular, if never an easy, occurrence. The New Testament encouraged church members to "confess your sins to one another, and pray for one another, that you may be healed" (Jas 5:16).

Every family that is a safe and nourishing place for its members includes confessing/forgiving in the rhythm of its life. Any small community that stays together for a long time develops rituals acknowledging faults and requesting forgiveness. A group may hardly be aware of the formulas it regularly uses to heal hurt feelings or of notes that are left on the refrigerator door accepting responsibility for a task undone. A church sacrament makes sense to people only when it sanctifies a practice that is part of ordinary experience.

In a church of circles within circles, confessing/forgiving would be a communal experience linked to other communities. The larger church's need for forgiveness would be focused on the structural failures in the world: the church's failure to act for a better neighborhood or nation, the failure to protest economic unfairness, racial bias, or militarism. The representative official who would speak for forgiveness would act for a church responding to a speaking and forgiving God. Forgiveness would not be directed to an isolated individual, but to a person within a communal and corporate church.

Forgiveness is the reaction to confession, but it is not a reaction that can be demanded. Avishai Margalit points out that in the Bible (the Old Testament) there is no duty to forgive.[28] Jews and Christians have a different emphasis regarding forgiveness. To Jewish ears the Christian profession of forgiveness often comes too quickly to be realistic. Where Jews and Christians can agree is that forgiveness is the opposite of vengeance, something not advocated in the Bible.[29] Between forgiveness and vengeance there are many other responses, including the demand for justice.[30] But justice can also take a variety of forms, either emphasizing punishment for the offender or restoring and healing the community.

The preaching of Jesus of Nazareth, drawing on a strand of Jewish tradition, emphasized doing good to one's enemies. The secular Jewish philoso-

---

28. Avishai Margalit, *The Ethics of Memory* (Cambridge, MA: Harvard University Press, 2002), 193.

29. Hannah Arendt, *The Human Condition* (New York: Doubleday, 1959), 240.

30. Martha Minow, *Between Vengeance and Forgiveness* (Boston: Beacon Press, 1998), 15.

pher Hannah Arendt credits Jesus of Nazareth with bringing forgiveness into the world of ideas and institutions.[31] For Arendt it is the only way to break the bonds of fate and open up an unpredictable future. The process of forgiving can begin apart from whatever may be the reasons for existing hostility. Such a gift of forgiveness can be extraordinarily powerful. David Sloan Wilson regards forgiveness the reason for the flourishing of early Christianity.[32] Enemies can be overcome by the conquering sword, but that is only a temporary victory. Enemies can also be overcome by a generous spirit that is not naive about human aggression but takes the first step in the process of reconciliation.

An extraordinary example of confession/forgiveness was provided to the world by South Africa's Truth and Reconciliation Commission. The churches, to their shame, had been deeply implicated in the scandal of apartheid. In a country so deeply influenced by Christianity, it was fitting that the commission for truth and reconciliation was designed and presided over by two church leaders, Alex Boraine and Desmond Tutu. There were other key figures in the commission's success, especially Nelson Mandela, who survived twenty-seven years in prison without becoming bitter.

The process is captured in microcosm by an interview Alex Boraine recounts. A woman who has just heard testimony from the killer of her husband is asked if she can forgive him. "Speaking slowly in one of the native languages her message through an interpreter was: 'No government can forgive.' Pause. 'No commission can forgive.' Pause. 'Only I can forgive.' Pause. 'And I am not ready to forgive.' "[33]

This woman got it just about right. God does the forgiving. As for the human who expresses the forgiving, the Spirit of God and the personal conscience determine the time and manner. Forgiveness takes time and involves other communal conditions so that whatever healing does occur is personal-corporate and not simply how an individual feels.

Forgiveness is something Christian people should show a mastery of. The secular world is severely limited in the resources it has for working out genuine apology and effective forgiveness. Jesus exemplified forgiveness and taught an extraordinary doctrine of forgiving. Some of his followers, inside and outside the church, have continued to manifest in their lives extraordinary

31. Arendt, *The Human Condition,* 241.

32. David Sloan Wilson, *Darwin's Cathedral: Religion and the Nature of Society* (Chicago: University of Chicago Press, 2002).

33. Amy Gutman and Dennis Thompson, "The Moral Foundation of Truth Commissions," 22–44, in *Truth vs. Justice,* ed. Robert Rotberg and Dennis Thompson (Princeton, NJ: Princeton University Press, 2000), 31.

examples of forgiving one's enemies. However, the Christian church's record on forgiving enemies is mixed. Too often the church has joined forces with those intent on killing their enemies.

In 1986 the United Church of Canada officially apologized to the native peoples: "We ask you to forgive us. These are not just words. It is one of the most important actions ever taken by the church." In response, Edith Memnock, representing the native peoples, acknowledged the apology but did not accept it.[34] It was not the right time. More important than native people saying "we forgive you" was that the Christian church and the native peoples could begin a new journey of gradual reconciliation.

---

34. Nicholas Tavuchis, *Mea Culpa: A Sociology of Apology and Reconciliation* (Stanford, CA: Stanford University Press, 1991), 109–11.

Chapter Five

Christian Interpretation of Divine Revelation

The relation between the local and the universal church discussed in chapter 3 is one piece of a bigger puzzle: the relation between what is particular and what is universal. The principle of this relation, that the two are not opposites but are reciprocally related, is a theme that runs throughout this book. This chapter on interreligious dialogue and the following chapter on an aesthetic appreciation of believing in a revealing God are especially concerned with how the relation of particular to universal situates Christianity in a plurality of religions today and describes the devotional and artistic life within Christianity. These two chapters form a single unit.

The plurality or manyness of religions is simply a fact. Acknowledging the presence of other religions does not imply "relativism," an ideology that says truth is relative to a particular situation, so that no truth applies in all situations. Relativism is often embraced in the name of tolerance. However, the trouble with that assumption, writes Kwame Appiah, is "that if we cannot learn from one another what is right to think and feel and do, then conversation between us will be pointless. Relativism of that kind isn't a way to encourage conversation; it's just a reason to fall silent."[1]

Every statement of truth is relative to the personal and cultural situation of the speaker, but that does not exclude a relevance to other speakers who affirm the truth as they understand it. Truths are always relative to other truths. The opposite of a great truth may be another great truth. In order to avoid relativism, we need to place the particular statements of truth in relation to other particulars. Every *statement* of truth is open to challenge by other statements of truth that

1. Kwame Appiah, *Cosmopolitanism: Ethics in a World of Strangers* (New York: W.W. Norton, 2007), 31.

might improve the original formula. No statement of truth is universal, because there is no universal language in which to express the truth.

The present chapter is about a particular expression of divine revelation and human believing in God. It cannot lay claim to universality, but it is an attempt to embody and signal what is universal in revelation and faith. For achieving a deeper, richer particularity, and hence a closer relation to universality, this one particular language has to engage other particulars. The Christian idea of believing in a revealing God finds its closest counterparts in Jewish and Muslim interpretations of faith and revelation. In genuine interreligious dialogue the Christian becomes more deeply Christian in the attempt to understand, however imperfectly, Jewish and Muslim interpretations of believing in a revealing God.

This chapter does not present Jewish, Christian, and Muslim versions of faith and revelation. My ambition is more modest. The presentation is from a Christian perspective. Within that limitation my question is twofold: How can the Christian position be stated so as to make dialogue possible? What insights might a Christian gather from appreciating Jewish and Muslim interpretations of faith and revelation?

A Christian relation to Judaism and Islam is not new. There have been borrowings among all three of the religions of Abraham, but mutual sharing and understanding have been rare throughout most of history. Christians borrowed much of their language from the Jews. In early Christianity the process was mainly one of defining Christianity against Judaism. Christianity appropriated the Scripture of the Jews, calling it the Old Testament. Christians are only now discovering that they can learn from the Jewish reading of the Old Testament. Even a reading of the New Testament can be helped by Jews who have a feel for the language and context.[2]

In its relation to the origins of Islam, Christianity was in a nearly opposite position. Muslims took over elements of the New Testament and made them their own. Christians do not like being told by Muslims what the Gospel is or who Jesus was. Jews know the feeling. Throughout the early Middle Ages, Christianity was indebted to Muslim scholars for knowledge of medicine, philosophy, and science. Then for many centuries there was an almost total blackout of reciprocal learning. Discovering a new framework for Muslim-Christian dialogue is urgently needed, but it is not an easy task in the twenty-first century.

2. See, for example, Pinchas Lapide, *Sermon on the Mount* (Maryknoll, NY: Orbis Books, 1986); Amy-Jill Levine, *The Misunderstood Jew* (San Francisco: HarperSan Francisco, 2006).

Interreligious or Interfaith?

As a first step it would he helpful to refer to interreligious rather than interfaith dialogue, despite the drawbacks I will later acknowledge. Faith is ultimately the more important term, but what is discussable about Jewish, Christian, and Muslim traditions is their religious elements. Religion connotes externality. That attribute is limiting, but religious beliefs and practices are the public basis for discussion, understanding, and cooperation. The richest aspect of faith, believing in, is a deeply personal act not readily transparent to oneself, let alone to others. A project of "interfaith" dialogue promises too much if faith means the interior act of believing in; it promises too little if faith means beliefs, which are only one element in the face religions turn toward the world.

Interreligious dialogue does not neglect faith; it begins with the presumption that one's dialogue partner is faithful. The alternative is to assume a lack of faith. Faith is a fundamental attitude toward God in Jewish and Christian Bibles as well as the Qur'an. Faith is an attitude that can be shared by Christians, Muslims, and Jews. When Christians and Jews or Christians and Muslims converse, it is *intra*faith dialogue. No one of the three groups can claim to possess the idea or the word "faith." It is a word used with universal intent and therefore it should be used with an openness to other people's participation. Christians, like Jews and Muslims, have interpreted believing in God so that there are Christian beliefs that differ from Jewish beliefs and Muslim beliefs.

In many attempts today to open dialogue one finds this kind of statement: "If we understand human historicity in the sense I am urging here, Christian faith (like every other faith) will be seen as one perspective, one worldview, which has developed in and through a long history alongside other traditions. . . ."[3] I do not think this approach is either accurate or practical. I doubt that Christians will ever accept that "Christian faith" is a perspective or worldview alongside other faiths. Christian faith is not part of a collection called faiths; it is commitment to God in and through the Christ figure, a particular form of faith with universal intent. Almost certainly, a Muslim will not talk about "Muslim faith." At the heart of each tradition is the act of believing in God who reveals; it is not a perspective that parallels other perspectives.

---

3. Gordon Kaufman, "Religious Diversity, Historical Consciousness, and Christian Theology," in *The Myth of Christian Uniqueness*, ed. John Hick and Paul Knitter, 3–15 (Maryknoll, NY: Orbis Books, 1987), at 9.

There have been many books and conferences under the title "three faiths, one God" for opening a dialogue among Christians, Muslims, and Jews.[4] It would be just as accurate and perhaps more challenging to consider "one faith, three gods." Jews, Christians, and Muslims share faith directed at the only God there is. They differ because they have to struggle with a revealing God, which inevitably includes incompleteness and imperfection in the image of God within each tradition.

It is not blasphemous to refer to three gods. Whatever human beings name and lay claim to is not the God of the universe. The Hasidic teacher points out that the Bible does not say the God of Abraham, Isaac, and Jacob; it says the God of Abraham, the God of Isaac, the God of Jacob.[5] Individuals and generations find God in their own way and within their own limits. "One faith, three (images of) God" would express a bond in the depths of our souls and focus attention on the fact that our differences are not in faith but in "doctrines of the faith."

The one faith that Christians, Jews, and Muslims share in is directed toward one divine revelation. There are multiple images and doctrines of God, but the activity of God revealing is unitary. If "revelation" is a word pointing to the ultimate basis of religion, then no one religious group has possession of divine revelation. Every human formula is a *consequence* of believing in a God revealing. Since the sixteenth century, Christian writers have used some clumsy and inaccurate phrases that collapse the mystery of God revealing and preclude serious dialogue with other religions.

If, in contrast, there is a divine revelation that Jews, Christians, and Muslims are responding to, then dialogue is not an extra frill, but an imperative for each religious community. The Christian church has every right to claim that its understanding of divine revelation is accurate, life-giving, and open to all truth wherever it is to be found. The Christian is one who professes that to be so. The central doctrines of Christianity are never going to be abandoned, but even they might be formulated better as a result of interreligious dialogue.

"Revealed truths," a phrase casually and constantly used in official documents, makes the claim that certain truths came directly from God. This body of material includes biblical texts and numerous official doctrines. Modern biblical scholarship that affirms the Bible's human authorship under divine inspiration has done little to shake the claim to "revealed truths."

---

4. John Hick and Edmund Meltzer, eds., *Three Faiths—One God* (Albany, NY: SUNY Press, 1989).

5. Cited in Michael Rosenak, *Commandment and Concerns: Jewish Religious Education in Secular Society* (Philadelphia: Jewish Publication Society, 1987), 265.

Religion and Religions

In saying that we need interreligious rather than interfaith dialogue, I am mindful that "religion" is not unambiguous, neutral, or universal. The Christian who is enthusiastic about interreligious dialogue should not be surprised if there is not comparable enthusiasm from Jews and Muslims, let alone Buddhists, Hindus, or Sikhs. "Religion" is biased by its Christian origins so that, while it may be the best available word, the Christian should remember that it is not a neutral word.

"Religion" was coined by the Romans to describe ceremonies and devotions concerned with the gods. Cicero boasted that "in religion and the worship of the gods we are preeminent."[6] The early church borrowed "religion" along with many related terms such as piety, reverence, devotion, and ritual. The word "religion" became a Christian fixture when Jerome used it in the Latin translation of the New Testament for referring to observances, rituals, and ways of worship. The Old Testament does not have the word.

From a variety of devotions and practices that surrounded the early church, the Christians laid claim to having "true religion" as opposed to "false religion." Augustine assumed this contrast in his book *De Vera Religione*, which could be translated as *On Genuine Devotion*. Augustine wrote that "what today is called Christian religion existed among the ancients and has never ceased to exist from the origin of the human race until the time when Christ himself came and men began to call Christian the true religion which already existed beforehand."[7] For a thousand years afterward, Christianity laid claim to the ownership of religion: not "the true religion" as opposed to other religions, but "true religion" as opposed to false devotion.

In 1474, Marsilio Ficino wrote that "every religion has something good in it; as it is directed toward God, the creator of all things, it is true Christian religion."[8] Ficino's usage hints at the modern meaning of religion and religions, but it took the Protestant Reformation to bring about a near-reversal in their meaning. John Calvin was still employing the ancient meaning of religion in his great work usually referred to as *The Institutes of the Christian Religion*, which could also be called *Instruction in Christian Devotion*. Ulrich Zwingli introduced something new when he began his book on true

---

6. Cicero, *The Nature of the Gods* (New York: Oxford University Press, 2008), II, 7.

7. Augustine, *The Retractions* (Washington, DC: Catholic University of America Press, 1968), I. 13.3.

8. Marsilio Ficino, *De Christiana Religione*, quoted in Peter Harrison, *"Religion" and the Religions in the English Enlightenment* (Cambridge: Cambridge University Press, 1990), 13.

and false religion by saying that he would deal with the true and false religion of Christians. The battles of the Reformation were about who was practicing (true) Christian religion.

The modern meaning of "religion"—plural in concept even when used in the singular—comes toward the end of the sixteenth century. When Catholics and Protestants had fought to a standstill in some European countries there appears reference to "Catholic and Protestant religions," a first step toward religious tolerance. Very soon, Catholic and Protestant were folded into one Christian religion—Christianity—but the word "religion" was now available to refer to other "religions": Jewish and Muslim, at least, and then many other groups. A 1614 text says that there are four religions in the world: Christian, Jewish, Muslim, and Idolaters.[9]

This modern meaning of "religion" was therefore biased from the start. One could almost say that the first two religions were called "Catholic" and "Protestant." Whether or not contemporary Jews know the history of the term, most Jews do not especially care for "religion." They tend to think of it as something Christians have. While Christians have religion, Jews are a people, a community, a nation; being Jewish is a way of life. Franz Rosenzweig avoided the word "religion" in his monumental work, *The Star of Redemption*: "The good Lord did not create religion, he created the world."[10] Any dialogue between Christians and Jews is made difficult but not impossible by this history of "religion." Jews are often willing to talk about religion if Christians show an interest in mutual understanding, including political concerns of Jews in countries where Christianity is dominant.

Dialogue with Islam is in some ways easier than with Judaism. At least that is true insofar as Muslims more easily recognize "religion." While the Hebrew Bible does not have the word, the Qur'an uses it a number of times. I said before that Christians practically owned "religion" until the sixteenth century; that is, the Latin word was theirs. Islam represents a qualification of the Christian control of the term with an Arabic word that has been translated as "religion." The meaning of religion in the Qur'an is the ancient meaning of devotion—the true devotion of Islam that has existed from the beginning of the world.

Still, there is a hint of the modern meaning of religion in that Muhammad self-consciously proclaimed the way of Islam in a setting where well-formed

9. Cited in Jonathan Z. Smith, "Religion, Religions, Religious," in *Critical Terms for Religious Studies*, ed. Mark Taylor, 269–84 (Chicago: University of Chicago Press, 1998), at 275.

10. See Emmanuel Levinas, *Difficult Freedom* (Baltimore: Johns Hopkins University Press, 1990), 186.

Jewish and Christian communities existed. Unusually for religious reformers, Muhammad laid out a whole systematic approach to Islam as true religion. In the twentieth century, but scarcely before that, "Islam" became in the West the name of the system, a religion. For Muslims the primary meaning of "Islam" is still the attitude of submission to God. "Verily *the* religion in the eyes of God is Islam."[11] That meaning of Islam is not necessarily opposed to Judaism and Christianity; a devout Christian could be said to practice Islam.

For reasons that are different from those of Jews, Muslims are wary about a dialogue with Christians. The history of the two religions is one of military battles or sullen silence. Muslims are never going to criticize or negotiate about Islam (the attitude), a fact that confuses and stymies Christians about any proposed dialogue between Christianity and Islam (the historical institution). Nonetheless, there is increasing recognition that these two great missionary religions had better find some mutual understanding for the sake of world peace.

Beyond Jewish and Muslim religions, the application of "religion" becomes much more problematic. Does Confucianism or Buddhism constitute a religion? Some characteristics are shared with the religions of Abraham's children, but overall the fit is not very good. It is widely admitted that "Hinduism" is not the name for a religion, but for a wildly diverse heritage of devotional practices in India. These problems do not deter textbooks in many countries from listing as the main religions of the world Christianity, Judaism, Islam, Buddhism, Hinduism, and sometimes one or two others.

What is bizarre is a Christian tendency to impose the word "religion" on every group *except* Christianity. The phrase "Christian faith and world religions" is common. There can be no dialogue and little understanding between Christian faith and world religions. Christians since the Reformation have perceived a danger in a religion of externals without a vibrant faith within. The danger is there, but religious beliefs and rituals can also be expressive of believing in. In any case, Christians should not assume that Jews, Muslims, Buddhists, and others are only about externals while the Christian is the one who believes in God. Either interfaith dialogue or interreligious dialogue is defensible, but not a conversation in which Christians start by defining themselves as the only true believers.

11. Qur'an 3:19.

Jewish Insights for Christians

Christian reform movements that spur a "return to sources" inevitably include a reexamination of the Jewish roots of Christianity. In defining themselves as a separate community, early Christians in their writings tended to be negative about Jews so as to be positive about Christians. Some of the dichotomy is already evident in New Testament accounts that were written as the synagogue and the nascent church were clashing. In recent times Christian-Jewish conflict has at least been softened. From the time of its origin Christianity has claimed to have added a new dimension to Judaism, and there is obviously some truth to that assertion. Christians nonetheless have to examine whether anything was lost along with the addition.

Christians and Jews since the first century CE have had different images of time. In both communities "revelation" has been mainly imagined as happening in the past, but Jewish writers have an easier time rethinking revelation as present event. When Christians say revelation reached its fullness and completion in Christ they tend to identify that statement with the life of Jesus and the founding of the church. The church thus has "revealed truths" that tell about the redemption of the world by Christ's death and resurrection.

The Jew is not tied to such an event and thinks of "redemption" as still to happen. "It is the newspaper which separates Judaism from Christianity. . . . The Jew looks at his newspaper and asks himself: 'Is this a picture of a redeemed world?' "[12] The Christian and Jewish understandings of redemption are not contradictory, but the Christian idea of future redemption is buried in obscure discussions of various "eschatologies." Christians have to learn to talk more simply of their belief that Jesus' life, death, and resurrection worked a decisive shift in history with the full results still in the future. There is no theological reason why Christians and Jews cannot join in the struggle to achieve a just and redeemed world.[13]

Christians cannot speak simply and effectively of a present struggle for justice without an understanding of revelation as the present encounter with the divine in all of creation. There are Jewish groups that identify revelation with truths delivered in the past, but there is a rich stream of Jewish writing and practice that recognizes God's speaking to Jews of each generation as

12. Lionel Blue, *To Heaven with Scribes and Pharisees* (New York: Oxford University Press, 1976), 98.

13. Abraham Heschel, *The Earth Is the Lord's* and *The Sabbath* (New York: Harper Torch, 1962), 72.

if they were at Sinai with Moses.[14] In a real sense Sinai is in the present for a Jew, which a Christian with a sacramental sense should be able to recognize. "Instead of one act of Revelation, there is a constant repetition of this act."[15] The sense of present revelation is contained in Jewish ritual, the heart of the religion.

Modern thinkers such as Martin Buber and Franz Rosenzweig speak of creation as the origin, redemption as the goal, and revelation in the present as the connection.[16] "The past creation is demonstrated from out of the living, present revelation."[17] Buber and Rosenzweig accuse Christianity of disrupting the unity of creation, revelation, and redemption. "The living truth," says Buber, "is that they actually coincide, that God every day renews the work of the beginning but also every day anticipates the work of the end."[18] The single word Rosenzweig identifies with revelation is "orientation," the present encounter that sets a direction for one's life.[19]

For revelation in the present, Jewish thought provides a corresponding meaning of faith as the response to divine revealing. "When was the Torah given? It is given whenever a person receives it."[20] This theme is especially strong in the mystical strand of Judaism. Faith is not accepting doctrines as true but accepting God into one's life. "Man receives, and what he receives is not a 'content' but a presence, a presence as strength."[21] Believing in a revealing God involves active engagement. "For we know it only when we *do* . . . . One hears differently when one hears in the doing."[22] God is revealed only as one takes part in the revelation.[23]

Christians could learn a lesson from Jews: that believing in is a communal act. Christianity cannot duplicate the sense of Jewish community; the history,

---

14. Yosef Yerushalmi, *Zakhor: Jewish History and Jewish Memory* (Seattle: University of Washington Press, 1982), 45.

15. Gershom Scholem, *Major Trends in Jewish Mysticism* (New York: Schocken Books, 1961), 9.

16. Martin Buber, "The Man of Today and the Jewish Bible," in his *On the Bible: 18 Studies*, ed. Nahum Glatzer (New York: Schocken Books, 1968), 6.

17. Franz Rosenzweig, *The Star of Redemption* (New York: Holt, Rinehart and Winston, 1970), 182.

18. Buber, "The Man of Today and the Jewish Bible," 8.

19. Franz Rosenzweig and Eugen Rosenstock-Huessy, *Judaism Despite Christianity* (Birmingham: University of Alabama Press, 1969), 119.

20. Emil Fackenheim, *What Is Judaism?* (New York: Collier Books, 1987), 28.

21. Martin Buber, *I and Thou* (New York: Scribner's, 1970), 158.

22. Franz Rosenzweig, in Nahum Glatzer, *Franz Rosenzweig: His Life and Thought* (Philadelphia: Jewish Publication Society, 1953), 245.

23. Martin Buber, *The Eclipse of God* (New York: Harper, 1957), 36.

size, and composition of the two groups are radically different. Nevertheless, something can be learned apart from simple imitation. I have argued in previous chapters that the structure of the church should be small communities gathered around a center. Christians should readily understand Buber's description of community: "The true community does not arise through people having feelings for one another (though indeed not without it), but through first, their taking their stand in living relation with a living Center. . . . The community is built up out of living mutual relations, but the builder is the living Center."[24]

Jewish community is based on the family, something Roman Catholics in the past could understand. Both Catholics and Jews are today faced with retaining a strong emphasis on family while acknowledging other groupings besides that of mother, father, and children. Catholics and Jews are having to accept that their religion is not automatically transmitted by the family. Catholic and Protestant Christians can be reminded by Jews that family and community loyalty are not out of date.

The Jewish community is not constituted by agreement about doctrines. There is always a minority view. The Talmud says that in the midst of a doctrinal dispute, "Moses pleaded with the Lord to reveal the final truth. . . . The Lord replied: There are no pre-existent final truths in doctrine or law. The truth is the considered judgment of the majority of authoritative interpreters in every generation."[25] Perhaps Vatican II in contrast to previous councils was a step in the direction of a Jewish attitude of not excommunicating the minority for their view. The faith of the Jew is expressed not as a body of doctrine but in devotion to the community's struggle for justice.

Martin Buber finishes his rather stark contrast of two types of faith by saying: "An Israel striving after the renewal of its faith through rebirth of the person and a Christianity striving for a renewal of its faith by the rebirth of the nation would have something yet unsaid to say to each other—hardly to be conceived at the present time."[26] The present time Buber here refers to was before the Holocaust and the state of Israel. Since he wrote that passage there are new obstacles to mutual understanding, but more urgency.

Finally, as an offshoot of community there has always been a difference between Christians and Jews as to the place of bodiliness, pleasure, and humor. Christianity has engendered wonderful flights of spirituality. Its danger

---

24. Buber, *I and Thou,* 45.

25. *y. Sanh.* 4:2 in *The Essential Talmud*, ed. Adin Steinsaltz (New York: Basic Books, 1984).

26. Martin Buber, *Two Types of Faith* (New York: Harper Torchbooks, 1961), 174.

lies in the neglect of the body and the material world. Unhealthy ascetical practices have often accompanied attempts to ascend to God above or to bring on the revelation of the last day. Jewish religion has for the most part been free of these dangers by being rooted in the ordinariness of the moment. As a Jewish saying puts it: there are four things one should avoid speculating about: what is in front, what is behind, what is above, and what is below.[27]

The Jewish attitude to the body comes out in traditional teaching about simple pleasures. According to the Talmud, at the final judgment "a man will have to give an account concerning everything in which his eye delighted, but the enjoyment of which he nevertheless denied himself."[28] While some Christian groups, such as the Puritans, forbade all pleasure on the Sabbath, the Jewish Sabbath was for enjoying simple pleasures—conversation, eating, sex—saved from the distractions of the workaday world.[29]

Humor abounds in Jewish tradition. Not just the Puritans but the whole Christian tradition could use a lighter touch and some ironic self-deprecation. Sometimes humor can be just a moment of relief, or it can be a cover-up of serious issues. But at its best, Jewish humor rattles the philosophic and religious foundations of the world. There are probably many places in the New Testament where the appropriate response is laughter, but Christians need Jewish help to get the joke.

Because of their confidence in being God's chosen, Jews can mock their own claim to self-importance. That allows startling reversals at times in the respective positions of the chosen and the Gentiles. A story in the Seder service recounts that when the Israelites were fleeing the Egyptian army, the Red Sea swallowed the pursuing soldiers. The angels in heaven began to sing, but God rebuked the angels and said: Stop your singing; don't you know that my people are drowning?[30] Even at this solemn moment when the survival of the community is at stake, the Jew is reminded that the earth is the Lord's and the chosen people are people. The Hasidic master prayed: "I beseech thee that thou mayest redeem Israel. And if thou willest not, redeem the Gentiles."[31]

Believing in a revealing God means believing in a God revealed in all of creation, material as well as spiritual, among all people and all creatures.

27. Jakob Petuchowski, *Our Masters Taught: Rabbinic Stories and Sayings* (New York: Crossroad, 1982).

28. *Qidd.* IV, 12, in Petuchowski, *Our Masters Taught*, 32.

29. *Ketub.* 62b, in David Feldman, *Health and Medicine in Jewish Tradition* (New York: Crossroad, 1986), 67.

30. *Meg.* 10b, in Avivah Gottlieb Zornberg, *The Particulars of Rapture* (New York: Doubleday, 2001), 215.

31. Buber, *Two Types of Faith*, 77.

Faith is a deeply personal act in the present surrounded by a tradition of witnesses from the past and with a hunger for justice yet to be realized.

Muslim Insights for Christians

When the Christian turns from Judaism to Islam for insight, the first reaction might be that dialogue is impossible. The two parties seem thoroughly alienated; few friendly exchanges have occurred for more than five centuries. A glimmer of hope can be found in the fact that Christian-Jewish conversation has made most of its progress in the short space of sixty years. Something comparable can occur in Muslim-Christian relations; the world certainly needs it.

If Islam looks unapproachable to the Christian, it might help to consider Islam as a reform movement from Judaism. That means, on the one hand, that Islam is structurally similar to Judaism; on the other hand, Islam and Christianity are siblings in the family of Abraham. Perhaps the most difficult part of Christians learning from Islam is that no religious group is very receptive to a group that claims to be its successor. Christians have borrowed from Jewish religion, which they imagined to be their predecessor; the positions are reversed in Christianity's stance toward Islam. However, Islam does not consider itself to be a reformed Christianity; it has distinctive insights to offer its sibling.

Faith for a Muslim has some of the same texture as it does for a Jew. Here, as in many places, the similarity extends to language. In the Qur'an the word *iman,* used more than five hundred times, is the positive response of the believer. The Arabic word is closely related to the Hebrew word (*aman*) that gives us the English word "amen." In the Qur'an the word for infidel (*kafir*) means ingratitude. A Muslim is someone who responds to the gift of the revealing God with gratitude and complete submission or *islam.*

As in Jewish religion, the true believer or Muslim shows faith by the evidence of practice rather than by statements of belief. The practice is summed up in the five pillars: the testimony of belief in Allah, the recitation of prayer five times daily, fasting during Ramadan, the giving of alms, and a pilgrimage to Mecca. There is no elaborate system of belief; instead, there is remembrance of one's faith in the daily observance of prayer, dietary laws, and family practice. Even more than for Judaism, Islam is an aural/oral and tactile religion. "The ultimate aim of the ego is not to *see* something but to *be* something."[32]

32. Muhammad Iqbal, *The Reconstruction of Religious Thought in Islam* (Lahore: Institute of Islamic Culture, 1986), 198.

Wilfred Cantwell Smith, who is Christian, asks the provocative question: If Jesus returned today, would he recognize himself more clearly in Christianity or in Islam?[33] Smith does not directly answer the question, but his context of comparing a Semitic outlook and Western philosophy points to the fact that Jesus is still a historical figure in Islam (and Judaism) and has not been swallowed up in the "divinity of Christ." Christians do not have to agree with Muslims or Jews on this point, but they do need reminding that Christ is a title to Jesus and it is a complicated theological idea that can obscure simple piety and imitation of Jesus.

Islam has never separated religion and politics as has Christianity, for better and for worse. The Christian church can function as a private enclave within the modern nation, submitting to the laws of the nation-state. Although tolerance of religious diversity has its price in compromise, most Christians think the compromise is worth the price. The Muslim ideal of "community" is a worldwide movement that can clash with modern secular law and the ultimacy of the nation-state. The call in many countries to establish the Muslim *Sharia* as the basis of law has problems, but it is a reminder that humanly made laws are not ultimate.

Difficult times lie ahead for the whole world as Islam is "modernized." Christians in the West should not assume that their path is the only one possible.[34] The need is to distinguish the original direction of the religion from cultural traditions that are distorting accretions. Like Christianity, Islam needs some structural changes that create checks and balances in government and allow for a vital return to sources, especially before the tenth century CE.

The Christian might recognize and appreciate a Muslim meaning of faith but still be stymied by the Muslim use of "revelation." Unlike the Bible, which is said to be the result of inspired human authorship, Muslims believe that the text of the Qur'an was dictated to Muhammad. Wilfred Cantwell Smith asks: Is the Qur'an the Word of God? The answer within Islam is "yes," and perhaps in some sense of the phrase it can be yes for Christians too.[35] An outsider might be willing to apply the phrase "word of God" while retaining a metaphorical sense.

At a first glance there seems to be no room to negotiate in Christian and Muslim interpretations of divine revelation. The Qur'an exists only in Arabic; anything called a translation is not accepted as the "word of God." Christianity,

---

33. Wilfred Cantwell Smith, *On Understanding Islam* (The Hague: Mouton, 1981), 259.
34. Reza Aslan, *No God but God* (New York: Random House, 2005), 117–39.
35. Wilfred Cantwell Smith, *On Understanding Islam*, 282–300.

in contrast, was a mix of languages at its origin and the New Testament has been translated into hundreds, even thousands, of languages. There is no imitating Islam on this point, but there may be something to learn about reverence for a sacred text and the value of recitation. "Qur'an" itself means recitation, the speaking aloud of a text that transcends any earthly book. The real Qur'an is a heavenly Qur'an. The revelation of God exists in the dialogue with the believer. "Not the text in itself is the revelation but that which the believer discovers every time afresh while reading it."[36]

Christianity has great flexibility in the way reforms are undertaken. Christian groups have often been ready to jettison beliefs that no longer fit today's cultural assumptions. Islam is not likely to proceed that way. I think it is unrealistic to say that "any real reconstruction of religious thought in Islam needs to be based on the principle that the area of unquestioned revealed truth needs to be narrowed, but not diluted."[37] Reform in Islam is not going to proceed by choosing among "revealed truths," nor is the questioning of "revealed truth" a dilution.

The "revealed truth" in Islam (if that is a meaningful phrase at all) is not a series of truths found in the scripture or in doctrines aligned with scripture. The "revealed truth" is the truth of the Qur'an as it speaks to the believer and receives in response an "amen." That may seem terribly confining to an outsider, but the dialogue via the text of the Qur'an has no preordained boundaries. The text is set, but the *meaning* of the text has to be sought for. What did the Arabic words mean at the time of Muhammad? What do the words mean to the Muslim today? Muhammad Iqbal says that "as the reading and reciting of Qur'an is a dialogue with God, the true speaker of the Word, the possibilities are as infinite as is God Himself."[38]

Muslim concentration on one text as revelatory of God might seem to be a denial of a wider revelation. Islam, like Christianity and Judaism, has its share of individuals who think they have the revealed God within the book they possess. The depth of human believing, however, is fully compatible with the breadth of divine revealing. Christian acceptance of a "revealed religion" as opposed to "natural religion" is unknown in Islam. "One of the characteristics of the Qur'an as the last Revelation is that at times it becomes as it were transparent in order that the first Revelation may shine through its verses; and this first revelation, namely, the Book of Nature, belongs to everyone.[39]

36. Aziz Lahbabi, as quoted in Annemarie Schimmel, *Deciphering the Signs of God* (Albany, NY: SUNY Press, 1994), 165.

37. G. H. Jansen, *Militant Islam* (San Francisco: Harper & Row, 1979), 201.

38. Muhammad Iqbal in Schimmel, *Deciphering the Signs of God*, 163.

39. Martin Lings, *What Is Sufism?* (Berkeley: University of California Press, 1975).

A religion that can seem legalistic, moralistic, and narrow-minded can turn out to be a religion that embraces universality and sees the universe in a grain of sand. Similar to Jewish mysticism that can spring from reflection on a single letter of the Hebrew alphabet,[40] the rational and the logical in Islam are never far from a mystical attitude. A God who can seem far beyond the heavens is "closer than the great vein in your neck." Christian and Muslim mysticisms are not variations on a common essence, but there are points of overlap. Although they differ as to whether the Spirit of God is a person within divine communion, Christians and Muslims can share in mystical prayer to the One whose final name is silence.

Uniqueness

The topic of uniqueness can be helpful to understanding the relations of Christian and Jew, Christian and Muslim. If claims of uniqueness are scattered through Christian writing and left unexplained, "uniqueness" becomes an insuperable obstacle to Christian-Jewish and Christian-Muslim conversations.

Jewish and Muslim writers occasionally use the term "unique," and it fits quite well as a description of the logic implied by their religions. However, it is Christianity that is mainly responsible for the word being applied to religion in the nineteenth century and for a constant repetition of the term in recent decades. It sometimes seems that "the uniqueness of Christ" has absorbed all the titles the church had applied to Jesus in the past. "The uniqueness of Jesus Christ" has become an unchallengeable dogma within the Catholic Church.

Writers who recognize that there is a peculiarity in the claim gingerly try to explore what "the uniqueness of Jesus Christ" means while not taking issue with the doctrine. They usually look for a way the word can be inclusive rather than exclusive, but that still sounds imperialistic. They then invent some phrase or add a qualifier, but the whole argument comes across as ad hoc and unpersuasive. Avoidance of the word is advocated by some Christian writers.[41] But the widespread use of "unique" almost guarantees that the word will not go away. One thing is certain: An explanation of the "uniqueness of Jesus Christ" will not get far unless it is intelligible within the ordinary use of the English word "unique." There is no persuasiveness in inventing a meaning for uniqueness that only applies to Christ or Jesus Christ.

---

40. *The Early Kabbalah*, ed. Joseph Dan (New York: Paulist Press, 1986), 10.

41. Jonathan Smith in *Drudgery Divine* (Chicago: University of Chicago Press, 1990), 36.

The meanings of "unique" and the way the word is used in ordinary speech are puzzling, but the word is fairly common, especially in discussion of the arts. "Unique" has a double meaning that makes it a word rich in significance for some people and for other people almost empty. A historian may say that of course every event is unique; it happens once and does not happen again; unique adds nothing. Another historian may say that if something were unique it would not be part of history; every event in history has similarities with other events. A connecting link in the two different meanings is the assumption that "unique" excludes comparison.

There has been intense debate among Jewish writers about whether the Holocaust is unique. Some writers think that unless the Holocaust is said to be unique its significance is not appreciated. Other Jewish writers declare that the claim to uniqueness is ridiculous, fatuous, unintelligible.[42] The argument cannot go anywhere unless two nearly opposite meanings of "unique" are acknowledged. The question of the "uniqueness of the Holocaust" is addressed to Christians as well as Jews. I will refer back to this example after sorting out the two meanings of "unique."

Words do not have opposite meanings; there is always a common root that can sharply diverge. Unique has a root meaning of "different from all others." In a first meaning one can imagine the difference as excluding all common characteristics with every other thing. In a nearly opposite meaning, uniqueness can also be imagined as "different from all others" by including the characteristics of all the others.

In imagining a movement toward uniqueness in either direction, the process is never complete. A process of excluding characteristics cannot be completed because everything in history has some common notes. A unique thing would not be a thing; anything at least has the note of thing. In the other direction, no one thing includes the notes of all other things. So long as history continues, there is otherness that is not (yet) included. Thus, besides recognizing the nearly opposite meanings of "unique," one must always be aware that in neither direction is uniqueness complete.

I am not positing a theory of how "unique" should be used. I am describing its regular use in ordinary conversations. Some people might assume that the second meaning—different from all others by a process of increasing inclusiveness—is very unusual. I would say that it is at least as common as the first. The two meanings constantly intermingle when the topic is human affairs.

People do recognize the incompleteness of uniqueness in that they almost always use qualifiers. Generations of grammar teachers have insisted that a

42. Peter Novick, *The Holocaust in American Life* (New York: Mariner, 2000), 9, 196.

thing is either unique or it is not; there cannot be a "very unique" or a "more unique." The panel of experts at the American Heritage Dictionary seems miffed that people do not understand how to use the word. According to the rules, unique does not admit of comparison. In ordinary usage, however, people recognize that the word unique *always* implies comparison. Things are more or less unique, that is, they are more or less nearly unique.

The first meaning of uniqueness—differing by a process of increasing exclusion—applies in the world of space and time. A thing exists by excluding others from its own territory. If one goes down to the smallest particle, it still has its own space while sharing a few notes with other things. Similarly with time: the movement of time imagined as physical happenings can be sliced into smaller and smaller units but there remain units that share characteristics with other units of time. In this first meaning of unique, no thing is simply and completely unique.

The second meaning—differing by a process of increasing inclusion—pertains to the meaning of humans and their affairs. Humans are the workshop of creation; they constitute the species in which the whole world can enter. As Theodosius Dobzhansky playfully puts the matter, "All species are unique but humans are the uniquest." But what is so confusing is that a human being is a combination of the two uniquenesses—a being that asserts its difference by fending off intrusions into its bodily space and a being open to the whole universe. Human life cannot collapse the tension between open and closed.

The (near) uniqueness of things is a fact, but not as interesting as a person's uniqueness of openness. Every human being is born unique, that is, very unique or more nearly unique than the other animals. Among human beings, some are more unique than others. Persons incorporate their people and their place to varying degrees. Studying some individuals of another time and another place can be revelatory of a whole world of meaning. Great art provides such a lens of understanding and so do portraits of the historical past.

Within each person's life some experiences are more unique than others. William Wordsworth refers to "spots" of memory, moments that include greater meaning than was realized at the time.[43] There are decisive choices that bring the person's whole life into play; one's life has led to that moment, and the choice may provide direction for the future of one's life.

Dying is the most unique experience; it alone can be open to the meaning of one's entire life. One of the few points on which all religions agree is that

---

43. William Wordsworth, *The Prelude* (New York: Penguin Books, 1986).

death is *not* the last in a series of points called "life." Dying recapitulates the life. If people have experienced an increasing uniqueness throughout life, they cannot believe that the process does not continue in some form. Reincarnation has been and still is the most common way of imagining the process continuing. Resurrection of the person is another way to imagine a continuing (process of) uniqueness.

The word "event" is employed to signify something richer than physical occurrences in space-time. Events can be more or less unique depending on their meaning for understanding the past and the direction of the present. Vatican officials have recently been arguing against calling Vatican II an event.[44] They seem to assume that the word means a break with the past. Were 1962–1965 just another three years in the smooth continuity of Catholic Church history? The Vatican would do better in arguing what kind of event it was. The greatness of Vatican II was its return to sources, an attempt to examine the whole tradition with as much openness as they could muster, so that the event would be very unique. Vatican II was a more unique event than Vatican I.

In the United States, the date September 11, 2001, immediately became the name of a very unique event called 9/11. For people in the United States the date has more meaning than does September 10 of that year. The claim almost immediately heard that "9/11 has changed everything" could not be true, but the event did change much. The three thousand people who died took on a special, almost sacred meaning. Because of the peculiar position of the United States, the event had considerable meaning across the world. In time, however, people who are unsympathetic to the United States have found the obsession with 9/11 irritating. Why is there such concern with those three thousand, a number that is about the same as the number of children who die *each day* of malaria?

People directly involved in the event may have found it the most unique event of their lives. Other people close to the event found it more unique than people who were at a distance. Physical proximity, however, is not the only criterion; personal involvement is always more important for how uniquely significant an event is. Even at present, people who live or work in lower Manhattan find the World Trade Center site to be a bothersome traffic impediment. At the same time the area holds thousands of people from far away who are visiting a shrine, or at least a place that has taken on a very unique meaning.

---

44. Joseph Komonchak, "Vatican II as an 'Event,'" in *Vatican II: Did Anything Happen?* ed. David Schultenover, 24–51 (New York: Continuum, 2007); Nicholas Lash, "What Happened at Vatican II?" in *Theology for Pilgrims* (Grand Rapids, MI: Eerdmans, 2008), 240–48.

For Jews, the Holocaust is a very unique event. Certainly "remember the six million" has a greater impact than "remember the three thousand." Still, there are critics of what they take to be a Jewish obsession. World War II took more than fifty million lives, not just six million. The meaning of human events, however, is not dependent on numbers alone.[45] For most Jews who were alive in the latter decades of the twentieth century the Holocaust was the most unique event of their lives. For other people it is not likely to be more unique than all other events, but it surely can be recognized as very unique.

One could say that the Holocaust became very unique in the 1960s when "Holocaust" was borrowed from the Bible and given only one meaning. In contrast to the word "genocide," which was also coined to describe the destruction of European Jewry but includes other mass murders of peoples, "Holocaust" with a capital *H* is used of only one event. That signifies a uniqueness beyond any ordinary measurements; comparisons are not welcome. That attitude is understandable, but there is a danger that the event can become so isolated as not to allow some comparison of factors that led to the event and some analyzing of how the event transpired. The attempt to understand facets of what happened takes nothing away from the uniqueness of the Holocaust. It adds to the possibility that Gentiles around the world would realize that the Holocaust is very unique for others besides Jews.

Unique Jesus? Unique Christ?

The above clarifications of the meanings of unique throw light on the use of the term in Christian writing. One always has to ask which meaning of unique is assumed and to what degree uniqueness can be affirmed. Uniqueness when applied to things, including ideas and institutions, implies a process of increasing exclusion. If there were a thing, a body of truths under Christian church control, that constituted "the Christian revelation," it would be unique in an exclusivistic way and to a very high degree. The claim that there exists a unique Christian revelation is a major obstacle to Christian-Jewish or Christian-Muslim conversation. But if there is no "Christian revelation," there is no "unique Christian revelation."

Is there a unique revelation of God? Because divine revelation is neither a thing nor a person, that question cannot be directly addressed. But faith as "believing in" is unique. Believing in a revealing God, as a deeply personal

---

45. Gabriel Moran, *Uniqueness* (Maryknoll, NY: Orbis Books, 1992), 34–40.

act, can be very unique in an increasingly inclusive way. The act of believing in negates no one else, and it opens the person to increasing engagement with other people and the things of God's world.

The statement "Jesus Christ is unique" is a conversation stopper. Jews and Muslims do not reject the claim; it is not intelligible to them. When something is unintelligible to Jews and Muslims, Christian writers ought to wonder if it makes sense to Christians. What Christians have to keep in mind when speaking with Jews or Muslims, and perhaps among themselves, is that Jesus is the name of someone.

Christ is a title Christians give to Jesus of Nazareth, the central element of their belief system. Jews have no difficulty discussing Jesus or Yeshua from Nazareth; he is one of their own. Muslims do not have the same level of familiarity with Jesus, but they give him an honored place. Jews have no interest in discussing "Christ," because it is a Christian belief. I am not suggesting that Christians give up belief that Jesus is the Christ. But if Christians, with a little help from Muslims and Jews, are to sort out the meanings of "unique" and how they apply, they must recognize that a person is different from a belief about that person.

The starting point for a Christian use of the term is "Jesus is unique." There were many men before and there have been many men since Jesus of Nazareth with the name Jesus; the name is not (very) unique. The uniqueness of Jesus of Nazareth is based on his position in world history, the record of his life, death, and resurrection, and the effect he has had on the whole world.

At a first level no one denies that Jesus is unique insofar as every human being is born unique, that is, with an openness to the world. At a second level the claim that "Jesus is very unique in comparison to other human beings" would be readily accepted by most Jews, Muslims, and other fair-minded people. At a third level the statement "Jesus is the most unique human who has ever lived" is a claim that involves community belief, supported by historical evidence. The title "Christ" is a statement of that belief; the life, death, and resurrection of Jesus are the Christian focus or scope of believing in a revealing God.

"Christ" by itself is not unique in the meaning of increasing inclusiveness. The word "Christ" as a title or idea is (exclusively) unique in that no one else controls the term. However, when it is combined with Jesus, "Christ" affirms a living presence and a greater future. But even if Christians are correct in the claim that Jesus is the most unique human there has ever been, he is not totally unique while history continues. Only at the end of history is there a uniqueness that is not of an idea called Christ but of the universally realized Christ.

Jesus-Christ as unique is indeed the Christian belief, but when the words are used as if they were the name of someone in the past, the whole point of the process of Jesus' resurrection as the beginning of the resurrection of the total Christ is lost. And in this context when the name "Jesus" is omitted, the belief of Christians is further obscured. "Christ is unique" is unintelligible except in the sense that the word and the idea are almost exclusively a church possession.

A claim that Jesus is called Christ because he is so unique is an invitation to study the people and the times in which that uniqueness was formed. Christians cannot believe in Jesus-Christ as very unique unless they have some knowledge of Jewish history and the religious ideas the church adopted from Jewish religion. Muslim writing on Jesus is less integral to Christian believing, but the Muslim appreciation of Jesus could enhance a Christian understanding of the uniqueness of Jesus as Christ.

The uniqueness of Jesus-Christ is badly distorted by the twentieth-century phrase "Christ event." I noted earlier that "event" can be a way of referring to the human meaning of physical happenings. Thus, events in Jerusalem near the year 30 CE were of more than passing significance to future history. "Christ event" may seem like catchy shorthand for what happened in the life, death, and resurrection of Jesus, but it collapses any helpful grasp of a very unique Jesus in relation to Christ.

Oscar Cullman was one of the main theologians responsible for the phrase "Christ event"; it became part of theological jargon and is assumed to be clear. Cullman's *Christ and Time* is about the "Christ event." Part 2 of the book is headed: "The unique character of the Christ-Deed at the Midpoint."[46] He later had second thoughts about locating the Christ event at the "midpoint" of history. The problem remained: locating "Christ event" in the past, instead of "Christ" linking past events in Jesus' life with the church of today and the future resurrection of the whole body.

The question is sometimes asked: Why is there only one Christ? If "Christ" is the Christian way of affirming the salvation of all peoples, it makes no logical sense to talk of a second Christ. It has to be admitted that there does remain a problem of seeming intolerance when Christians say that only Christ can save. I will return in the next chapter to that issue.

A similar logic applies to the question "why only one incarnation?" If "incarnation" is identified with a "Christ event" in the past, the singularity of incarnation is a problem. But if "incarnation" is about God's presence carnally, expressed in the most unique way in the life, death, and resurrection

46. Oscar Cullman, *Christ and Time* (Philadelphia: Westminster, 1950), 121–74.

of Jesus, then one incarnation makes logical sense whether or not people share this Christian belief.[47]

The question behind those two questions may be "why is there only one person, Jesus, said to be the Christ?" An answer to that question is not so logically simple. Every true Christian—that is, every follower of the Christ way—shares in the meaning of Christ. Only one person was needed to make the breakthrough for everyone else.

The answer can be put in the form of a paradox about the origin of "person." In Christian theological language Jesus is not a person; that is, he does not possess human personhood. He was so uniquely human that he was taken up by the personhood of the Son of God. Outside of that technical language everyone thinks of him as a human person, a very unique person. Jesus is not only perceived as a person, but it was in early church reflection on him that the idea and the word "person" emerged.

Uniqueness as a process of increasing inclusiveness existed before the time of Jesus, as did a word "person," but unique personhood became conceptualized in large part because of Jesus. The one who had no person gave us the idea of person. There did not have to be a second Jesus-Christ because unique personhood had to be introduced only once. This argument for the centrality of christological disputes in constituting the meaning of person is debatable, but Christians can offer historical evidence as well as theological concepts about the origin of unique personhood.

Christians need not and ought not to give up any of their beliefs in order to converse with Jews or Muslims. But some of those beliefs are encased in nearly impenetrable theological language. The language has to be made intelligible to outsiders. The changes needed may sometimes seem minor, but they can be the difference between a conversation starting or not starting. In the effort to explain Christian teaching to an outsider, Christians may get a better understanding of that teaching for themselves. A Christian interpretation of believing in a revealing God is best situated within an interreligious dialogue.

---

47. Jacob Neusner, *The Incarnation of God: The Character of Diversity in Formative Judaism* (Philadelphia: Fortress Press, 1988).

Chapter Six

Aesthetic Understanding
of Believing in a Revealing God

The key to understanding religion is the relation between the particular and the universal. This involves an aesthetic understanding, by which I mean seeing that the universal is found in the particular and only in the particular. And the particular is particular insofar as it conveys in its concreteness an intimation of universality. When something gives no signal of the universal, it is a mere part of a whole. It does not invite entering into a depth of understanding.

In this chapter I continue the last chapter's concern with how Jewish, Christian, and Muslim religions provide examples of this aesthetic logic. I also supply examples from the arts, illustrating the logic in the works of Flannery O'Connor and Samuel Beckett. Finally, I examine Christian liturgy as a profound embodiment of the joining of word and action for understanding believing in a revealing God.

The Logic of Particular-Universal

Logic in the modern world is generally assumed to refer either to using induction from many individual cases or else deduction from a general rule. In either direction, the assumption is that there is a world of individual cases from which the human mind can abstract laws or rules. The natural image for such a movement is up and down. The general rule leaves behind the messiness of individual differences for an *idea* that comprehends many cases. This kind of thinking in individual cases and general ideas occurs in all areas of life, including art, history, and religion. Every phenomenon can be examined from the outside. But to study the religious experience, the artistic production, or the historical event solely as an outsider is to miss the heart of the matter.

The natural image for aesthetic or religious thinking is a movement that circles an activity in order to reach a depth of appreciation. Instead of building a larger and larger system with a clear top and bottom, an aesthetic way of thinking does not pursue width, length, and height; it keeps turning toward the center. Ludwig Wittgenstein asks: How does one understand a piece of music by Brahms? His answer: Listen to it and then listen to it again. After repeated listenings one can compare it to other pieces by Brahms and then to works by Mozart or Beethoven.[1]

A particular work of art cannot be universal; it can only approach the universal. Like the word "unique," the "universal" is never fully achieved. The difference between minor works of art and the "classics" is the degree to which they approach universality. We know that Bach, Mozart, and Beethoven have a high degree of universality. They continue to speak profoundly to millions of people. When a work of art cuts across gender, race, culture, and other divides of the human race, it lays claim to approaching universality.

Thomas Merton once wrote that he had a dream about Karl Barth's love of Mozart's music. Addressing Barth, Merton wrote: "Your books (and mine) matter less than we might think! There is in us a Mozart that will be our salvation."[2] When I looked at the front page of the *New York Times* on December 11, 1968, and saw that Barth and Merton had both died on the day previous, my first thought was that they were listening to Mozart.

The religions of Abraham give a special place to words and the artistic use of words. Words play such a constant role in daily life that the power of their particularity can be lost sight of. Especially with our modern media, we can get "in touch" with anyone, anywhere, at any time; that ability has obvious advantages. But lacking any restraints, the words touch only the surface rather than sound the depths.

The precision of poetic speech lies in its ambiguity; concrete meanings of descriptions are used that point beyond themselves. A variety of literary genres can convey the (nearly) universal truth by the crafting of a few words. The truth of human experience is not always best conveyed by trying to say prosaically what happened. The poet, novelist, or playwright might get closer by zeroing in on a particular person or event. Regarding Shakespeare's *Macbeth*, Northrop Frye writes: "If you wish to know the history of eleventh-

---

1. Ludwig Wittgenstein, *Wittgenstein's Lectures 1930–33*, ed. G. E. Moore (London: Allen and Unwin, 1959), 278.

2. Thomas Merton, *Conjectures of a Guilty Bystander* (Garden City, NY: Doubleday Image Books, 1968), 12.

century Scotland, look elsewhere; if you wish to know what it means to gain a kingdom and lose one's soul, look here."[3]

The artist does not usually have in mind a universal truth when working with particular materials. In fact, the conscious attempt to speak to the ages tends to distract from the moment at hand. What is constructed to attract millions of onlookers may get immediate attention but is not likely to last. Not only the artist but also the person experiencing the work of art cannot be first interested in what has universal application. A person who leaves the particular work of art for a supposed universal meaning usually finds only the general and the sentimental. Of great poetry, Goethe wrote, "Whoever grasps this particular in a living way will simultaneously realize the universal, too, without becoming aware of it—or realize it only later."[4]

Art museums around the world have two kinds of visitors. Some people are dashing from one room to another so as not to miss anything. Others save their eyes for a few paintings or sculptures so as to absorb their impact in depth. Edwin Schlossberg, who has created museums that invite a sense of community and a personal response, says that he hopes his designs get a person to turn to the next person and say: "What does this mean?"[5]

A reaction of puzzled questioning, Schlossberg thinks, is not a bad first response to a profound work of art. Repeated viewing, listening, or reading would then help a person to slowly comprehend. Any good book bears repeated readings; each time it can reveal more of its truth as the reader matures. I read Martin Buber's *I and Thou* when it first appeared in English and did not understand either its form or its content. Each of the dozen or more times I have read it since then, I discover something I have previously missed. What great writers do is shake up our sense of language to help us see beyond the humdrum of our lives. Of Kafka's strange tales it has been said that "he created symbols which through their paradoxical form expressed the inexpressible without betraying it."[6]

---

3. Northrop Frye, *Educated Imagination* (Bloomington, IN: Indiana University Press, 1964), 64.

4. Johann Wolfgang von Goethe, "Maxims and Reflections," in Walter Kaufman, *From Shakespeare to Existentialism* (New York: Doubleday Anchor Books, 1959), 54.

5. Elizabeth Ellsworth, *Places of Learning: Media, Architecture, Pedagogy* (New York: Routledge, 2004), 140.

6. Heinz Politzer, quoted in John Dominic Crossan, *Raid on the Articulate: Cosmic Eschatology in Jesus and Borges* (New York: Harper, 1976), 95.

Jewish, Christian, and Muslim Particularity

What I have said about artistic literature applies especially to Jewish and Christian Bibles, as well as the Qur'an. This profound literature is capable of conveying a (nearly) universal truth if it is received in the right way. However, when misunderstood, the claims in the Bibles and the Qur'an are an endless source of trouble and intolerance. The understanding of the Bibles has been helped by libraries filled with books of criticism. The Qur'an has not been subjected to the same kind of historical and literary criticism, but it has been commented upon, interpreted, and analyzed at great length over the centuries.

For the purpose of examining the logic of particularity in the three Abrahamic religions, I will concentrate on a single issue: According to each tradition, who has a share in the life to come? It is obvious that the answer to this question reveals much about the tradition as a whole. If a religious group says disparaging things about anyone outside its boundaries, that would show intolerance. If the group thinks that outsiders go to hell, that would be a case of ultimate intolerance.

Jews in the past, and probably most Jews in the present, routinely refer to Christians believing that all Jews are closed off from the hereafter. Some Christians apparently do hold such a belief. I cannot imagine a greater insult than to believe that my Jewish colleagues are damned to hell for following their best intellectual lights and moral convictions. Christians need to be reminded that the clearest criterion in the New Testament for judgment of one's life is found in Matthew 25. The criterion is whether one has practiced the works of mercy: giving food to the hungry, clothing the naked, visiting the imprisoned.

Emil Fackenheim writes: "Judaism is 'universalistic' for it teaches that the righteous of all nations enter the Kingdom of Heaven. Christianity is 'particularistic' for it bars from the Kingdom all unsaved non-Christians, no matter how great their righteousness."[7] Most Christians would be bewildered by this contrast. It has always been central to Christian thinking that Christianity was a movement from the particular religion of the Jewish people to a universal or catholic religion. ("In Christ there is neither Jew nor Gentile . . . .") How could anyone think that the fifteen million Jews constitute a universal religion while the billion-plus Christians are particularistic?

---

7. Emil Fackenheim, *To Mend the World: Foundations of Future Jewish Thought* (New York: Schocken Books, 1982), 39.

What Jews say of Christians is a perfect mirror of what Christians have regularly said of Jews. Each has accused the other of affirming the particular while asserting that its own position is universal. The polemic against the other prevents both parties from recognizing that the universal can only be realized as embodied in the particular.

The sad irony is that from the outside Christian, Jewish, and Muslim religions appear to be remarkably similar in the intolerance of their respective languages. All three religions believe there is one God, creator of all, who is good and just. Each religion also believes that this God of the universe spoke to their particular group at particular times and particular places. The paradox is obvious to everyone in the world who is neither Jewish, Christian, nor Muslim. How can a just and benevolent God condemn people who through no fault of their own do not accept or practice Jewish, Christian, or Muslim religions?

Each religion has to make an attempt to show how its logic works. That is, when one religion uses a term with the intention of speaking universally, it has to acknowledge that its particular way of speaking leaves room for other particular forms that have universal intent. This task is quite novel in the history of religions.

Christian Language for Who Is Saved

Within Christianity, "Christ," "church," and "baptism" have particular references. Christianity has control of these terms; no one else is arguing for possession of them. The meaning of each term is mainly set by Christian usage, but these days outsiders may take more than a passing interest in these terms. From early in its history the church has maintained that "Christ is the one savior," "outside the church there is no salvation," and baptism is necessary to be saved.

From just as early in Christian history, thinkers have wrestled with the question of what these beliefs imply about the salvation of the non-Christian. Augustine, for example, posited a place called limbo for the unbaptized. What he had described as the *limbus* or edge of hell became over the centuries more like the edge of heaven. When the Roman Catholic Church finally acknowledged limbo to be a bad idea, the general reaction was mostly amusement. But Augustine's problem was not thereby solved. Is the Catholic Church now saying that baptism is not important?

Most of the fathers of the church, despite a fiercely held belief that Christ with his church is the ark of salvation, also imply or accept that God has his own ways. In the Fourth Gospel, the later Pauline letters, and the philosophical thrusts of Justin Martyr and Clement of Alexandria, there is a connecting of belief in Christ to the very order of the universe and every individual.[8] Thomas Aquinas thought that an angel might be sent to someone dying in Africa who had not heard the Gospel. The solutions were often clumsy and only partially developed, but they were a recognition of the tension built into Christian claims.

Christian doctrines that affirmed the necessity of Christ-church-baptism were addressed to Christian church members, not to outsiders. There is no denying, however, that these doctrines were lifted from their context and applied to outsiders. It is understandable, if tragic, that ordinary Christians drew the conclusion that Jews or Muslims were damned because "Christ is my savior," the Bible or my catechism tells me so. What is truly scandalous is that the Catholic Church in its official teaching left the same impression until Vatican II made it clear that Catholic Church doctrine does not say Jews or Muslims are damned, but rather that those who "seek God with a sincere heart, and, moved by grace, try in their actions to do his will as they know it through the dictates of their conscience—those too may achieve eternal salvation" (*LG* 16).

From the very coining of the term "Christ," translating the Hebrew "messiah" but drawing in other connotations, there was an intent to link a particular person and a grand divine plan of the universe that is still operative today. "Christ" refers both to Jesus of Nazareth and also to the foundation and end of the world. In the inner language of the church, "Christ" is by definition the only way. Anyone who is saved—something humans cannot judge—is by definition saved by, through, and in Christ. Wilfred Cantwell Smith makes the provocative statement that there are no non-Christians because "strictly speaking, no outsider can possibly reject Christ; he rejects only Jesus. What makes him an outsider is precisely that he has not seen the latter is indeed the former."[9]

A Christian church member who would say to a Jew or a Muslim that "you are saved by Christ" might intend a compliment, but the statement is likely to be received as an insult. The Christian using the inner language of his or her community is trying to say to the Jew or Muslim: You and I are traveling on different paths but guided by what in my language is called "Christ." But given the connotations that "Christ" has for Jews, the Jew can

---

8. Gerald O'Collins, *Salvation for God's Other Peoples* (New York: Oxford University Press, 2008), 215–16.

9. Wilfred Cantwell Smith, *The Meaning and End of Religion* (New York: Macmillan, 1963), 299, n. 108.

hardly be expected to accept that "Christ" is a pointer to universality. A Buddhist, in contrast, might accept it as a compliment to be told that he or she is a follower of Christ, especially if the Christian is willing to acknowledge his or her own Buddha-nature.

The best known formula in recent theology that addresses this issue is Karl Rahner's phrase "anonymous Christian."[10] The most notable thing about Rahner's use of the phrase was that he intended it as inner-church language. The phrase, he often repeated, was a challenge to church members' smugness; it is "a profound admission of the fact that God is greater than man and the Church."[11] When he was asked whether he would accept being called an "anonymous Buddhist," he said he had no problem with that.[12]

Many Christian writers who have ridiculed the phrase as nonsensical or offensive do not offer an alternative for what is a central problem of Christian language. George Lindbeck writes that "the notion of an anonymous Christianity present in the depths of other religions is from this [linguistic-cultural] perspective nonsense, and a theory of the salvation of non-Christians built upon it seems thoroughly unreal."[13] Some people may have used "anonymous Christian" that way, but Lindbeck's harsh judgment misses Rahner's point. Rahner did not posit an anonymous Christianity buried in other religions. He was interested in what he called the "anonymous Christian," a follower of Christ. The implication is that the name "Christ-ian" applies to a true follower of Christ as well as to a member of the sociohistorical institution of Christianity. That is why he said his intention was to shake up Christians (= church members) with another meaning of Christian.

If Rahner had wanted to be more provocative (and at the same time more traditional), he could have dropped the word "anonymous." In Christian intramural language only a true Christian can be saved, but a true Christian can be a Jew or a Muslim or a Buddhist or an atheist. Not every Christian church member who proclaims that Christ is his savior is a true Christian. Rahner, far from wanting to make Jews or Muslims anonymous members of the existing church, repeatedly pointed out that "anyone who courageously accepts

---

10. Karl Rahner, "Christianity and the Non-Christian Religions," *Theological Investigations,* vol. 5 (Baltimore, MD: Helicon, 1966), 115–34; also, "On the Importance of the Non-Christian Religions for Salvation," *Theological Investigations,* vol. 18 (London: Darton, Longman and Todd, 1984), 288–95.

11. Rahner, "Christianity and the Non-Christian Religions," 134.

12. Rahner, *Theological Investigations*, vol. 16 (New York: Crossroad, 1983), 219.

13. George Lindbeck, *The Nature of Religious Doctrine* (Philadelphia: Westminster, 1984), 62.

life—even a shortsighted, primitive positivist who apparently bears patiently with the poverty of the superficial—has really accepted God."[14]

The doctrine that "outside the church there is no salvation," sounds embarrassing these days, but it is based on the same principle of particular-universal. As "Christ" is used for both concrete historical reference and a universal ideal, so "church" is used for a historical institution and a "heavenly Jerusalem." The necessity of baptism is a correlative belief. Baptism (by water) is necessary to enter the existing church; in Christian language, a baptism implicitly desired provides admission to the heavenly church.

The existence of hundreds of Christian churches is sometimes called a scandal, but it can be a reminder of the church's incompleteness. Each church has a right to assert that its particular form is the best expression of universality so long as it does not fill in the difference between particular and universal with its own language. Tiny churches that call themselves "the church of God" or "the church of Christ" do not pose a threat of domination. A large and powerful church that calls itself Catholic (universal) should regularly use a qualifier in front of "Catholic." All Christians believe in the one, true, catholic church, but that is an ideal still to be realized.

Parallels to the Christian Language of Particular-Universal

I do not presume to know in detail how the internal logic of Judaism and Islam works. That explanation is best left to an insider of each tradition. However, it is important for a Christian to see an outline of the parallel. Christians have some sense of Jewish religion from adopting the Jewish Scripture and some central categories from Jewish history. The more urgent and in some ways more interesting parallel is Islam. If Christians understood the logic of Islam they would better understand their own Christianity.

Muslim Language for Who Is Saved

It is hardly surprising that Christians who do not grasp the logic of their own religion find Islam to be intolerant. Of course, there are intolerant members of Islam just as there are intolerant church members. But Muslim tradition has the resources and the language to avoid oppressing outsiders, those who do not accept Islam as *a* religion. Muslims often quote the text from the Qur'an that "there is no compulsion in religion" (2:256). Muslims

---

14. Karl Rahner, "Thoughts on the Possibility of Belief Today," *Theological Investigations*, vol. 5 (New York: Crossroad, 1980), 7.

have not always lived up to that ideal. However, in comparison to Christian history, the Muslim record can hold its own. When Christians lived under Muslim rule in medieval Spain or sixteenth-century India they were treated as "protected peoples."[15] Contemporary religious and political conflicts cloud that history but do not prove that Islam is an intolerant religion.

Islam is a missionary religion that spread across the world faster than did Christianity. Islam represents a threat to Christian identity by claiming to be the last word. Muslims did not negate Christianity. In fact, Muhammad saw Torah, Gospel, and Qur'an as a single narrative (42:13). Islam is the capstone of the religion that runs from Abraham through Moses and the prophets. Islam has one extra prophet, Jesus of Nazareth, before Muhammad, the seal of the prophets.

The Qur'an thus claims to be the fullness of revelation. The paradox is that the Qur'an itself says that every people has its own messenger (10:47) and the messenger speaks with the language of his people (14:4). Like Christianity, Islam affirms a particular set of writings as incomparable, but those writings include moments in which the writings point beyond themselves.

Like the Christian claim of Christ and church as necessary for salvation, the Muslim claim is refracted through the terms "Islam" and "Muslim." Only a true Muslim can be saved; Islam is necessary for salvation. What makes Islam as a religion powerful to insiders and confusing to outsiders is that the same word is used for the religion and the practice of religion. "Islam" thus manages to unite both the ancient meaning of religion as genuine devotion and the modern meaning of religion as a sociohistorical institution. The institution of Islam gives concrete and powerful force to the particular practice of the true religion, Islam. Muslims who practice Islam embody the universal ideal of Islam. A non-Muslim is an infidel by definition.

Islam is no more intolerant than any other religion; its condemnation of the infidel is intramural language. A non-Muslim is someone who rejects the gift God offers and refuses to submit to the will of God. The warning of God's condemnation is meant for one who acknowledges the gift of Islam and then renounces it. For that reason conversion away from Islam to another religion is literally unthinkable. The challenge that modernity offers to the religious institution of Islam is to recognize genuine forms of religious subjection that have a different name than Islam.

---

15. Robert Burns, *Muslims, Christians and Jews in the Crusader Kingdom of Valencia* (Cambridge: Cambridge University Press, 1984); Jorge Flores, *Goa and the Great Mughal* (New York: Scala, 2004).

"Every child is born a Muslim."[16] By naming the religion that existed from the beginning of the world as Islam, Muslim language implies that each human being is offered a gift that is consonant with its very being. Every child starts with the presence of this gift and thus to become an unbeliever (*kafir*) requires an act of ingratitude. The doctrine that only a true Muslim can be saved is a consequence of the fact that in Muslim language Islam is the fulfillment of the human vocation.

Jewish Language for Who Is Saved

Jewish religion does not pose the same problem as does Christianity or Islam in that the number of Jews is relatively small and Judaism is not a missionary religion. Nevertheless, it can convey to an outsider arrogance if not the danger of political oppression. The claim to be the "chosen people" sounds like an inflation of self-importance. Some modern Jewish reformers, such as Mordecai Kaplan and the Reconstructionist movement, have tried to eliminate the claim to be God's chosen. Many Jews try to play down the phrase. The words and the idea are not likely to disappear, and the claim cannot just be smoothed over.

Jews, Christians, Muslims, and perhaps all religious groups claim a kind of special calling. The test of the claim is whether the group turns in on itself, intent only on claiming a higher status, or whether it thinks of itself as a demonstration of something profound in all human life. As a demonstration community its concern is all humanity. The fulfillment of that belief is the recognition that the human community itself is a demonstration of the character of the universe as a whole. Because "chosen people" is not a technical term belonging to only one religious tradition, Jews have to allow that there may be others who can lay claim to be the "chosen people."

As I noted in chapter 5, Jews acknowledge the relation of particular and universal with self-deprecating humor. "Chosen people" can be treated as an ironic joke in the face of terrible suffering. Chosenness is not something won through merit or something to glory in. It is either a burden that Jews accepted after God had offered it to every other people, or it has been laid upon the Jews without their choice.[17] In either case "chosen people" is not a higher plane; it is more like a central place in suffering humanity. "The

---

16. The parallel in Christianity is Horace Bushnell's principle that "every child is born a Christian" in his influential book *Christian Nurture* (New Haven: Yale University Press, 1988).

17. Jakob Petuchowski, *Our Masters Taught: Rabbinic Stories and Sayings* (New York: Crossroad, 1982), 35.

death camps ended forever one argument of history—whether the Jews are a chosen people. They are chosen, unmistakably, extremely, utterly."[18]

Two terms that Jews use to link the particular and the universal are "Torah" and "covenant." Each of them has a particular and concrete reference in Jewish history, but each is a way to point to what is universal in humanity. "Torah," like "Christ" and "Islam," is a term that has not migrated to other religions; it remains an intramural term with universal intent. "Covenant" has a different history because the Christian movement laid claim to being the true or new covenant, jarring the word loose from its Jewish moorings.

"Torah" is a term that starts out as instruction given by a parent to a child. It becomes the name for God's revelation to Moses, then the first five books of the Bible, and thereby the center of Jewish life.[19] In today's language it is better translated as "teaching" rather than "law." Although "Torah" is a term unknown to most non-Jews, the Talmud promises salvation to those who "engage in Torah."[20] How can someone engage in Torah who has never heard of Torah? "Torah," like "Christ" in Christianity, is a Jewish way of affirming universal truth. The righteous of all nations who are following their best lights are, in Jewish language, following the way of Torah.

A similar point is made with the term "covenant." In this case the term became central to the conflict of Jewish and Christian religions. The word also moved out to a variety of religious and secular uses. "Covenant" started out as a secular term describing the relation of a landowner and workers on the land. The Jews stamped the word with a religious meaning, the agreement between God and "his people." The covenant henceforth referred to an historical moment, a particular place, and a community that said yes to God.

Over time, Jewish tradition itself extended covenant to what was there from the beginning of time. In Genesis the covenant begins to take form with Noah. To the question of how Gentiles are saved, the Jewish answer is "by following the covenant with Noah." Most Gentiles have never heard of a covenant with Noah, and yet that is their way of salvation. People who follow the seven commandments in God's covenant with Noah (for example, avoiding murder, incest, and idolatry) are in Jewish language following the covenant and will find salvation.[21]

---

18. Arthur Cohen, *Tremendum: A Theological Interpretation of the Holocaust* (New York: Crossroad, 1988), 11.

19. Frank Crüsemann, *The Torah* (Philadelphia: Fortress Press, 1996), 4.

20. *The Essential Talmud*, ed. Adin Steinsaltz (New York: Basic Books, 1984), 209.

21. *Sanh.* 56a-56b.

The covenant with Moses at Sinai remains the particular meaning at the center of Jewish religion. To the extent that "covenant" has universal meaning, other forms of covenant have to be allowed. Within the Bible itself there are many renewals or reforms of the covenant, but not a second covenant.

Some recent Christian-Jewish discussion about "covenant" seems to miss the logic of particular and universal. The choice is sometimes assumed to be between one covenant (Jewish versus Christian) or two covenants (Jewish plus Christian). If one understands "covenant" as a universal ideal that has particular embodiments, neither of those answers is to the point. There cannot be two covenants any more than there are two Christs or two Islams. Neither is there a single covenant that Jews own or Christianity fulfilled. Instead, there are numerous (particular) covenants that attempt to embody a universal covenant.

In conclusion, someone might understandably ask why these three religions use a language, logic, and grammar that are so easily misunderstood. Why not just say "anyone who is good goes to heaven"? Is that not what all these doctrines finally come to? That kind of generalization would not help anyone, and it would undermine religion's resistance to destructive tendencies within the human. People live in particular places and particular times and they speak particular languages. Religion is a poetry that lives on the passionate commitment to particular events, peoples, beliefs, and causes as the way to universal truth. If the three Abrahamic religions were to disappear, they would be replaced by movements that could be equally or more dangerous insofar as they would lack deep roots. What has saved Jewish, Christian, and Muslim religions is the play of ritual and story, and a willingness to tolerate the paradoxical.

Two Revelatory Writers

Before examining Christian liturgy for its union of the particular and universal I approach the liturgical use of words with two twentieth-century examples of the powerful crafting of words. The liturgical proclaiming of the "word of God" needs a context of other revelations in human life. All great literature prepares the way for reading and hearing literature that is said to be sacred.

I choose two writers who gather up the tensions and contradictions of the twentieth century: Flannery O'Connor and Samuel Beckett. O'Connor was a conservative Roman Catholic who never went far from her home in rural Georgia. Beckett was an Irish Protestant who wrote strange plays in French; he is often assumed to be an atheist because he was attuned to the silence of God. From almost opposite ends in their striking particularity, Flannery O'Connor and Samuel Beckett illuminate a (nearly) universal meaning for the act of believing in a revealing God.

Flannery O'Connor

Flannery O'Connor wrote a fairly small body of work before her always frail health gave out when she was thirty-nine. I will focus on the short story "Revelation" and the novella *Wise Blood* for my examples. The paradox of O'Connor is that her work brims with traditional Catholic belief but is also a cauldron of modern violence. Her peculiar and particular stories, by means of their skillful craftsmanship, manage to touch (nearly) universal feelings. In the book *Do You Believe?* author Michael Cunningham writes: "O'Connor, in her fiction and her letters and essays, is the best argument I know against dismissing Catholicism outright."[22]

O'Connor's short story "Revelation" is a deadly serious but humorous insight into who is called to the heavenly banquet.[23] The central character, Mrs. Turpin, is a self-satisfied, ostentatiously Christian woman. There are two revelatory moments for Mrs. Turpin: the first turns her life around, and the second is a vision of the final judgment.

While sitting in a physician's office, Mrs. Turpin compares herself to an unhappy young woman across from her named Mary Grace. "If it's one thing I am, Mrs. Turpin said with feelings, it's grateful. When I think who all I could have been besides myself and what all I got, a little of everything, and a good disposition besides, I just feel like shouting, 'Thank you, Jesus, for making everything the way it is.' "

At that moment she is struck above the eye by a book thrown by the girl, followed by the girl herself, "whose fingers sank like clamps into the soft flesh of her neck." There was no doubt in Mrs. Turpin's mind "that the girl did know her, knew her in some intense and personal way, beyond time and place and condition. 'What you got to say to me?' she asked hoarsely and held her breath, waiting as for a revelation. The girl raised her head. Her gaze locked with Mrs. Turpin. 'Go back to hell where you came from, you old wart hog' " (p. 500).

This revelation was not at all what Mrs. Turpin had expected or desired to hear. But the suddenness and the violence of it succeed in puncturing her

22. Michael Cunningham in *Do You Believe? Conversations on God and Religion*, ed. Antonio Monda (New York: Vintage Books, 2007), 44.

23. Flannery O'Connor, "Revelation," in *The Complete Stories* (New York: Farrar, Straus and Giroux, 1971), 499–508.

complacent self-satisfaction. At the very end of the story Mrs. Turpin, while hosing down a pigpen, has a vision of a "vast swinging bridge extending upward from the earth." A great horde of freakish-looking people are rumbling toward heaven. At the very end of the procession are Mrs. Turpin and her husband. "They were marching behind the others with great dignity, accountable as they had always been for good order and common sense. They alone were on key. Yet she could see by their shocked and altered faces that even their virtues were being burned away" (p. 508).

O'Connor's novel *Wise Blood* has a central character who is a mirror image to Mrs. Turpin.[24] Hazel Motes is a Christian in spite of himself. His integrity, O'Connor says, lies in "not being able to escape the ragged figure who moves from tree to tree in the back of his mind" (p. 8). Enoch, a blind man, warns Hazel that "you can't run away from Jesus. Jesus is a fact" (p. 32). Hazel insists that he is not a Christian: "Do you think I believe in Jesus? Well I wouldn't even if he existed" (p. 13). The more he protests that he is not waiting for the judgment, "he was waiting on nothing," the more evident becomes his obsession with Jesus. "Nothing matters but that Jesus don't exist" (p. 33).

Hazel meets a modern-day preacher, Omnie Jay Holy, who urges membership in a church in which "you don't have to believe nothing you don't understand and approve of. If you don't understand it, it ain't true and that's all there is to it" (p. 84). In opposition to such complacent Christian churches, Hazel founds his own church as a bizarre inversion: "I preach the church without Christ. I'm member and preacher to that church where the blind don't see and the lame don't walk and what's dead stays that way. Ask me about that church and I'll tell you it's that church that the blood of Jesus don't foul with redemption" (p. 60).

As happens with many of O'Connor's characters, Hazel's life does not have a happy ending. His violent contortions in reaction to the faith he cannot leave involve wearing torturous instruments and blinding himself. He has no place on earth and dies a violent death. Hazel Motes, as the one man in the story who sees something beyond the cultural and religious complacency of his world, is blinded by his vision and ends life in a ditch.

Samuel Beckett

A *New York Times* reviewer of a book on Samuel Beckett said that the two people most written about in the twentieth century were Adolph Hitler

---

24. Flannery O'Connor, *Three by Flannery O'Connor* (New York: New American Library, 1962).

and Samuel Beckett. I do not know if that is provable, but the comment suggests the extraordinary influence of the novelist and playwright Samuel Beckett. The irony is that so many words would be written about an author who used words more and more sparingly in the course of his life. He went from writing 1930s novels in the style of James Joyce to a 1965 play of two pages that lasts four minutes.[25] The revelation in Beckett is as much in silence as in the words.

I will comment mainly on what are widely judged to be his two greatest plays: *Endgame* and *Waiting for Godot*.[26] I cite Beckett as revelatory of the situation of the modern individual in a desolate environment. Similar to Flannery O'Connor's, Beckett's characters are misfits in today's world, frozen in time and waiting to die. What is revealed is nothingness, which may not seem to be a religious theme, but I think most mystics would understand a religious experience of nothingness.

The characters in Beckett's plays can achieve nothing, but they stubbornly exist, carrying on a dialogue within their own heads or with an estranged partner. At the center of Beckett's plays is the recognition that time is not a series of points with the past behind us and the future before us. As in religious revelation, there is only the present, but for Beckett's characters the present is without the depth in which the past supplies wisdom and the future offers hope. The chief image of time in Beckett is the ground coming up to bury us. In *Happy Days* the major character, Winnie, tries to keep up optimistic chatter even though in the first act she is covered in sand up to her waist and in the second act up to her neck. Soon it will be "saying any old thing with sand in your mouth."

In *Endgame* Clov asks: "Do you believe in the life to come"? Hamm answers: "Mine was always that . . . . Moment by moment pattering down like the millet grains . . . and all life long you wait for that to mount up to a life" (pp. 49, 70). Time offers no salvation. "You're on earth; there's no cure for that" (p. 53). The religious symbol for escape from time as a series of points is a circular or spherical movement. Beckett's characters are in search of a circle they cannot locate. In *Endgame* the dialogue goes: "Am I right in the center?" "I'm more or less in the center?" "I'd say so." "You'd say so. Put me right in the center" (pp. 26–27).

---

25. Samuel Beckett, "Come and Go," in *Collected Shorter Plays of Samuel Beckett* (London: Faber and Faber, 1984).

26. Samuel Beckett, *Endgame* (New York: Grove Press, 1958); *Waiting for Godot* (New York: Grove Press, 1954).

Endgame is mainly a dialogue between a blind man and a crippled man in a destroyed world, possibly after Noah's flood or perhaps after a nuclear war. The dialogue includes a grim humor, which is the way to keep going on. At one point there is an attempt at prayer: "Our Father, which art . . ." followed by silence and then Hamm's response: "The bastard! He doesn't exist" (p. 55). Clov adds: "Not yet." Whatever Hamm's blasphemous outburst means, it cannot be classified as atheism. The closest Beckett comes to despair is a line in *Endgame*: "There are no more coffins" (p. 77). The abrogation of death and burial as a human ritual would be final despair. The most religious line in the play is: "To think perhaps it won't all have been for nothing" (p. 33). Beckett's own summary of Hamm is that "he says no to nothingness."

Waiting for Godot is one of the masterpieces of twentieth-century literature. Like *Endgame*, it is mainly two ragged men keeping the conversation going while they wait. "What are we doing here, *that* is the question. And we are blessed in this, that we happen to know the answer. Yes, in this immense confusion one thing alone is clear. We are waiting for Godot to come" (p. 52).

Word and deed have become separated. Both of the play's acts finish with "yes, let's go," but no one moves. The disjunction is part of what creates humor in the play. When I first taught this play through reading the text, students found it difficult to grasp the meaning. When I brought in a filmed version of the play, students could immediately relate to it as similar to an Abbot and Costello or Marx Brothers routine.

The original title of the play was *Waiting*. What are they waiting for? Probably nothing. Godot is not a character so much as a forlorn hope of the two characters that their lives will eventually mean something. The only direct reference to Christianity is: " 'You're not going to compare yourself to Christ!' 'All my life I've compared myself to him. Where he lived it was warm; it was dry. Yes, and they crucified quick' " (p. 34). Beckett was often asked if Godot was God. His response was: "If I had known who Godot is, I would have said."[27]

While the two characters wait, they try to pass the time, which in Beckett's world does not pass; "it piles up all about you" (*The Unnameable*). They keep up the conversation, although ultimately it is presence that counts the most. "Don't touch me! Don't question me! Don't speak to me! Stay with me!" (p. 37). They cannot find a meaning in their lives, but they recognize

---

27. Quoted in Richard Gilman, *The Making of Modern Drama* (New York: Da Capo Press, 1987), 246.

the absence. Vladimir says: "We are not saints but we have our appointments. How many people can boast as much?" Estragon's deflating response is: "billions" (p. 51). Instead of becoming saints, people cover over emptiness by rushing from one appointment to another. "They give birth astride of a grave, the light gleams an instant, then it's night once more" (p. 57).

Samuel Beckett, like Flannery O'Connor, reminds us that those who think themselves to be high and mighty are no better off when it comes to finding the meaning of life. People who construct elaborate systems of ideas do not come up with an answer. The disenfranchised of the world are more likely to hear a word from God in the midst of daily chatter. God may be revealed in unlikely places, including the ironic bantering that recognizes human frailties and accepts the human as it is. As Winnie says in *Happy Days*, "How can one better magnify the Almighty than by sniggering with him at his little jokes, particularly the poorer ones?"

Christian Liturgy

There are hundreds of fine books on Christian liturgy. My specific concern is the way liturgy fulfills the principle of particular-universal and is thereby the most profound expression of believing in a revealing God. At issue in this chapter is the relation between the documents on the liturgy and on revelation. The Constitution on Divine Revelation speaks of revelation as something from the past that is handed down and preserved in official teachings. The Constitution on the Liturgy says that "in the liturgy God speaks to his people and Christ is still proclaiming his Gospel. And the people reply to God both by song and by prayer" (*SC* 33).

My question is whether this liturgical language is to be taken seriously. Does God speak (rather than only having spoken)? Does Christ proclaim (rather than having proclaimed)? Are the songs and prayers of the people a reply to what is happening or to what happened? What is happening can include what happened, but not vice versa. Is there a "presence of Christ" in the liturgy and in the assembly, or only a believing in a doctrine about Christ?

One of the best-known statements of the Constitution on the Liturgy is that "the liturgy is the summit toward which the activity of the Church is directed; it is also the fount from which all her power flows" (*SC* 10). As in many places, the council put together two images that do not quite fit with each other. "Fount" or "fountain" works better than "summit." Liturgy ought to be a source of life near the center of church life. The movement of the liturgy ought to be an overflow into works of justice, which is then followed by a flowing back toward the center. The reform of the church's structure away from bureaucracy toward particular communities embodying a universal church is one of the main things needed before the liturgical reform advocated by the council can achieve fruition.

Godfrey Diekmann, one of the great leaders of liturgical reform in the twentieth century, wrote that "the liberalizing revisions and the successive overwhelming votes on the liturgy schema were the first great convincing proof to a skeptical world, non-catholic as well as Catholic, that Vatican II was courageously facing the issue of *Ecclesia semper reformanda* [the church always in need of reform]."[28]

As the first document approved by Vatican II, the Constitution on the Liturgy became a standard for subsequent documents. When the first draft of the document on the church was introduced, the objection raised was that it did not fit with the idea of the church implied by the Constitution on the Liturgy.[29] The council as a whole was invigorated by cooperative effort on the liturgy document, resulting in a work with theoretical depth and immediate practical effects.

There remains a gap between liturgical language and what the liturgical assembly experiences. The council says that "the full and active participation by all the people is the aim to be considered before all else" (*SC* 14). That is an impressive statement, but the calls for "active and intelligent participation" have been made since Pope Pius X at the beginning of the twentieth century. Vatican II did take a few giant leaps to make feasible "active participation," but initial practical steps did not continue. There was much enthusiasm for the introduction of the vernacular, though Anglicans warned at the time that English alone was no panacea. A new generation of Catholics does not get any thrill because the priest speaks in English; a few are even fascinated by using Latin as a connection to the tradition. The kiss of peace and the amen of response at communion are profound symbols, but they can be overshadowed in their meaning by the often uninspiring setting of Sunday morning.

The Constitution on the Liturgy urged active participation, but Godfrey Diekmann puts his finger on a problem so obvious that it escaped notice: "No lay person, so far as I know, was directly asked to give advice. . . . This, I believe, is the most flagrant flaw of the Constitution: a house was

---

28. Godfrey Diekmann, "The Constitution on the Sacred Liturgy," in *Vatican II: An Interfaith Appraisal*, ed. John Miller, 17–30 (Notre Dame, IN: University of Notre Dame Press, 1966), 18.

29. Diekmann, "The Constitution on the Sacred Liturgy," 19.

built without consulting the persons who are to live in it."[30] The house was built for "the faithful," but as I pointed out in chapter 3, the bishops keep excluding themselves from "the faithful." There is a clear, stark choice here: In a church that is the sacramental presence of Christ, the minister of the liturgy is at the center, not the top; the minister looks out from within the people rather than delivering a message down to the people.

The constitution shows the ambivalence of the bishops in speaking about themselves: "The bishop is to be considered as the High Priest of his flock. . . . All should hold in the greatest esteem the liturgical life of the diocese centered around the bishop" (*SC* 41). Mary Collins rightly refers to this article as a mixed metaphor.[31] If bishops wish to be at the center of the diocese's liturgical life, they have to give up the title of "high priest." A concern of bishops at Vatican II and since then has been to share in some of the power that moved to the top after Vatican I. Trying to get higher, however, is not the way to do it. A shift is needed toward a sacramental church, sacramental in structure as well as practice. Power radiates to and from the center; the college of bishops represents the power of Christ's presence within the body of the faithful.

Vatican II did open the door to the possibility of more radical changes in liturgy. "Provision should be made, when revising the liturgical books, for legitimate variations and adaptations to different groups, regions, and peoples, especially in mission countries" (*SC* 38). The Constitution on the Liturgy encouraged the arts for the shaping and expression of belief in the divine presence. Special attention was given to music. "The musical tradition of the universal Church is a treasure of inestimable value, greater even than any other art" (*SC* 112). Catholics could learn from Protestant practice about popular participation in music. The Catholic Church's special contribution to liturgical music is the preservation of ancient chant, which never goes out of date.

Modern Christianity has not been especially welcoming to artists and consequently not attractive to artistic attention. It will take a long and concerted effort to convince musicians and other artists that the church is ready to be challenged by art. "The enthusiasm of our artists cannot be awakened through dry laws; it must emerge out of the general religious consciousness of the universal church."[32] The council called for clearing away much of the

30. Diekmann, "The Constitution on the Sacred Liturgy," 20.

31. Mary Collins, "On Becoming a Sacramental Church Again," in *Open Catholicism*, ed. David Efroymson and John Raines, 111–28 (Collegeville, MN: Liturgical Press, 1997), 122.

32. Quoted in Josef Jungmann, "Constitution on the Sacred Liturgy," in *Commentary on the Documents of Vatican II*, ed. Herbert Vorgrimler, vol. 1, 1–87 (New York: Herder & Herder, 1967–69), 81.

clutter in the Catholic Church in the name of a "noble simplicity" (*SC* 34). It did not call for getting rid of all images and statues, but that "their number should be moderate and their relative positions should reflect right order" (*SC* 125). The point of artistic simplicity is to restore the primary meaning of church to the gathering of the members.

The church exists most fully where the word is preached and the sacramental actions are performed. In Christian history after the Reformation, word and deed were split apart. Protestants celebrated the presence of Christ in the proclaiming of the word; the Roman Catholic Church focused on "the holy sacrifice of the Mass." Both sides were hurt by this dichotomy. The Second Vatican Council was a magnificent effort to restore the union of word and act. In eucharistic worship the liturgy of the word and the liturgy of the meal constitute a unity. The Roman Catholic Church's embracing of the Bible might release Protestants from overemphasizing the Bible to the near exclusion of other sacramental practices.

The administration of the sacraments before Vatican II did involve words. No words were more honored than "this is my body . . . this is my blood." Other formulas, "I baptize thee . . ." or "I absolve you . . ." also carried powerful meaning. However, with little attention to the biblical narrative, words of consecration or forgiveness tended toward the magical. A sacrament became an "instrument of grace" rather than the culmination of the personal act of believing in and the expression of a community fully engaged in history.

Human actions require an adequate linguistic context for their meaning to emerge. Language itself has to be understood as an action if it is to be a sacramental expression. Language is not an object that acts as an instrument to convey thoughts. Language has to mediate, but not as an intermediary object.

"Mediate" has two nearly opposite meanings, joined in both being the opposite of im-mediate. In a first meaning there are two separate objects and a third party intervenes between them. This intermediary substitutes its actions on behalf of both parties. Third-party intermediaries may become necessary when, for example, union-management negotiations stall or when two warring nations distrust each other.

The second meaning of mediation takes place within a person or a community. One's thoughts become fully one's own only as they are mediated by bodily and communal expression. In communicating with others, a person's thoughts and desires are mediated by speech and other behavior. Language is not an object used as an instrument for one's thoughts. Language re-presents one's thoughts as one's own.

It is understandable that love seeks immediacy. The paradox is that the immediacy proper to love can only be achieved when one kind of mediation (an intervening object) is eliminated by a different kind of mediation (language). The mediation of the instrumental object is eliminated by the mediation of word-gesture. If we were angels, our thoughts and emotions might not need mediation. As we are humans, our bodily, social, temporal existence is mediated, and the attempt to escape this kind of mediation is our greatest temptation.

Our relation to the divine is mediated. We do not need a "middleman" or objects between the divine and the human. The sacramental principle is a profound recognition that our relation to God is always mediated by bodily actions, including language. And the most profound instance of such a sacrament is Jesus-Christ as the sacrament of God's presence.

Christian belief is not directed to an intermediary between God and humanity, but to one who embodies divine revealing and human believing. Appropriately, the Christian tradition came to speak of Jesus the Christ as the Word of God, but it should not be forgotten that he is also the word of humanity, Son of Man. The church is the sacrament of Christ's presence as human response to the divine mediated by bodily symbols. "The sacraments thus serve as a *buffer* which repels every temptation Christians might have to ignore body, history, society in order to enter without any mediation into communion with God."[33]

Implied in this strange and mysterious liturgical language is a metaphysics of time and being. In recent centuries there has been a relentless push toward seeing the universe as unimaginably large in the extension of space and time. Corresponding to this greatness of the universe has been a claim that humans are an insignificant speck of dust in a span of billions of years (though the people who make this claim seem to think that their findings are significant).

The Christian liturgy and the presence of Christ in the liturgical assembly affirm a time that begins with presence. This particular presence recapitulates all former presences. The repetition of the liturgical word-deed is not an addition of an object, but an opening to let the past-present be present. The depth of the present is what provides an attitude of hope toward the future beyond our imagination. Believing in a revealing God is always a present and communal act. The community believes in Christ's presence and, it can also be said, Christ is present because there is a believing community.

33. Louis-Marie Chauvet, *The Sacraments: The Word of God at the Mercy of the Body* (Collegeville, MN: Liturgical Press, 2001), 114; see also Mary Douglas, *Natural Symbols* (New York: Vintage Books, 1973), 51.

The council affirmed the traditional doctrine that Christ is present in three ways: in the assembly, in the word, and in the meal (*SC* 7). Unfortunately, the council's language reverses the order that prevailed until the twelfth century. In the early church the (real) presence of Christ was in the community. Following on that presence is the presence of the word and finally the (mystical) presence of Christ in the consecrated bread and wine.[34] Medieval disputes over whether Christ is *really* present in the eucharistic bread and wine led to a dichotomy and a different language. The church community became the (mere) mystical body of Christ. The Eucharist became the (real) body, but separated from the context of Christ's presence in the word and the assembly's belief. The Reformation and Counter-Reformation hardened the lines of this split.

Roman Catholics referred to "holy communion," a beautiful image for what the presence of Christ in the Holy Spirit means. But without the context of the (real) presence of Christ in the community, holy communion can become the name of an object one takes in one's mouth or hand.[35] At its most profound, holy communion is a name for the Christian grasp of being itself as communion. The presence of Christ through the workings of his Spirit reveals that the ultimate mystery of the universe is communion.[36] Humans participate in the divine and holy communion. Each particular Eucharist celebrates this universal communion. "It is to what you are that you reply *Amen*, and so replying you express your assent."[37]

Another hallmark of Roman Catholic language was "sacrifice of the Mass." This language of "making sacred" has roots in the early church. The Christian church tried to give its own stamp to how the world is made sacred. It made a valiant effort at nearly reversing the pre-Christian meaning of sacrifice. However, there was a rather rapid reversion to the earlier meaning of sacrifice that was tied to interlocking beliefs about sin, guilt, reparation, revenge, evil, and judgment. If the church has not succeeded in two thousand years in salvaging "sacrifice," perhaps the attempt should be abandoned. That seems to have been the thinking of some of the bishops at Vatican II and many people since then. As a result of compromise at the council, "sac-

---

34. Edward Kilmartin, *The Eucharist in the West: History and Theology* (Collegeville, MN: Liturgical Press, 1999), 183; Chauvet, *The Sacraments,* 139.

35. Kevin Seasoltz, *God's Gift Giving* (New York: Continuum, 2007), 76.

36. Dennis Edwards, *Breath of Life: A Theology of the Creator Spirit* (New York: Orbis Books, 2004), 26.

37. Augustine, Sermon 272, quoted in Seasoltz, *God's Gift Giving,* 29.

rifice" was added somewhat awkwardly to article six of the constitution, an addition opposed by 150 bishops.[38]

One good reason for the church to continue using "sacrifice" is to resist the widespread use to which the word is now put in secular usage. It is amazing how often a word that means "to make sacred" is used in secular contexts. When a young soldier's body is shipped home from war there is a ready political line that he sacrificed his life for his country. At that particular moment of a family's grief it would be callous to protest. Nonetheless, the constant invoking of "sacrifice" for the horrible deaths of young people as a cover-up for the incompetence and lies of government officials is truly obscene. Those who have first-hand experience of war do not think of it as making anything sacred. Ernest Hemingway's soldier of World War I speaks for millions of others caught in the insanity of war: "I was always embarrassed by the words sacred, glorious and sacrifice. . . . I had seen nothing sacred and the things that were glorious had no glory and the sacrifices were like the stockyards in Chicago if nothing was done with the meat except to bury it."[39]

The Christian story is that killing or revenge for previous disrespect is part of a hopeless cycle that can never right the wrong. The Christian story is that a cycle dominated by hatred, guilt, and fear is broken through by openness to God's love for us. Unearthing the best of Christian tradition, Edward Kilmartin writes: "In the New Testament sacrifice is, in the first place, the self-offering of the Father in the gift of his Son, and in the second place the unique response of the Son in his humanity to the Father, and in the third place, the self-offering of believers in union with Christ by which they share in his covenant relation with the Father."[40]

What then of the widespread understanding of sacrifice as involving violent destruction, a meaning that has often provided an explanation for the sufferings of Jesus? René Girard has provided some of the most thoughtful reflection on guilt, atonement, and violence. He writes: "God doesn't sacrifice his Son to quell God's anger. God through the suffering of Jesus Christ reveals the violence at the heart of all human culture, a violence which scapegoats and manifests itself through victimization."[41] Thus the revelation of the cross was and is that human violence attempts to obliterate God's gifts.

38. Jungmann, "Constitution on the Sacred Liturgy," *Commentary on the Documents of Vatican II*, 1:12.

39. Ernest Hemingway, *A Farewell to Arms* (New York: Scribner's, 1957), 137.

40. Kilmartin, *The Eucharist in the West*, 381–82.

41. René Girard, quoted in Seasoltz, *God's Gift Giving*, 108.

This meaning of sacrifice has ecumenical possibilities for healing a breach between Protestant and Roman Catholic forms of worship. A united Christian front is needed against trivial and obscene uses of "sacrifice." A Christian protest for "making sacred" by love, not war, has only a limited chance of success. But that, sadly, is true not because the world has moved beyond an outdated Christianity's primitive notions. Rather, it is because we are in constant danger of reverting to a barbarous pre-Christian idea of sacrifice.

As was true of the documents on church and revelation, the Constitution on the Liturgy could have used a more integral approach to the Holy Spirit. The liturgy is perhaps the logical place for the Western church to begin a thorough rethinking of the Spirit. As a result of criticism, three references to the Holy Spirit were added to the liturgy document, but what is needed is a language in which the Holy Spirit makes the church to be and is thereby understood as "always and everywhere graciously present in self-offering to human beings."[42]

References to "Christ" without the Holy Spirit are always in danger of just referring to a god-man sacrificed on a cross a long time ago. Instead, Jesus raised by his Father becomes a living and present Christ by the Holy Spirit. The Christ-Spirit is present in the liturgical assembly, the speaking of the word, and the enactment of the eucharistic meal. The Spirit makes sacred the whole world. The breath of the Spirit provides an experience of opening to a present love, human and divine.

42. Edwards, *Breath of Life*, 50; see also John Ziziolas, *Being as Communion* (New York: St. Vladimir's Seminary Press, 1985), 132.

Chapter Seven

Revealing-Believing
as Teaching-Learning

All attempts to speak of God reach the limits of human language very quickly. Karl Barth is right that only God can speak of God. But that principle, if not followed by silence, may lead to a claim to possess words that come directly from God. Such a belief became known as fundamentalism in the twentieth century. Barth tried carefully to avoid this idolatry while still referring to the "word of God."

The Christian church lays claim to have writing that was inspired by God and is its chief source for reflection on the relation between divine and human. The New Testament is centered on testimony to the life, death, and resurrection of Jesus of Nazareth, who is called the Christ. Unlike other religious believers, Christians usually have a definite image in mind when they refer to God. Christians consider this anchoring of imagery and language in the portrait of Jesus to be a great advantage. In some ways it is, but the Christian imagination can too quickly shut down when the mystery of God has barely begun to be explored.

Jesus is portrayed in the New Testament as saying that he has to leave in order for the Holy Spirit to take over. The revealing of God cannot be confined to what Jesus said in his lifetime. God is revealed today in the Spirit-filled Christ. This chapter draws together many themes from the previous chapters, such as church structure, the moral life, and liturgy. How should the Christian church engage in education if it believes in a revealing God?

Metaphors for a Divine Revealer

The history of religions contains dozens of images for God. The images inevitably reflect the social and political situation of the particular religious group. The correspondence need not mean a simple replicating of the human arrangement: a warrior god for soldiers, a sovereign god for a monarchy, a capitalist god for capitalism. Religious rituals and beliefs might sometimes introduce an element of change into these political systems. Jewish, Christian, and Muslim religions can make the case that, instead of simply affirming existing societies, they introduced major changes. Of course, after an initial push to bring about radical change they have tended to shift attention to securing the part of the world they have succeeded in changing.

Christianity took over images of God that Jewish religion had arrived at from centuries of experience. Christianity also absorbed images from Greek philosophy and the many religions that were present at the time of the origin of the Jesus movement. Jews shared with many other religions the images of king and warrior. God had to be powerful to protect the people against the forces of the nonhuman world as well as against human enemies. The image of God as a loving father seems to have been a novel development within Jewish tradition. That God cares for each individual as a parent cares for a child is an extraordinary belief, but it has come down to the present. Jesus borrowed this Pharisaic image of "our father" and made it a centerpiece of his teaching.

It is often lamented that Christianity imported a meaning of God from Greek philosophy that conflicts with the biblical imagery. Although Greek and Jewish traditions do conflict, the Christian adoption of Greek concepts was probably inevitable and was not all bad. Alfred North Whitehead wrote that "Plato's discovery that the divine element in the world is to be conceived as a persuasive agency and not as a coercive agency was . . . one of the greatest intellectual discoveries in the history of religion."[1]

In modern times Christian thinkers are less enthusiastic than was the early church about the idea that Plato is a near-perfect fit with Christian doctrine. Nevertheless, Plato's philosophy is an inescapable influence on Christianity. Instead of trying to get rid of the influence of Plato, Aristotle, or Plotinus for the sake of a pure word of God, Christian thinking that has been influenced by Greek philosophy needs to seek its complement in other philosophic, scientific, and artistic thinking.

Divine Teacher

How, then, might Christianity imagine a divine revealer, using the Bible as the main source but not restricting the search to biblical words? Jewish

1. Alfred North Whitehead, *Adventure of Ideas* (Cambridge: Cambridge University Press, 1933), 213, 231.

religion introduced a dialogic element into the relation between divine and human. God speaks and humans speak back. Sometimes they only say "amen," but trusting God can include asking questions. "God has never stopped talking to his people and his people have never stopped answering back."[2] The reason they talk back, says a contemporary writer on the Holocaust, "is because of the unconvincing performance of divine providence in history."[3]

Thomas Aquinas, commenting on the book of Job, asks whether Job should have been arguing with God. Thomas's very Jewish answer is that if you are sure you are in the right you should keep arguing, even if it is with God. In Plato and Plotinus, God is perceived in a speechless vision. In Christianity with its Jewish roots and Christ as Word, believing in a revealing God is always a dialogue. "The incessant dialogue between God and the Jews has, since Abraham, exhibited every aspect of the magisterial relation with a people of adoring, mutinous, obedient but recalcitrant, but above all a questioning nature."[4] This "magisterial relation" places Jew and Christian in a position of listening and learning in dialogue.

The Christian churches have not generally shown a dialogical relation in either their structure or their educational practice. The Catholic Church is divided into the church teaching and the church taught. A small minority does the speaking; everyone else is to listen. When the teacher is a knowledgeable adult and the learner is an inexperienced child, one would expect the adult to do most of the speaking. However, that situation is the exception in education, and even when it exists, the youngest child has some experience from which to draw questions and indicate interests.

The favorite mode of church education is the sermon. Sermons, to be effective, require the consent of the listener. Stepping into a church is a sign of consent, although not consent to twenty minutes of rambling that pretends to be a sermon. The positive value of preaching sermons is undermined by the assumption that God teaches almost exclusively in this fashion. Preaching in Protestant churches is generally much better than in Catholic churches, but the Protestant preacher is asked to carry most of the liturgical performance. Preaching is asked to convey the presence of God as teacher.

2. Lionel Blue, *To Heaven with Scribes and Pharisees* (New York: Oxford University Press, 1976), 86.

3. Eliezer Berkovitz, *With God in Hell* (New York: Hebrew Publishing Company, 1979), 127.

4. George Steiner, *Lessons of the Masters* (Cambridge, MA: Harvard University Press, 2005).

Rudolf Bultmann writes that "Jesus Christ is the eschatological event not as an established fact of past time but as repeatedly present, as addressing you and me here and now in preaching."[5] Bultmann understandably wants the revelation of God not to be a fact of the past, but instead what God is doing now. But tying God's teaching exclusively to preaching is expecting too much. Perhaps Bultmann intended "preaching" to mean much more than the Sunday morning sermon. The word "preach" can be extended, but not very far. Politicians regularly preach as part of their work; advertisements on television are expensively produced thirty-second sermons ("buy this product . . . be happy forever"); parents hear themselves preaching while perhaps having vowed not to engage in that kind of speech.

The Christian church has rightly defended a positive role for preaching. The church can be said to preach the Gospel in season and out, by action as well as by word, by the lives of its members as well as from pulpits. Still, trying to fit believing in a revealing God exclusively within a metaphor of preaching is unduly restrictive. It creates an image of God as issuing proclamations.

Karl Barth, in his *Theology of John Calvin*, says that at the beginning of the Reformed church stands a schoolmaster. This fact, Barth says, shows both the strength and the weakness of the Reformation. Calvin did not merely *proclaim* Christianity but *expounded* it. Barth goes on to say that Calvin's work was tragic in its effects, that it "systematized and institutionalized the Reformation—and thereby ended it."[6]

Schoolmasters, like preachers, have their place within the church, but God is not best imagined as a schoolteacher. The metaphor of God as teacher is more appropriate. A distinction between God as teacher and God as schoolteacher should be clear enough. However, modern society has tended to collapse teaching into school teaching, a blurring of differences that is not helpful to schoolteachers and is a disaster for other teachers.

Jesus as Teacher, Christ as Teacher

The Christian turns to the New Testament portrait of Jesus to discover what God is like. Jesus is given a dozen or more titles, but none is as prominent as "teacher." English translations often hide that fact by translating the word for teacher as "master." Contemporaries of Jesus certainly identified him as a

---

5. Rudolf Bultmann, *History and Eschatology* (New York: Harper Torchbooks, 1957), 151–52.

6. Karl Barth, *The Theology of John Calvin* (Grand Rapids, MI: Eerdmans, 1995), 158.

teacher or rabbi. Jesus, like Moses, Gautama, Socrates, and Muhammad, worked with a few disciples (learners) who subsequently tried to spread the teachings of the master.

Jesus as teacher has had an effect well beyond the Christian church. "The unique impression of Jesus," Emerson wrote, "is not so much written as ploughed into the history of this world."[7] Jesus taught by his words and the example of his life. Like any rabbi, he asked a lot of questions, argued with his opponents, and told stories. His parables are recognized as literary gems even by most non-Christians. He apparently preached, although his long sermons are probably compilations of preaching done on several occasions.

Jesus' teaching in words was integrally related to the perception of who he was. Gandhi testified that "I refuse to believe that there now exists or has ever existed a person that has not made use of his (Jesus') example to lessen his sins, though he may have done so without realizing it. . . . The lives of all have, in some greater or lesser degree, been changed by his presence, his actions, and the words spoken by his divine voice."[8]

Especially on the question of passive resistance to violence, the teaching of Jesus has, if anything, gained in prominence over the past century.[9] Even many people who want nothing to do with the Christian church are inspired by Jesus' teaching on nonviolence and forgiveness. Christians who call for repentance by the church make their appeal to the teacher who founded the Christian way.

A change from Jesus as teacher began with the resurrection. In the process that followed, something was lost or at least obscured; something was also gained, although its potential has never been fully realized. What was lost was a picture of Jesus as a fairly typical first-century rabbi. What was potentially gained was the Christ as contemporary teacher through the work of the Holy Spirit.

In Jaroslav Pelikan's book *Jesus through the Centuries* the first chapter is titled "The Rabbi." Pelikan writes that "to the Christian disciples of the first century the conception of Jesus as a rabbi was self-evident, to the Christian disciples of the second century it was embarrassing, to the Christian disciples of the third century and beyond it was obscure."[10] The most obvious

---

7. Ralph Waldo Emerson in *Three Prophets of Liberalism*, ed. Conrad Wright (New York: Skinner House Books, 1986), 95.

8. Quoted in James Douglass, *The Non-Violent Cross* (New York: Macmillan, 1966), 56.

9. Gabriel Moran, "Roman Catholic Tradition and Passive Resistance," in *Religion, Terror and Globalization*, ed. K. K. Kuriakose (New York: Nova Science, 2006), 203–14.

10. Jaroslav Pelikan, *Jesus through the Centuries* (New Haven: Yale University Press, 1985), 7.

reason for deemphasizing the title "rabbi" was the early church's struggle to define itself in opposition to Judaism. The last title they wanted Jesus to be known by was the one that was used for a Jewish leader.

The decline of Jesus as teacher is not entirely explained by this fact of Jewish-Christian enmity. From the very beginning the disciples understood their mission as continuing not the teaching, but the life of the teacher. Søren Kierkegaard notes in his comparison of Socrates and Jesus that in the contemporary world Socrates' teaching is important, while it is Jesus' person that remains important.[11]

The most commonly used name for a founder of a religious group is "teacher." What is passed down over the centuries is a body of teachings (doctrines). The Christian movement claimed to be distinctive. Its main focus was not on a great teacher of the distant past who left some beautiful teachings. Its more comprehensive and vital scope was God being revealed in the present by the teaching of the Spirit-filled Christ. The transition between these two outlooks was and is perilous. Jesus the rabbi can never be forgotten, but the main focus should not be there. While church reformers always have to return to Jesus' teachings, those teachings have to be part of a larger project that Christianity initiated.

The return to a pure Jesus, unencumbered by what has followed, is neither possible nor desirable. Even for smoothing out Christian-Jewish relations, simply reinstating Jesus the rabbi is not the route to go. Jacob Neusner, criticizing the liberal Christianity of the nineteenth century, warns that "Judaism did not in the end benefit and Christianity was injured by the conception of Jesus as a reforming rabbi, and Christianity as an improvement on Judaism in continuity with Judaism."[12]

For better and for worse, Christianity attempted a radical transformation of religion. The New Testament is written from the standpoint of Jesus having already become Christ, and a transformation of the world having begun. To this day this transformation has not been completed. Jesus, the Christ, transformed by the Holy Spirit, continues to be the presence of God revealing or teaching. The Christian is asked not to believe in teachings, but in the teacher.

The master teacher is revealed not only by teachings from the past but also by the events of the present. It is not an exaggeration or a banality to

---

11. Søren Kierkegaard, *Philosophical Fragments* (Princeton, NJ: Princeton University Press, 1962), 28–45.

12. Jacob Neusner and Andrew Greeley, *The Bible and Us* (New York: Warner Books, 1992), 215.

say that God's teaching extends to the whole universe. A Christian view of teaching has to be thoroughly incarnational or sacramental. Every act of teaching is a symbolic expression of God's presence through Christ and the Spirit in body, history, and society.

Augustine versus Aquinas

Augustine of Hippo (354–430) and Thomas Aquinas (1225–1274) are the two intellectual giants who shaped the theology of the Western church. On matters of doctrine central to Christianity they are usually close together. In reference to "teaching," their differences are covered over by Thomas's unwillingness to contradict Augustine. Augustine and Thomas are in complete agreement that God is the ultimate teacher. From that premise they draw opposite conclusions. For Augustine, God as teacher means that no one else should be called teacher. For Thomas, God as teacher means that everyone and everything can be a teacher.

Augustine

Augustine in *Christian Teaching* has some wonderful insights on teaching.[13] Themes that dominated his life, such as dialogue, friendship, and classical rhetoric, capture important elements of teaching-learning. He was for many centuries the great teacher of Christian scholars. Like many other great teachers, he did not reflect at length on the activity of teaching. He has two short treatises, *First Catechetical Instruction* and *The Teacher*, that contain practical guidelines for teaching and reflections on being a teacher. The latter, however, contains a negative view of teaching and teachers.[14]

What came to buttress Augustine's experience was a philosophy that valued the inner over the outer, spirit over matter, and ascent as the way to truth. Some of Augustine's best-known lines refer to God in the interior of the soul, "deeper than my most inward being," and God as "closer to me than I was to myself."[15] For Augustine the road that first leads inward then leads upward. The result is that God is found above the mere material world and consequently the soul does not need to be nourished by interaction with an external world.

13. Augustine, *De Doctrina Christiana*, which I refer to in the text as *Christian Teaching*. The recent edition is published with the title *Teaching Christianity*, ed. John Rotelle (Hyde Park, NY: New City Press, 1996).

14. Augustine, *The First Catechetical Instruction* (New York: Paulist Press, 1978); *Against the Academics* and *The Teacher* (Indianapolis: Hackett Publishing, 1995).

15. Augustine, *The Teacher,* X. 8. 15, III. 6. 11.

The most compact summary of *The Teacher* was written by Augustine himself. At the end of his life he wrote in *Reconsiderations*: "I wrote a work entitled *The Teacher*. There it is debated, sought and found that there is no teacher giving knowledge to man other than God. This also is in accordance with what is written by the Evangelist: 'Your teacher, Christ, is unique.' "[16] His view of teaching, he says, is based on Matthew 23: "But you are not to be called rabbi, for you have one teacher, and you are all students" (v. 8). "And call no one your father on earth, for you have one Father—the one in heaven" (v. 9). "Nor are you to be called instructors (*didaskaloi*), for you have one instructor, the Messiah" (v. 10).

Contemporary exegetes agree that Jesus is speaking here to an inner circle of his followers. He is warning them, the future leaders of the Christian community, to avoid the trappings and honorific titles, including teacher, current at the time. Jesus wished his disciples to be servants within the community, not leaders above the community.

Augustine says that the human teacher has nothing but words to remind us of the reality within. By making language only an instrument to signify things and ideas, Augustine makes teaching a reminder to look within the soul. The treatise ends with a frontal attack on the schoolteachers of the time: "Who is so foolishly curious as to send his son to school to learn what the teacher thinks?" After the teachers "have explained by means of words the disciplines they profess to teach," the students have to look upon the Inner Truth. "That is therefore the point at which they learn."

Thomas

Thomas Aquinas's opposition to Augustine's view of teaching is a model of respectful disagreement. In fact, it is expressed with such courtesy that a quick reading of chapter 11 of *Truth* could miss the fact that the two writers have diametrically opposite positions. Thomas's view of teaching flows from his brilliant synthesis of the New Testament and church fathers with Neoplatonic and Aristotelian philosophy.

Thomas's philosophy is one of participation in the "act of 'to be.'" Knowing is a way of be-ing, rather than the having of ideas. For Augustine, human knowledge participates in divine ideas; for Thomas, human knowledge participates in divine knowing. That makes a difference in understanding teaching. Humans and other creatures participate in divine creativity, includ-

---

16. Augustine, *The Retractions* (Washington, DC: Catholic University of America Press, 1968). This is an alternative English title for *Reconsiderations*.

ing teaching. God works through "secondary causes." There is no competition between divine and human. The human teacher is not the ultimate source of being, knowing, and teaching but nevertheless is a true teacher by participating in divine teaching.

Related to the principle of participation is Thomas's resistance to up/down imagery. In Augustine, the movement to the inner is the first rung on a ladder leading upward. Knowledge becomes a search for the pure idea above material and sensual elements. In contrast, Thomas describes the creaturely journey as movement out, around, and back.[17] The movement of knowing is a kind of "circulation."

Thomas begins with the question: is only God a teacher or are humans also teachers? He has thus already agreed with Augustine that God is the ultimate teacher. He says that "when Augustine proves that only God teaches, he does not intend to exclude man from teaching exteriorly, but intends to say that God alone teaches interiorly." Actually, Augustine does not make such a distinction; he does in fact exclude humans from teaching.

Thomas's metaphor for teaching-learning is the human body's natural power of healing, assisted by an external agent. "Thus in healing, the physician assists nature, which is the principal agent, by strengthening nature and prescribing medicines, which nature uses as instruments for healing." His analogy holds up very well in today's understanding of sickness and the healing powers of the body. He concludes his analogy that "just as the physician is said to heal a patient through the activity of nature, so a man is said to cause knowledge in another through the activity of the learner's own natural reason, and this is teaching. So one is said to teach another and be his teacher."

This comparison between teaching and healing has been used by writers as far back as the Sophists.[18] Augustine also employs this comparison, but his version brings out the difference between him and Thomas. Augustine writes that "medicines for the body, after all, only do good to those whose health is restored by God and he can cure them, while they cannot do so without Him."[19] In comparing healing to God's action with or without medicine, Augustine has left out the healing powers of the body itself. In Augustine's version of the relations among physician, medicine, illness, body, and

---

17. Thomas Aquinas, *Commentary on the Sentences of Peter Lombard*, quoted in Josef Pieper, *Guide to Thomas Aquinas* (San Francisco: Ignatius Press, 1991), 101.

18. W. K. C. Guthrie, *The Sophists* (Cambridge: Cambridge University Press, 1971), 168–69.

19. Augustine, *Teaching Christianity*, Book IV.

God, the interaction of the physician with the healing capacities of the body is subverted. God can cure without medicine and, similarly, learning can occur without human teachers.

Thomas Aquinas, in contrast to Augustine, posits a modest but realistic place for human teachers. Teaching is a humble activity, central to humans and extending at least to all living beings. The human teacher remains dependent on the natural powers of the learner and the environment; the teacher has to listen and respond to the learning situation. The teacher can only perform certain movements, none of which is guaranteed to bring about learning in the student. Teaching-learning is a single activity, but there is always a gap between a human teacher's *intention* to teach and the teaching-learning that actually occurs.

The Modern Flight from Teaching

In twentieth-century writing on teaching and learning, Augustine's view is easy to recognize: humans do not teach. Thomas Aquinas's view does not get much play in theory, but the theories are incomplete. In the full expanse of teaching-learning by all human beings and other creatures as well, Thomas's incarnational or sacramental view of teaching is right at home.

The idea of teaching itself has played badly in the modern world, especially in the United States as the child of the Enlightenment. The opposition to teaching crystallized in the late eighteenth century as the United States was being founded, although the theoretical attack was centered in France and Germany. It is no coincidence that the flight from teaching and the flight from the Christian religion have been intertwined. The Christian church may have played down the title of teacher for Jesus, but teaching (or doctrine) remained closely associated with Christianity. So also was the idea of tradition. The modern West has been intent on escaping from teaching and tradition.

Immanuel Kant is probably the most influential thinker in the modern Western world. Kant provided the motto of the Enlightenment: "Dare to be wise. Have courage to use your own understanding." Kant consciously borrowed language from St. Paul's letter to the Romans. We need to get free of the "pedagogue" that has held us in bondage. For Paul, the teacher was the Law; for Kant, the teacher is the human race's submission to religious tradition. "Enlightenment is man's emergence from his self-incurred immaturity."[20] The enemy was the pedagogue and all forms of tradition.

---

20. Immanuel Kant, "What Is Enlightenment?" in *Kant's Political Writings* (Cambridge: Cambridge University Press, 1991), 54.

In the language of the Enlightenment, education's aim was to free the child from the prejudices of the father (they did not think to add "mother"). To this day, progress and tradition are assumed to be opposites. To be an enlightened person is to leave behind the prejudices (or prejudgments) every child acquires from its parents.

The contemporary philosopher Hans-Georg Gadamer has brilliantly encapsulated the problem in his principle that "the fundamental problem of the Enlightenment was the prejudice against prejudice." Gadamer posits instead that education should include examining our childhood prejudices to decide which ones are worth keeping. Gadamer has offered the most sustained and comprehensive defense of tradition as something that exists only as it becomes other than itself.[21]

The world could not get along without teaching and tradition. It required a delicate move in the nineteenth century to leave tradition in the family and restrict teaching to the school. Teaching was henceforth to be understood as rational explanation to "school age" children. That meaning of teaching, which seems so self-evident today, runs counter to the etymology and history of the term. The modern meaning of teaching is extremely narrow, leaving schoolteachers no ground to stand on. In former times, and in much of the world today, a teacher is one who represents the community and its tradition. The teacher's job, carried out with the wholehearted support of the community, is to show people how to live (and die) according to the best lights of the tradition.

Tradition and teaching should not be romanticized. Progress is desirable and it involves reforming a tradition. However, the attempt to overthrow tradition rather than reform it leads to disaster. Adolescence, which simply means becoming adult, was identified in the nineteenth century with the teen years, when young people would rebel against teachers and teaching. A period of rebellion is almost inevitable in the lives of young people (even the Amish take that into account). But when teaching is identified as only for children in classrooms it can produce a society of endless adolescence.[22]

The nineteenth century gave us the language we still use: education is what happens in school; school is a place for six- to sixteen-year-olds; teachers are people who instruct school pupils until they can think for themselves. There have been many attempts at reforming education, but they have not included a rethinking of tradition and teaching. When universal schooling

21. Hans-Georg Gadamer, *Truth and Method* (New York: Crossroad, 1982), 241–53.

22. Nicholas Lash, *The Beginning and the End of Religion* (Cambridge: Cambridge University Press, 1996), 87.

for the young was initiated, there were immediate calls for educational centers that would be open day and night for a community's teaching-learning. The public library is a reduced version of that hope. The Internet offers new hope and possibilities, but its ability to sustain community and tradition is limited by its mode of teaching.

The adult education movement was the largest effort to sustain the late-nineteenth-century hope for community education, and the movement has produced some good results. The practical benefits have been achieved despite inadequate theoretical underpinnings of the movement. Instead of defending education as belonging to people of every age, theorists of adult education set "adult education" in opposition to (child) education. Part of the contrast often made was that children need teaching but adults do not. A bad theory of education was made worse.[23]

A myth of adult education, which has sometimes infiltrated church circles, is that education has been too concerned with children, not enough with adults. Actually, the worst part of modern educational theory since the nineteenth century has been its exclusion of children in their most formative years. The primary education is not in primary schools but in the "preschool" years. Politicians and school officials routinely invoke the cliché of the parent as the first and most important teacher. That rhetorical gesture has no effect at all on educational language and practice, especially when power and money are at stake. The adult education movement, far from challenging educational language, found its comfortable niche in an entrepreneurial society.

Teaching-Learning in a Sacramental Universe

The Christian church needs to be both teacher and learner in relation to modern education's powerful but narrow ideal of enlightenment. The forces of historical, scientific, and philosophical enlightenment affect the great majority of church members. Instead of trying to wall off the influence, a properly educational approach of the church would try to situate the value of enlightenment in a wide and deep context of other kinds of learning.

What is just as inadequate as trying to keep modernity outside the church is doing bad imitations of modern education. There is no point in running schools, clinics, or television shows if the resources are not there for doing them reasonably well. Many churches might combine their resources to do

---

23. Malcolm Knowles, *The Adult Learner: A Neglected Species* (Houston, TX: Gulf Publishing Company, 1990).

a few things well. Resources the church is more at home with can be used for exemplifying other kinds of education.

The starting principle for church involvement in education is that the revealing God teaches through everyone and everything. Every creature participates in the process of teaching-learning. The phrase "lifelong education" is often bandied about, but secular practice does not reflect a belief in such education. The Catholic sacramental system from baptism to the last anointing was lifelong education long before the phrase had to be invented as a protest. The possibilities for an education that would be thoroughly sacramental have not been realized, but the church does have more than a slogan.

What is less often said but is just as important as education being lifelong is that education has to be life-wide. Many people are not enthusiastic about lifelong education because it connotes to them endlessly sitting in high school. Through most of human history, school has played only a small role in education. In today's world, school is an indispensable part of education. Nonetheless, equating education with what schools do is not helpful for either education or school. When the school tries to do all of education, its one great strength is enveloped in dozens of tasks it is not designed for. The classroom of a school ought to be sacred space where one thing is all-important: opening the mind to the intellectual riches of the universe.

On that terrain the Christian church cannot sustain a system of elementary, secondary, and tertiary schools competing with the public sector. It does have to show that it is capable of not only allowing but also enthusiastically supporting some classrooms where minds are awakened and learning of all kinds is truly celebrated. In addition to having some examples of its own, the church should be a supporter of affordable schools for all people.

A person is educated Christianly by all the experiences of life, starting with family interaction in childhood. The church should do all that it can to help the family as educator. The church can be a big help by widening the scope of family life through providing interaction between a number of families and between families and nonfamilial groups.

The phrase "domestic church" has been used since Vatican II, but that phrase can be misleading. The Catholic Church should not try to imitate early Puritanism, which envisioned each family as a domestic church led by its own minister. The Catholic parish's rightful concern was community brought about by a gathering of families. However, the shape of community needs to be rethought today. Simply gathering families in suburban parishes for Sunday Mass does not adequately represent the reality of community today, either the mobility of people or their various living arrangements and work commitments.

A life-wide education involves one's work and leisure activities. The moral and liturgical life of a Christian is built upon the numerous personal examples and the organizational environment that shape one's life. The teaching occurs consciously and unconsciously in personal encounters and organizational decisions.

Unintended teaching is also done by nonhuman animals that have an important role in education. Humans teach their dogs, horses, or cats to behave in certain ways. Conversely, animals teach their "owners" more than most of these caretakers are likely to acknowledge. The exclusion of nonhuman living beings from the modern meaning of education is an unfortunate result of narrowing education to enlightenment.

Formation and Academic Instruction

Education as lifelong and life-wide is captured in a term with a long Christian history: formation. The forms of life (family, work, school, leisure activity) are the teachers. The humans who try to teach would best look at how to improve the forms. Forms of life are given to us by the past, but they are always in need of reform.

In secular literature the term most often associated with Christian and other religious education is "indoctrination." The assumption that church education is indoctrination is so widespread that it is seldom questioned. But it misses the point of how religious communities initially attract and then form their members.

From the early church's "see how they love one another" to the Unification Church's practice of "love bombing," new and old members are shaped by examples of care, love, curiosity, wisdom, and stability in a community. Some religious groups do go on to indoctrinate—that is, use coercive methods to put particular doctrines into people's heads. Even then, indoctrination is secondary, and where there is real community formation, indoctrination is simply unnecessary.

John Keegan, a historian of war who teaches in a military college, distinguishes between two kinds of education: formation and academic instruction.[24] I was at first surprised to find this distinction used by a war historian. But it is perhaps not surprising in that preparing for war is a kind of religious education. Everyone's education is through formation, but a soldier or a monk is most conscious of the process and of the tension between formation and academic instruction. Church writers today often contrast formation and

24. John Keegan, *The Face of War* (New York: Penguin Books, 1983).

information. That is a linguistically inviting pair, but it is too easy. Formation in the church meets its serious competitor in good classroom instruction.

Keegan says that formation "aims if not to close the student's mind to unorthodox or difficult ideas, at least to stop it down to a fairly short focal length."[25] The army lieutenant in the midst of battle has to concentrate the mind not on how the war is going but on how to withstand this battle. For Christian formation, the time to pray is not the time for biblical criticism; the place for feeding the hungry is not the place to study the origins of poverty. Formation is a bracketing of academic matters.

A classroom, in contrast, is not a place for consciously seeking formation; it is the place that challenges what that formation means. Keegan says academic education "aims to offer the student not a single but a variety of angles of vision."[26] He then lists what he calls valid and documented points of view (officer, private soldier, statesman, and so forth). His most interesting viewpoint on the list is "professional pacifist." Should a military officer take seriously the view of the pacifist? On the battlefield that consideration would be dangerous, but in the classroom it is necessary. The teacher in a military college has to realize that examining pacifism is a risk; the student of military matters might decide to change careers. But if that *risk* is not there, then what happens in the classroom is indoctrination, not academic instruction.

The church has to be secure enough not only to allow but also to sponsor a view from the outside. Christians as well as non-Christians can view the church and its history from the outside. If church programs do not allow for a variety of voices, then the field is left entirely to unfriendly critics.

Formation of Christians

The teacher in the community of church is literally everyone and everything. A constant theme in Jewish and Christian traditions is that God is revealed in the small, the vulnerable, and the weak to remind us that our ways of measuring greatness are faulty. Rabbi Joshua ben Qarehah was asked: "Why of all things did God choose the humble thorn bush as the place from which to speak to Moses?" He replied: "God chose the humble thorn bush to teach you that there is no place on earth bereft of Divine Presence, not even a thorn bush."[27] The theme is central to the theology of Thomas Aquinas and is echoed in mystical writers such as Julian of Norwich: "God

25. Ibid., 22.
26. Ibid., 23.
27. *Exodus Rabbah* II.5, in Jakob Petuchowski, *Our Masters Taught* (New York: Crossroad, 1982), 2.

wants us to know that not only does he care for great and noble things, but equally for little and small, lovely and simple things as well."[28]

The Roman Catholic Church shares with most institutions an overly restricted imagination for its idea of teaching. Its storehouse of teachings in the form of doctrines is an invaluable element that surrounds the tradition, but to neglect the teaching that occurs in liturgy, family life, artistic works, leisurely play, and political protest is myopic.

The Catholic Church is hindered from exploring its own wealth of resources and forms of teaching by its use of the term *magisterium*. In the Middle Ages this Latin word described an "office of teaching" and applied to the academic work of the theologian as well as the "pastoral teaching" of bishops.[29] Only in the nineteenth century did teaching almost disappear into an abstraction called "the *magisterium*." In a carefully detailed history of the term, Yves Congar concluded that " 'the magisterium' seems to us to be of recent usage. It appears first with Gregory XVI and Pius IX and it is contemporary with the series of encyclicals generally considered to begin with *Mirari vos* (August 15, 1832)."[30]

Vatican I repeatedly used "the *magisterium*," most prominently in referring to "the infallible *magisterium* of the Roman Pontiff." Unfortunately, Vatican II's move away from nineteenth-century authoritarianism did not include the nineteenth-century language of "the *magisterium*." In fact, the author of a book titled *Magisterium* says he wrote the book because since Vatican II "much has happened to focus attention on the magisterium to the extent that it has become practically a household word."[31]

One could doubt that there are many households in which "the *magisterium*" is discussed. However, it is a term that constantly obscures a discussion of teaching-learning in the Catholic Church. Criticism of the usefulness of "the *magisterium*" is not a denial that the body of bishops has a teaching office in the Catholic Church. To be a Catholic is to accept the teachings or doctrines that are central to the tradition. However, the term *magisterium* creates an abstraction outside the historical process that teaching-learning involves. Raymond Brown notes that "to use properly the teaching role that

---

28. Julian of Norwich, *Revelations of Divine Love* (New York: Dover Publications, 2006), ch. 32.

29. Thomas Aquinas, *Quodl.* III, 9, ad 3.

30. Yves Congar, "A Semantic History of the Term 'Magisterium,' " in *The Magisterium and Morality*, ed. Charles Curran and Richard McCormick, 297–313 (New York: Paulist Press, 1983), 309–10.

31. Francis Sullivan, *Magisterium: Teaching Authority in the Catholic Church* (New York: Paulist Press, 1983), 1.

is theirs by the charism of their office bishops must take the step of learning about what they are teaching. That is not only common sense; it is the age-old understanding of the Church."[32]

Teaching does not consist in telling people what to think. When humans teach by words they have to show someone how to use the words. It is a dialogical process involving a series of steps. The teacher has to show why some ways of speaking are better than others. Teachings that are formulated truths from the past need to be explored, if only to convey the continuing validity of those truths. When human teaching-learning is the issue, the questions are who is teaching, who is the recipient of the intended teaching, on what basis is something taught, and what procedures are used in teaching. The current use of the term *magisterium* is simply an obstacle to thinking about teaching in the Catholic Church.

The main teaching by a bishop is not as an enforcer of orthodox beliefs but as the center of liturgical life in a diocese. Liturgists sometimes are uneasy when "education" and "teaching" are used in a discussion of liturgy. They are rightly wary of turning liturgical prayer into an object of instruction. Because of society's reductionistic use of education and teaching, that danger is real. But precisely because of society's exclusivistic use of "teach" for instructing school-age children, the liturgy has to be affirmed as the community's lifelong and life-wide education. The homily or sermon, which is designed to be more directly instructive than the rest of the liturgy, ought not to be a school lesson, but it is a teaching moment nonetheless.

The General Directory for Catechesis says that the liturgy must be regarded as "an eminent kind of catechesis."[33] For the liturgist who is resistant to this claim "catechesis" likely connotes a kind of Sunday School instruction. But if "catechesis" belongs anywhere, it belongs with liturgy. Catholic Church people who frequently use this language can forget that "catechesis" and its cognates are peculiar words, practically unheard of beyond the Catholic Church and not very familiar even to most Catholics. Except for "catechism," which has centuries behind it and is familiar to Catholic and non-Catholic (Luther was the main inventor), the associated words—catechesis, catechetics, catechize, catechetical—are English-language imports mostly from after 1960.

The fact that catechetical language is practically unknown outside the Catholic Church is not an argument against its use. The language has an

---

32. Raymond Brown, "The Magisterium vs. the Theologians," in *The Magisterium and Morality*, eds. Curran and McCormick, 277–96, at 280.

33. Congregation for the Clergy, *General Directory for Catechesis* (Washington, DC: U.S. Conference of Catholic Bishops, 1997), no. 71.

ancient Christian heritage that deserves to be preserved. Those who use the language, however, should not forget they are speaking in a strange tongue to most people and that the language should be precisely used in an appropriate setting. The swallowing of the church's education by "catechesis" undermines the full range of education and does no service to the liturgical place of catechesis. A frequently made claim that "the catechist is not a mere teacher" is a disastrous misunderstanding of teacher and teaching. Catechizing can be very effective as teaching, though it is only one form of church teaching.

The catechetical and liturgical movements grew up together. Liturgy and catechetics are part of the inner language of formation. Their language is made for insiders. A stranger who drops in on a liturgy should *not* be able to understand everything being said and done. The stranger should feel welcomed by the community and should not find the action offensive or boring. But insiders, those who can appreciate the activities at some depth, have more knowledgeable experiences of the inner life of the community than a stranger can have.

The study of liturgy produced what may be the most successful educational innovation in the Catholic Church, namely, the Rite of Christian Initiation of Adults. This educational formation properly links catechetical instruction and the liturgy. It is most impressive when the process leads up to the reception of new members at the Easter vigil. The process gives serious attention to the initiate's need to understand what being a church member entails. Just as important, the whole community is given a burst of new energy as the ritual of admission unfolds. The "catechumenate" is for every church member, from recent convert to "born Catholic."

The catechumenate obviously concerns the catechetical in the context of liturgy. Many other programs that are intended to show Roman Catholics what the beliefs of the tradition are and how to practice these beliefs are part of the church's catechetical mission. This important function of the church should not be put on the shoulders of untrained volunteers. The work of unpaid volunteers is a wonderful part of the church's history that should be preserved. For example, many retired people who had good-paying careers and have good pension plans are willing and able to give of their abilities and time to church work. However, aspects of church education that involve extensive knowledge of the tradition and skills of presenting it require professional competence and training. If the work is full time, simple justice calls for at least a living wage.

A group called "catechists" should not be assigned the whole task of church education. In one respect that implies too much and in another direction it is too little. For carrying on education from inside, catechists should be joined by theologians for catechetical/theological formation. The relation of theologians and catechists is similar to that of college professors and schoolteachers. A dichotomy is not helpful. Catechists need the direct support of theologians; both are part of the church's educational mission.

Academic Teaching

Catechetical/theological language does not encompass all the education the church should be engaged in. The church's educational mission can and should include a distinct setting and an aim that is academic in nature. This teaching is an examination of the church done by Christians and with Christian tools of scholarship, but from the view of the outsider. It is neither theology nor the secular study of religion. This academic approach to the church's history and practice has no well-defined existence, but it is one of the church's urgent needs.

This kind of teaching-learning does happen in many college and high school classrooms. It can also be found in some parish and diocesan centers. Because this kind of teaching-learning is not protected by clear signs of what game is being played, it is vulnerable to interference by outsiders who should not have the right to censor what is taught. Teachers in church-related universities usually have some protection; teachers in church-sponsored high schools have almost none. A teacher in a parish, even after giving clear signals that he or she is providing an academic course, is still likely to be closed down.

Part of this problem is that church officials consider "theology" to be an ecclesiastical and not an academic term. At least in the United States they have general usage on their side. Most Catholic universities—that is, universities having some relation to the Catholic Church—have departments of religion or religious studies. That should be a bridge for clarifying that when a theologian is teaching in a university classroom, he or she is an academic instructor in Catholicism or other religions. In a classroom, orthodoxy and heterodoxy are irrelevant terms, except perhaps that academic teaching in any area should be skeptical of all orthodoxies.

Some church officials might think that the Catholic Church sponsorship of seminars, workshops, and courses that are not kept within orthodox limits is quixotic or suicidal. But the paradox is that the door has to be open for the believer as well as the unbeliever to look at the church from the outside. A person needs at times to have an imagined distance from his or her community to appreciate it more fully. Does that encourage doubt? It would encourage facing doubts that every reasonable person has. As Rabbi Simon Greenberg says, "The ability to doubt is indispensable to one who wants to remain a believer without going insane or becoming a fanatic."[34] Believing in a revealing God requires a certitude that has been "tested and sustained in full exposure to the hazards and uncertainties of our existence."[35]

I am not denying the need for a church concern with orthodoxy, and even more so orthopraxy (right practice). Without them there is no functioning Christian tradition. Boundaries of what is not acceptable should be set by practicing Christians, including church officials. However, the classroom is not the place for setting such boundaries. The classroom is a place for challenging boundaries.

Catholic Church officials might invite Protestant leaders to join with them in discussing the boundaries of Christian tradition. Christians have to ask whether some groups—for example, the White Aryan Nation—are beyond the pale of the tradition. Even if consensus could not be reached, the discussion would be worthwhile. Protestant and Catholic leaders could also reflect together on how Christian tradition should be reformed.

Internal to the Catholic Church, bishops should be concerned about whether people in official positions are clearly at odds with orthopraxy. A Catholic priest who has sex with a fifteen-year-old is destroying the credibility of the church. A person's reputation should be protected from an isolated accusation without evidence. But if there is clear evidence of disgraceful behavior, something has to be done other than requiring a quick stint in a rehabilitation facility or transferring the person to another setting.

Some public policies should be criticized as contrary to Catholic doctrine. Whether Catholic Church officials should organize opposition to such policies is a legitimate question, but such action goes beyond the border of orthopraxy. If church officials do issue a condemnation of public policies, the language has to be clear and formulated in terms intelligible to outsiders.

Joseph Ratzinger, before becoming pope, wrote: "There may be a legitimate diversity of opinion about waging war and applying the death penalty, but not however with regard to abortion and euthanasia."[36] The statement is muddled on all counts. On the first half of the statement, there may be some "diversity of opinion" about war insofar as the term now carries more

34. Quoted in Eugene Bianchi, *Aging as a Spiritual Journey* (New York: Crossroad, 1982), 110.

35. Nicholas Lash, *Believing Three Ways in One God* (Notre Dame, IN: University of Notre Dame Press, 1993), 19.

36. Robert Moynihan, ed., *Let God's Light Shine Forth: The Spiritual Vision of Pope Benedict XVI* (New York: Doubleday, 2005), 155.

ambiguity than it formerly did. The ambiguity is not so great that the church cannot say that almost anything that is clearly war is immoral. As for the "death penalty," it is a euphemism for the state execution of prisoners, and I fail to see how the state execution of prisoners can be judged other than blatantly immoral and sacrilegious.

On the other side of Ratzinger's contrast, practically no one thinks that abortion is a good thing, but that does not resolve the problem of public policies. The majority of Catholics in the United States believe that attempts to outlaw abortion are counterproductive to actually lessening abortion through better sexual education, more adequate health care for the poor, and a change of economic policies. Accusing tens of millions of one's fellow citizens of being murderers is not a way to bring about change. There is no church diversity of opinion about abortion being wrong; there is legitimate disagreement about what to do about the practice.

As for euthanasia, the Catholic Church has been a leading light in dealing with care of the dying. But to say that there is no diversity of opinion on "euthanasia" is simply incorrect. Fifty years ago the meaning of the term "euthanasia" was clear ("mercy killing") and the practice was condemned by nearly all medical authorities and ethicists. In recent decades the meaning of the term "euthanasia" has changed. I think the change is unfortunate, but it has happened. The term now usually if not always includes what the Catholic Church has consistently approved: namely, that no extraordinary means are required to prolong the process of dying. The Catholic Church has many well-informed thinkers who need to be in this discussion. For bishops or the Vatican simply to issue condemnations of euthanasia is not facing up to the ambiguities of language and the extraordinary complexity of what goes on in hospitals and nursing homes today.

As for church officials condemning writers for "propositions" in their writing, I would think the embarrassing example of Archbishop Etienne Tempier would be enough to steer them away. Tempier was the archbishop of Paris who in 1277 condemned 219 propositions he found in the writings of Thomas Aquinas. The archbishop, to put it mildly, was the one who was wrong.

Something similar happened to Meister Eckhart in 1327. Thomas Merton said of Eckhart's condemnation: "He was ruined, after his death, in twenty-eight propositions which doubtless might be found somewhere in him, but which had none of his joy, his energy, his freedom."[37] It was not until the

---

37. Thomas Merton, *Conjectures of a Guilty Bystander* (Garden City, NY: Doubleday Image Books, 1968), 54.

twentieth century that the Catholic Church could rediscover Eckhart, long after he had profoundly influenced the course of Western thinking. Church officials have still not learned who the enemies of the church are if their concern is finding unacceptable propositions by Jon Sobrino or Jacques Dupuis. It is not that orthodoxy does not need defending; it is that this means of defense is even more futile than it was in 1277.

The test of Christian orthodoxy and orthopraxy is the one offered by Jesus in Matthew 25: caring for the small, the weak, the suffering, the unjustly accused. Or as Jesus proclaimed in Matthew 5, the blessed are those who make peace, seek justice, hunger for righteousness, and are merciful. It is not as if church officials and others of the faithful have to look far afield for actions in support of justice, but it all depends in which direction one is looking. Martin Buber notes that "the encounter with God does not come to man in order that he may henceforth attend to God but in order that he may prove its meaning in action in the world. All revelation is a calling and a mission."[38]

Central to Thomas Aquinas's moral teaching is the principle that "the good is diffusive of itself." Believing in a revealing God manifests itself in an overflow of life. Thomas says that the most appropriate names for the third person of the Trinity are Gift and Love. Believing in a revealing God is shown by a loving justice that gives testimony that the Spirit of God still "over the bent World broods with warm breast and with ah! bright wings."[39]

38. Martin Buber, *I and Thou* (New York: Scribner's, 1970), 164.

39. Gerard Manley Hopkins, "God's Grandeur," in *Works of Gerard Manley Hopkins,* ed. N. MacKenzie (Oxford: Oxford University Press). By permission of Oxford University Press on behalf of the British Province of the Society of Jesus.

Bibliography

Abrashoff, Mike. *It's Your Ship*. New York: Business Plus, 2002.

Ahern, Barnabas. "The Eschatological Dimension of the Church." In *Vatican II: An Interfaith Appraisal*, edited by John Miller, 293–300. Notre Dame, IN: University of Notre Dame Press, 1966.

Alberigo, Giuseppe. "Transition to a New Age." In *History of Vatican II*. Vol. 5, *The Council and the Transition: The Fourth Session and the End of the Council, 1965*, edited by Giuseppe Alberigo and Joseph Komonchak, 573–652. New York: Orbis Books, 1995.

Allison, Dale. "The Eschatology of Jesus." In *The Encyclopedia of Apocalypticism*. Vol. 1, *The Origins of Apocalypticism in Judaism and Christianity*, edited by John Collins, 267–302. New York: Continuum, 1998.

Allison, Jay, and Dan Gediman, eds. *This I Believe*. New York: Holt, 2007.

Appiah, Kwame. *Cosmopolitanism: Ethics in a World of Strangers*. New York: W. W. Norton, 2007.

Arendt, Hannah. *Eichmann in Jerusalem*. New York: Penguin Books, 1994.

———. *The Human Condition*. New York: Doubleday, 1959.

———. *On Violence*. New York: Harvest Books, 1970.

Aslan, Reza. *No God but God*. New York: Random House, 2005.

Augustine of Hippo. *Against the Academics* and *The Teacher*. Indianapolis: Hackett Publishing, 1995.

———. *The City of God*. New York: Penguin Books, 2003.

———. *The Enchiridion: On Faith, Hope and Love*. Chicago: Regnery, 1961.

———. *First Catechetical Instruction*. New York: Paulist Press, 1978.

———. *The Retractions*. Washington, DC: Catholic University of America Press, 1968.

———. *Teaching Christianity*. Hyde Park, NY: New City Press, 1996.

Barkun, Michael. "Politics and Apocalypticism." In *The Encyclopedia of Apocalypticism*. Vol. 3, *Apocalypticism in the Modern Period and the Contemporary Age*, edited by Stephen Stein, 442–60. New York: Continuum, 1998.

Barth, Karl. *The Theology of John Calvin*. Grand Rapids, MI: Eerdmans, 1995.

Beckett, Samuel. *Collected Shorter Plays of Samuel Beckett.* London: Faber & Faber, 1984.

———. *Endgame.* New York: Grove Press, 1958.

———. *Waiting for Godot.* New York: Grove Press, 1954.

Benedict XVI, Pope. *Saved in Hope.* San Francisco: Ignatius Press, 2008.

Berkovits, Eliezer. *With God in Hell.* New York: Hebrew Publishing Company, 1979.

Bianchi, Eugene. *Aging as a Spiritual Journey.* New York: Crossroad, 1982.

Bickel, Alexander. *The Morality of Consent.* New Haven, CT: Yale University Press, 1975.

Blue, Lionel. *To Heaven with Scribes and Pharisees.* New York: Oxford University Press, 1976.

Boman, Thorlief. *Hebrew Thought Compared with Greek.* New York: W. W. Norton, 1960.

Bonhoeffer, Dietrich. *Ethics.* New York: Macmillan, 1965.

Boyle, Marjorie O'Rourke. *Erasmus on Language and Method in Theology.* Toronto: University of Toronto Press, 1977.

Brown, Peter. *Augustine of Hippo.* Berkeley: University of California Press, 1986.

Brown, Raymond E. "The Magisterium vs. the Theologians." In *The Magisterium and Morality,* edited by Charles Curran and Richard McCormick, 277–96. New York: Paulist Press, 1982.

Buber, Martin. *Eclipse of God.* New York: Harper Torchbooks, 1957.

———. *I and Thou.* New York: Scribner's, 1970.

———. "The Man of Today and the Jewish Bible." In *On the Bible: Eighteen Studies,* edited by Nahum Glatzer, 1–13. New York: Schocken Books, 1968.

———. *Two Types of Faith.* New York: Harper Torchbooks, 1961.

Bultmann, Rudolph. *History and Eschatology: The Presence of Eternity.* New York: Harper Torchbooks, 1957.

———. *Theology of the New Testament.* London: SCM Press, 1955.

Burns, Robert. *Muslims, Christians and Jews in the Crusader Kingdom of Valencia.* Cambridge: Cambridge University Press, 1984.

Bushnell, Horace. *Christian Nurture.* Grand Rapids, MI: Baker Book House, 1979.

Butler, Christopher. "Introduction" in *Constitution on the Church,* iii–vi. New York: Deus Books, 1965.

Bynum, Caroline Walker. *The Resurrection of the Body in Western Christianity 200–1336.* New York: Columbia University Press, 1995.

Calvin, John. *Institutes of the Christian Religion.* Philadelphia: Presbyterian Board of Christian Education, 1960.

Catechism of the Catholic Church. Washington, DC: United States Catholic Conference, 1994.

Chauvet, Louis-Marie. *The Sacraments: The Word of God at the Mercy of the Body.* Collegeville, MN: Liturgical Press, 2001.

Chenu, Marie-Dominique. *Nature, Man and Society in the Twelfth Century.* Toronto: University of Toronto Press, 1997.

Chesterton, Gilbert K. *Orthodoxy*. Garden City, NY: Doubleday Image Books, 1959.

Cicero. *The Nature of the Gods*. New York: Oxford University Press, 2008.

Cohen, Arthur. *Tremendum: A Theological Interpretation of the Holocaust*. New York: Crossroad, 1988.

Cohn, Norman. *Cosmos, Chaos and the World to Come*. New Haven, CT: Yale University Press, 1993.

———. *Pursuit of the Millennium: Revolutionary Millenarians and the Mystical Anarchists of the Middle Ages*. New York: Oxford University Press, 1970.

Collins, Adela Yarbo. *Crisis and Catharsis: The Power of the Apocalypse*. Louisville, KY: Westminster John Knox, 1984.

Collins, John. *The Apocalyptic Imagination*. New York: Crossroad, 1984.

Collins, John, Bernard McGinn, and Stephen Stein, eds. *Encyclopedia of Apocalypticism*. 3 vols. New York: Continuum, 1998.

Collins, Mary. "On Becoming a Sacramental Church Again." In *Open Catholicism*, edited by David Efroymson and John Raines, 111–28. Collegeville, MN: Liturgical Press, 1997.

Congar, Yves. "A Semantic History of the Term 'Magisterium.' " In *The Magisterium and Morality*, edited by Charles Curran and Richard McCormick, 297–313. New York: Paulist Press, 1982.

Congregation for the Clergy. *General Directory for Catechesis*. Washington, DC: United States Conference of Catholic Bishops, 1997.

Congregation for the Doctrine of the Faith. "Letter to the Bishops of the Catholic Church on Some Aspects of the Church Understood as Communion." *Origins* 22, no. 7 (June 25, 1992): 108–12.

———. "Notification on Two Books of Father Jon Sobrino." *Origins* 36, no. 41 (March 29, 2007): 1–5.

———. "Responses to Some Questions regarding Certain Aspects of the Doctrine on the Church." *Origins* 37, no. 9 (July 19, 2007): 134–36.

Crosby, Alfred. *The Measure of Reality: Quantification in Western Europe 1250–1600*. Cambridge: Cambridge University Press, 1997.

Crossan, John Dominic. *Raid on the Articulate*. New York: Harper, 1976.

Crüsemann, Frank. *The Torah*. Philadelphia: Fortress Press, 1996.

Cullmann, Oscar. *Christ and Time*. Philadelphia: Westminster, 1950.

Dan, Joseph, ed. *The Early Kabbalah*. New York: Paulist Press, 1986.

Daneels, Godfried. "Liturgy Forty Years after the Council." *America* 197, no. 5 (August 27–September 3, 2007): 13–16.

D'Antonio, William. *American Catholics: Gender, Generation and Commitment*. Lanham, MD: Rowman & Littlefield, 2001.

Decrees of the Ecumenical Councils, edited by Norman Tanner. Washington, DC: Georgetown University Press, 1990.

De Lubac, Henri. "Lumen Gentium and the Fathers." In *Vatican II: An Interfaith Appraisal*, edited by John Miller, 153–75. Notre Dame, IN: University of Notre Dame Press, 1966.

Dennett, Daniel. *Elbow Room: The Varieties of Free Will Worth Wanting.* New York: Bradford, 1984.

Dewey, John. *A Common Faith.* New Haven, CT: Yale University Press, 1930.

Diekmann, Godfrey. "The Constitution on the Sacred Liturgy." In *Vatican II: An Interfaith Appraisal,* edited by John Miller, 17–30. Notre Dame, IN: University of Notre Dame Press, 1966.

Documents of Vatican II. Translated by Austin Flannery. Grand Rapids, MI: Eerdmans, 1975.

Dodds, Eric. R. *Pagan and Christian in an Age of Anxiety.* Cambridge: Cambridge University Press, 1990.

Douglass, James. *The Non-Violent Cross.* New York: Macmillan, 1966.

Dupuis, Jacques. *Toward a Christian Theology of Pluralism.* New York: Orbis Books, 1997.

Durkheim, Emile. *Moral Education.* New York: Free Press, 1973.

Edwards, Dennis. *Breath of Life: A Theology of the Creator Spirit.* New York: Orbis Books, 2004.

Ellsworth, Elizabeth. *Places of Learning: Media, Architecture, Pedagogy.* New York: Routledge, 2005.

Emerson, Ralph Waldo. *Three Prophets of Liberalism,* edited by Conrad Wright. New York: Skinner House Books, 1986.

Fackenheim, Emil. *To Mend the World: Foundations of Future Jewish Thought.* New York: Schocken Books, 1982.

———. *What Is Judaism?* New York: Collins, 1987.

Feldman, David. *Health and Medicine in Jewish Tradition.* New York: Crossroad, 1986.

Feuerbach, Ludwig. *Essence of Christianity.* New York: Harper Torchbooks, 1957.

Flores, Jorge. *Goa and the Great Mughal.* New York: Scala, 2004.

Fowler, James. *Faith Development.* San Francisco: HarperSan Francisco, 1981.

French, Peter. *Collective and Corporate Responsibility.* New York: Columbia University Press, 1984.

Frye, Northrop. *Educated Imagination.* Indianapolis: Indiana University Press, 1964.

Gadamer, Hans-Georg. *Truth and Method.* 2nd ed. New York: Crossroad, 1989.

Gager, John. *Kingdom and Community.* Englewood Cliffs, NJ: Prentice Hall, 1975.

Gilman, Richard. *The Making of Modern Drama.* New York: Da Capo, 1987.

Glatzer, Nahum. *Franz Rosenzweig: His Life and Thought.* Philadelphia: Jewish Publication Society, 1953.

Graham, Patricia. *Progressive Education: From Arcady to Academe.* New York: Teachers College Press, 1967.

Greeley, Andrew, and Jacob Neusner. *The Bible and Us.* New York: Warner Books, 1990.

Grillmeier, Aloys. "Constitution on the Church." In *Commentary on the Documents of Vatican II.* General editor Herbert Vorgrimler. Vol. 1, *Constitution on the Sacred Liturgy. Decree on the instruments of social communication. Dogmatic Constitution on the Church. Decree on Eastern Catholic Churches*, 153–85. New York: Herder & Herder, 1967.

Gritsch, Eric. *Martin Luther: God's Court Jester*. Philadelphia: Fortress Press, 1983.

Gunton, Colin. *A Brief Theology of Revelation*. Edinburgh: T & T Clark, 1995.

Guthrie, William K. C. *The Sophists*. Cambridge: Cambridge University Press, 1971.

Gutman, Amy, and Dennis Thompson. "The Moral Foundations of Truth Commissions." In *Truth v. Justice*, edited by Robert Rotberg and Dennis Thompson, 22–44. Princeton, NJ: Princeton University Press, 2000.

Harris, Maria. *Dance of the Spirit*. New York: Bantam Press, 1989.

Harris, Sam. *The End of Faith*. New York: W. W. Norton, 2007.

Harrison, Peter. *"Religion" and the Religions in the English Enlightenment*. Cambridge: Cambridge University Press, 1990.

Hathaway, Ronald. *Hierarchy and the Definition of Order in the Letters of Pseudo-Dionysius*. The Hague: Nijhoff, 1969.

Haughton, Rosemary. *Images for Change: The Transformation of Society*. New York: Paulist Press, 1997.

Hearne, Vicki. *Adam's Task: Calling Animals by Name*. New York: Knopf, 1986.

Hemingway, Ernest. *A Farewell to Arms*. New York: Scribner's, 1957.

Heschel, Abraham Joshua. *The Earth Is the Lord's* and *The Sabbath*. New York: Harper Torchbooks, 1962.

Hick, John, and Edmund Meltzer, eds. *Three Faiths—One God*. Albany, NY: State University of New York Press, 1989.

Hopkins, Gerard Manley. *God's Grandeur and Other Poems*. New York: Dover Books, 1995.

Iqbal, Muhammad. *The Reconstruction of Religious Thought in Islam*. Lahore: Institute of Islamic Culture, 1986.

Jansen, Godfrey H. *Militant Islam*. San Francisco: Harper & Row, 1979.

Joachim of Fiore. *Enchiridion Super Apocalypsim*. Translated by Edmund Berger. Toronto: Pontifical Institute of Medieval Studies, 1986.

Johnson, Luke Timothy. "Human and Divine: Did Jesus Have Faith?" *Commonweal* 135, no. 3 (31 January 2008): 10–16.

Julian of Norwich. *Revelations of Divine Love*. New York: Dover Books, 2006.

Jungmann, Josef. "Constitution on the Sacred Liturgy." In *Commentary on the Documents of Vatican II*. General editor Herbert Vorgrimler. Vol. 1, *Constitution on the Sacred Liturgy. Decree on the instruments of social communication. Dogmatic Constitution on the Church. Decree on Eastern Catholic Churches*, 1–87. New York: Herder & Herder, 1967.

Kant, Immanuel. "What Is Enlightenment?" in *Kant's Political Writings*, edited by Hans Reiss, 54–60. Cambridge: Cambridge University Press, 1991.

Käsemann, Ernst. *New Testament Questions of Today*. Philadelphia: Fortress Press, 1969.

Kasper, Walter. "On the Church: A Friendly Reply to Cardinal Ratzinger." *America* 184, no. 14 (April 23, 2001): 8–14.

————. "Letter from the President of the Council for Promoting Christian Unity." *America* 185, no. 17 (November 26, 2001): 28–29.

Kaufman, Gordon. "Religious Diversity, Historical Consciousness, and Christian Theology." In *The Myth of Christian Uniqueness*, edited by John Hick and Paul Knitter, 3–15. New York: Orbis Books, 1987.

Kaufman, Walter. *From Shakespeare to Existentialism*. New York: Anchor Books, 1959.

Keegan, John. *The Face of War*. New York: Penguin Books, 1983.

Kierkegaard, Søren. *Philosophical Fragments*. Princeton, NJ: Princeton University Press, 1962.

Kilmartin, Edward. *The Eucharist in the West: History and Theology*. Collegeville, MN: Liturgical Press, 1999.

Knitter, Paul. *No Other Name*. New York: Orbis Books, 1985.

Knowles, Malcolm. *The Adult Learner: A Neglected Species*. Houston, TX: Gulf Publishing Company, 1990.

Komonchak, Joseph. "Vatican II as an 'Event.'" In *Vatican II: Did Anything Happen?* edited by David Schultenover, 24–51. New York: Continuum, 2007.

Kübler-Ross, Elisabeth. *On Death and Dying*. New York: Macmillan, 1969.

Landes, Richard. "The Apocalyptic Year 1000: Millennial Fever and the Origins of the Modern West." In *The Year 2000: Essays on the End*, edited by Charles Strozier and Michael Flynn, 13–29. New York: New York University Press, 1997.

Lapide, Pinchas. *The Sermon on the Mount*. New York: Orbis Books, 1986.

Lash, Nicholas. *Believing Three Ways in One God*. Notre Dame, IN: University of Notre Dame Press, 1993.

————. *The Beginning and the End of "Religion."* Cambridge: Cambridge University Press, 1996.

————. *Theology for Pilgrims*. Notre Dame, IN: University of Notre Dame Press, 2008.

Lawler, Michael, and Thomas Shannahan. *Church: A Spiritual Communion*. Collegeville, MN: Liturgical Press, 1995.

Lee, Bernard. *The Becoming of the Church*. New York: Paulist Press, 1974.

Levinas, Emmanuel. *Difficult Freedom*. Baltimore: Johns Hopkins University Press, 1990.

Levine, Amy-Jill. *The Misunderstood Jew*. San Francisco: HarperSanFrancisco, 2006.

Lilla, Mark. *The Stillborn God*. New York: Knopf, 2007.

Lindbeck, George. "A Protestant View." In *Vatican II: An Interfaith Appraisal*, edited by John Miller, 219–30. Notre Dame, IN: University of Notre Dame Press, 1966.

————. *The Nature of Religious Doctrine*. Philadelphia: Westminster, 1984.

Lings, Martin. *What Is Sufism?* Berkeley: University of California Press, 1975.

Locke, John. *An Essay Concerning Human Understanding*. Los Angeles: Pomona, 2007.

————. *The Reasonableness of Christianity*. Stanford, CA: Stanford University Press, 1958.

Luther, Martin. *Exposition of the 14ᵗʰ, 15ᵗʰ and 16ᵗʰ Chapters of the Gospel of John.* Vol. 24, *Luther's Works,* edited by Jaroslav Pelikan. St. Louis: Concordia Publishing House, 1961.

Lynch, William. *Images of Hope.* Notre Dame, IN: University of Notre Dame Press, 1974.

McDonnell, Kilian. "The Ratzinger/Kasper Debate: The Universal Churches and the Local Churches." *Theological Studies* 63, no. 2 (2002): 227–50.

———. "Walter Kasper on the Theology and Praxis of the Bishop's Office." *Theological Studies* 63, no. 4 (2002): 711–29.

McGinn, Bernard. *Visions of the End: Apocalyptic Traditions in the Middle Ages.* New York: Columbia University Press, 1979.

———. "Apocalypticism and Church Reform." In *Encyclopedia of Apocalypticism.* Vol. 2, *Apocalypticism in Western History and Culture,* edited by Bernard McGinn, 74–109. New York: Continuum, 2000.

Madsen, Catherine. *The Bones Reassemble.* Aurora, IL: Davies Group, 2005.

Marcel, Gabriel. *Homo Viator.* Chicago: Regnery, 1951.

———. *Philosophy of Existence.* New York: Citadel, 1961.

———. *The Mystery of Being.* New York: St. Augustine, 2001.

Margalit, Avishai. *The Ethics of Memory.* Cambridge, MA: Harvard University Press, 2002.

Marini, Piero. *A Challenging Reform.* Collegeville, MN: Liturgical Press, 2008.

Merton, Thomas. *Conjectures of a Guilty Bystander.* Garden City, NY: Doubleday Image Books, 1968.

Midgley, Mary. *Ethical Primate.* New York: Routledge, 1996.

Miller, John, ed. *Vatican II: An Interfaith Appraisal.* Notre Dame, IN: University of Notre Dame Press, 1966.

Minow, Martha. *Between Vengeance and Forgiveness.* Boston: Beacon Press, 1998.

Monda, Antonio, ed. *Do You Believe? Conversations on God and Religion.* New York: Vintage Books, 2007.

Moran, Gabriel. "Roman Catholic Tradition and Passive Resistance." In *Religion, Terror and Globalization,* edited by K. K. Kariakose, 203–14. New York: Nova Science, 2006.

———. *Uniqueness: Problem or Paradox in Jewish and Christian Traditions.* New York: Orbis Books, 1992.

Moynihan, Robert. *Let God's Light Shine Forth: The Spiritual Vision of Pope Benedict XVI.* New York: Doubleday, 2005.

Murray, John Courtney, and J. Leon Hooper. *Bridging the Secular and the Sacred: Selected Writings of John Courtney Murray.* Washington, DC: Georgetown University Press, 1994.

Neumann, Erich. *Depth Psychology and a New Ethic.* Boston: Shambhala, 1990.

Neusner, Jacob. *The Incarnation of God: The Character of Divinity in Formative Judaism.* Philadelphia: Fortress Press, 1988.

Newman, John Henry. *An Essay in Aid of a Grammar of Assent*. Garden City, NY: Doubleday Image Books, 1960.

Newman, Katherine. "Incipient Bureaucracy: The Development of Hierarchies in Egalitarian Organizations." In *Hierarchy and Society: Anthropological Perspectives on Bureaucracy*, edited by Gerald Britain and Ronald Cohen, 143–63. Philadelphia: Institute for the Study of Human Issues, 1980.

Nichols, Terence. *That All May Be One: Hierarchy and Participation in the Church*. Collegeville, MN: Liturgical Press, 1997.

Nietzsche, Friedrich. *Beyond Good and Evil*. London: Penguin, 1973.

Nissiotis, Nikos. "The Main Ecclesiological Problems of Vatican II." *Journal of Ecumenical Studies* 2, no. 1 (1965): 31–62.

O'Brien, Conor Cruise. *On the Eve of the Millennium*. New York: Free Press, 1995.

O'Collins, Gerald. *Salvation for God's Other Peoples*. New York: Oxford University Press, 2008.

O'Connor, Flannery. *Mystery and Manners*. New York: Farrar, Straus & Giroux, 1969.

———. *Three by Flannery O'Connor*. New York: New American Library, 1962.

———. *The Complete Stories*. New York: Farrar, Straus & Giroux, 1971.

Ong, Walter. *In the Human Grain*. New York: Macmillan, 1967.

O'Malley, John. "Did the Council Change Anything?" In *Vatican II: Did Anything Happen?* edited by David Schultenover, 52–91. New York: Continuum, 2007.

Osborne, Kenan. *Orders and Ministry*. New York: Orbis Books, 2006.

Ovitt, George. *The Restoration of Perfection*. New Brunswick, NJ: Rutgers University Press, 1986.

Peirce, Charles S. *The Writings of Charles S. Peirce*. Bloomington: Indiana University Press, 1982.

Pelikan, Jaroslav. *The Christian Tradition: A History of the Development of Doctrine*. Vol. 3, *The Emergence of the Catholic Tradition*. Chicago: University of Chicago Press, 1971.

———. *Jesus through the Centuries*. New Haven, CT: Yale University Press, 1985.

Petuchowski, Jakob, ed. *Our Masters Taught: Rabbinic Stories and Sayings*. New York: Crossroad, 1982.

Piaget, Jean. *The Moral Judgment of the Child*. New York: Collier Books, 1962.

Pieper, Josef. *Faith, Hope, Love*. San Francisco: Ignatius Press, 1997.

———. *Guide to Thomas Aquinas*. New York: Pantheon, 1962.

Pitkin, Hanna. *Wittgenstein and Justice*. Berkeley: University of California Press, 1992.

Polanyi, Karl. *Personal Knowledge*. Chicago: University of Chicago Press, 1974.

Prejean, Helen. *Dead Man Walking*. New York: Vintage Books, 1993.

Pseudo-Dionysius. "The Celestial Hierarchy." In *The Complete Works*, 143–93. New York: Paulist Press, 1987.

———. "The Letters." In *The Complete Works,* 261–89. New York: Paulist Press, 1987.

Rahner, Karl. *Theology of Death*. New York: Herder and Herder, 1964.

————. "Thoughts on the Possibility of Belief Today." In *Theological Investigations*. Vol. 5, *Later Works*, 3–22. Baltimore: Helicon, 1966.

————. "Christianity and Non-Christian Religions." In *Theological Investigations*. Vol. 5, *Later Works,* 115–34. London: Darton, Longman and Todd, 1966.

————. "The Universality of Salvation." In *Theological Investigations*. Vol. 16, *Experience of the Spirit: Source of Theology*, 199–224. London: Darton, Longman and Todd, 1979.

————. "Basic Theological Interpretation of the Second Vatican Council." In *Theological Investigations*. Vol. 20, *Concern for the Church*, 77–89. New York: Crossroad, 1981.

————. "The Dispute Concerning the Teaching Office of the Church." In *The Magisterium and Morality*, edited by Charles Curran and Richard McCormick, 113–28. New York: Paulist Press, 1982.

————. "On the Importance of the Non-Christian Religions for Salvation." In *Theological Investigations*. Vol. 18, *God and Revelation*, 288–95. London: Darton, Longman and Todd, 1984.

Ratzinger, Josef. "Constitution on Divine Revelation." In *Commentary on the Documents of Vatican II*. General editor Herbert Vorgrimler. Vol. 3, *Declaration on the relationship of the Church to non-Christian religions. Dogmatic Constitution on Divine Revelation. Decree on the Apostolate of the Laity*, 155–66; 181–98. New York: Herder & Herder, 1967.

————. *Gospel, Catechesis, Catechism*. San Francisco: Ignatius Press, 1997.

————. *Introduction to Christianity*. Revised edition. San Francisco: Ignatius Press, 2004.

————. "The Local Church and the Universal Church." *America* 185, no. 16 (November 19, 2001): 7–11.

————. *Salt of the Earth: The Church at the End of the Millennium*. San Francisco: Ignatius Press, 1997.

————. *The Theology of History in Saint Bonaventure*. Chicago: Franciscan Herald Press, 1971.

Reeves, Marjorie. *Joachim of Fiore*. New York: Harper Torchbooks, 1977.

Richardson, Herbert. "Martin Luther King, Jr.—Unsung Theologian." In *New Theology No. 6*, edited by Martin Marty and Dean Peerman, 174–84. New York: Macmillan, 1969.

Rist, John. *Augustine*. Cambridge: Cambridge University Press, 1996.

Robinson, Geoffrey. *Confronting Power and Sex in the Catholic Church*. Melbourne: John Garrett, 2007.

Rosenak, Michael. *Commandment and Concern: Jewish Religious Education and Secular Society*. Philadelphia: Jewish Publication Society, 1987.

Rosenzweig, Franz. *Star of Redemption*. New York: Holt, Rinehart and Winston, 1970.

Rosenzweig, Franz, and Eugen Rosestock-Huessy. *Judaism Despite Christianity*. Birmingham: University of Alabama Press, 1969.

Rousseau, Jean-Jacques. *Emile*. New York: Basic Books, 1979.

Rush, Ormond. *Still Interpreting Vatican II*. New York: Paulist Press, 2004.

Schillebeeckx, Edward. *On Christian Faith*. New York: Crossroad, 1987.

Schimmel, Annemarie. *Deciphering the Signs of God*. Albany: State University of New York Press, 1994.

Scholem, Gershom. *Major Trends in Jewish Mysticism*. New York: Schocken Books, 1961.

Schultenover, David, ed. *Vatican II: Did Anything Happen?* New York: Continuum, 2007.

Seasoltz, Kevin. *God's Gift Giving*. New York: Continuum, 2007.

Semmelroth, Otto. "Dogmatic Constitution on the Church, Chapter VII." In *Commentary on the Documents of Vatican II*. General editor Herbert Vorgrimler. Vol. I, *Constitution on the Sacred Liturgy. Decree on the instruments of social communication. Dogmatic Constitution on the Church. Decree on Eastern Catholic Churches*, 280–84. New York: Crossroad, 1967.

Sizer, Theodore. *Horace's School: Redesigning the American High School*. Boston: Houghton Mifflin, 1992.

Smith, Jonathan. *Drudgery Divine: On the Comparison of Early Christianities and the Religions of Late Antiquity*. Chicago: University of Chicago Press, 1990.

———. "Religion, Religions, Religious." In *Critical Terms for Religious Studies*, edited by Mark Taylor, 269–84. Chicago: University of Chicago Press, 1998.

Smith, Morton. "On the History of 'Apocalyptic' and 'Apocalypse.'" In *Apocalypticism in the Mediterranean World and the Near East*, edited by David Hellholm, 9–20. Tübingen: Mohr, 1983.

Smith, Wilfred Cantwell. *Faith and Belief*. Princeton, NJ: Princeton University Press, 1999.

———. *On Understanding Islam*. The Hague: Mouton, 1981.

Steiner, George. *Lessons of the Masters*. Cambridge, MA: Harvard University Press, 2005.

Steinsalz, Adin, ed. *The Essential Talmud*. New York: Basic Books, 1976.

Stout, Jeffrey. *Democracy and Tradition*. Princeton, NJ: Princeton University Press, 2005.

Sullivan, Francis. *Magisterium: Teaching Authority in the Catholic Church*. New York: Paulist Press, 1983.

Talmon, Yonina. "Millenarianism." In *The International Encyclopedia of Social Sciences*. Vol. 19, edited by David Sills, 349–62. New York: Macmillan, 1991.

Tavuchis, Nicholas. *Mea Culpa: A Sociology of Apology and Reconciliation*. Stanford, CA: Stanford University Press, 1991.

Taylor, Charles. *The Secular Age*. Cambridge, MA: Belknap Press, 2007.

Thomas Aquinas, *Summa Theologiae*. New York: McGraw-Hill, 1963.

———. *On Truth*. Indianapolis: Hackett, 1994.

Vanderkam, James, and William Adler. *The Jewish Apocalyptic Heritage in Early Christianity*. Philadelphia: Fortress Press, 1996.

Vorgrimler, Herbert, gen. ed. *Commentary on the Documents of Vatican II*. 5 vols. New York: Herder & Herder, 1967–69.

Wallis, Jim. *God's Politics*. San Francisco: HarperSanFrancisco, 2005.

Ward, Barbara. *Faith and Freedom*. Garden City, NY: Doubleday Image Books, 1962.

Walzer, Michael. *The Revolution of the Saints*. Cambridge, MA: Harvard University Press, 1965.

Weber, Max. "Politics as a Vocation." Chap. 4 in *From Max Weber: Essays in Sociology*, edited by Hans Gerth and C. Wright Mills, 77–128. New York: Oxford University Press, 1946.

Weick, Karl. *The Social Psychology of Organizations*. Reading, PA: Addison-Wesley, 1969.

Weil, Simone. *The Weil Reader*, edited by George Pinachas. Mt. Kisco, NY: Moyer Bell, 1977.

Welch, Jack. *Straight from the Gut*. New York: Warner Books, 2001.

White, Lynn. "The Historical Roots of Our Ecological Crisis." *Science* 155, no. 3767 (March 10, 1967): 1203–7.

———. *Medieval Religion and Technology*. Berkeley: University of California Press, 1986.

Whitehead, Alfred North. *Adventure of Ideas*. Cambridge: Cambridge University Press, 1933.

———. *Science and the Modern World*. New York: Free Press, 1997.

Wilde, Melissa. *Vatican II: A Sociological Analysis of Religious Change*. Princeton, NJ: Princeton University Press, 2007.

Wills, Garry. *St. Augustine*. New York: Penguin, 1999.

———. *What Jesus Meant*. New York: Viking, 2006.

Wilson, David Sloan. *Darwin's Cathedral: Religion and the Nature of Society*. Chicago: University of Chicago Press, 2002.

Wittgenstein, Ludwig. *Wittgenstein's Lectures 1930–33*, edited by G. E. Moore. London: Allen and Unwin, 1959.

Wordsworth, William. *The Prelude*. New York: Penguin, 1986.

Yerushalmi, Yosef. *Zakhor: Jewish History and Jewish Memory*. Seattle: University of Washington Press, 1982.

Zizioulas, John. *Being as Communion*. New York: St. Vladimir's Seminary Press, 1985.

Zornberg, Avivah Gottlieb. *The Particulars of Rapture: Reflections on Exodus*. New York: Doubleday Image Books, 2002.

Index